LINGUISTIC THEORY AND THE BIBLICAL TEXT

Linguistic Theory and the Biblical Text

Edited by
William A. Ross and Elizabeth Robar

https://www.openbookpublishers.com

© 2023 William A. Ross and Elizabeth Robar (editors).
Copyright of individual chapters is maintained by the chapters' authors.

This work is licensed under an Attribution-NonCommercial 4.0 International (CC BY-NC 4.0). This license allows you to share, copy, distribute, and transmit the text; to adapt the text for non-commercial purposes of the text providing attribution is made to the authors (but not in any way that suggests that they endorse you or your use of the work). Attribution should include the following information:

William A. Ross and Elizabeth Robar (eds), *Linguistic Theory and the Biblical Text*. Cambridge, UK: Open Book Publishers, 2023, https://doi.org/10.11647/OBP.0358

Further details about CC BY-NC licenses are available at http://creativecommons.org/licenses/by-nc/4.0/

All external links were active at the time of publication unless otherwise stated and have been archived via the Internet Archive Wayback Machine at https://archive.org/web

Any digital material and resources associated with this volume will be available at https://doi.org/10.11647/OBP.0358#resources

Semitic Languages and Cultures 20.

ISSN (print): 2632-6906
ISSN (digital): 2632-6914
ISBN Paperback: 978-1-80511-108-5
ISBN Hardback: 978-1-80511-109-2
ISBN Digital (PDF): 978-1-80511-110-8
DOI: 10.11647/OBP.0358

Cover image: A section of Cisneros' original complutensian polyglot Bible, https://en.wikipedia.org/wiki/File:Cisneros%27_original_complutensian_polyglot_Bible_-2.jpg; additional text and diagrams created by authors.

Cover design by Jeevanjot Kaur Nagpal

The main fonts used in this volume are SIL Charis, SBL Hebrew, and SBL Greek.

CONTENTS

Abbreviations and Symbols vii

Contributors.. xii

Preface.. xv

Abstracts and Keywords xvi

Elizabeth Robar

Introduction... 1

Jacobus A. Naudé and Cynthia L. Miller-Naudé

Generative Linguistics as a Theoretical Framework for the Explanation of Problematic Constructions in Biblical Hebrew 6

Randall Buth

Functional Grammar and the Pragmatics of Information Structure for Biblical Languages 67

William A. Ross

Cognitive Linguistic Theory and the Biblical Languages... 117

Kaspars Ozoliņš

Historical Linguistics and the Biblical Languages 172

Willem Th. van Peursen

Computational Linguistic Analysis
of the Biblical Text 223

Sophia L. Pitcher

Emerging from Silos of Analysis: A Complexity
Theory Approach to the Study of Biblical Texts 273

Glossary 324
Indices 337

ABBREVIATIONS AND SYMBOLS

φ	Intermediate phrase
ι	Intonational phrase
{x}	Graphic representation (e.g., {a})
/x/	Phonological representation (e.g., /a/)
[x]	Phonetic representation (e.g., [a])
x:	Lengthened vowel (e.g., a:)
ẋ	Consonant with emphatic articulation (e.g., ṣ)
x^j	Consonant with palatalised articulation (e.g., t^j)
x^h	Consonant with aspirated articulation (e.g., t^h)
*x > y	Segment x develops into segment y (e.g., *ā > ō)
ā	Indicates a lengthened vowel (e.g., ā)
ă	Indicates a short vowel (e.g., ă)
ā̆	Indicates a vowel with variable length
-	Morpheme boundary
x ~ y	Variation between segments x and y
*	Reconstructed element (no direct attestation)
$*h_1$ $*h_2$ $*h_3$	Laryngeal consonantal series reconstructed for Proto-Indo-European
$*k^w$	Voiceless labiovelar stop reconstructed for Proto-Indo-European
*ḱ	Voiceless palatal stop reconstructed for Proto-Indo-European

*ḏ	Voiced dental fricative reconstructed for Proto-Semitic
*ś	Voiceless lateral fricative reconstructed for Proto-Semitic
1	first person
2	second person
3	third person
A	Adjective/Adverb
AGR	Agreement
AI	Artificial Intelligence
AIBI	Association Bible et Informatique
ASCII	American Standard Code for Information Interchange
Asp	Aspect
BCE	Before Common Era
BH	Biblical Hebrew
BHSA	Biblia Hebraica Stuttgartensia Amstelodamensis
BNC	British National Corpus
C	Complementiser/Coordinator
CC	Contextualising Constituent
c	common gender
ca	*circa*, 'approximately'
CBGM	Coherence-Based Genealogical Method
CBLC	Center of Biblical Languages and Computing
cf.	*confer*, 'compare'

cons.	construct state
CP	Complementiser Phrase
CT	Complexity Theory
D	Determiner
D-structure	Underlying (deep) structure
dem. pron.	demonstrative pronoun
dir	direct
DP	Determiner Phrase
DSS	Dead Sea Scrolls
E-language	External language
e.g.	*exempli gratia*, 'for example'
ECM	Editio Critica Maior (Deutsche Bibelgesellschaft, 1997–)
EST	Extended Standard Theory
et al.	*et alia*, 'and others'
etc.	*et cetera*, 'and the rest'
ETCBC	Eep Talstra Centre for Bible and Computer
f	feminine
f.	feminine
FDG	Functional Discourse Grammar
FG	Functional Grammar
FSP	Functional Sentence Perspective
gen.	genitive
Ger.	German

Gk	Greek
HTML	HyperText Markup Language
I	Infinitive
I-language	Internal language
i.e.	*id est*, 'that is'
ind	indirect
INFL	Inflection
JArm.	Jewish Aramaic
LF	Logical Form
LM	Landmark
LXX.D	Septuaginta Deutsch
M	Mood
m	masculine
m.	masculine
Move α	Move alpha
MT	Masoretic Text
N	Noun
n.	footnote
NETS	*A New English Translation of the Septuagint*
NP	Noun Phrase
O	Object
P	Preposition
p	plural

PF	Phonetic Form
pl.	plural
PP	Preposition Phrase
PRON	Pronoun
rel. pron.	relative pronoun
REST	Revised Extended Standard Theory
S	Subject
s	singular
S-structure	Surface structure
sg.	singular
SHEBANQ	System for Hebrew text: Annotations for Queries and markup
T	Tense
TP	Tense Phrase
TR	Trajector
UG	Universal Grammar
Umbr.	Umbrian
V	Verb
viz.	*videlicet,* 'namely', 'that is to say'
VP	Verb Phrase
WIVU	Werkgroep Informatica Vrije Universiteit (previous name of ETCBC)
XML	Extensible Markup Language

CONTRIBUTORS

Randall Buth (PhD, University of California, Los Angeles, 1987) is academic provost at The Whole Word Institute in Jerusalem, where he runs programmes to train persons in the biblical languages through communicative language (immersion) pedagogies, particularly for persons involved in Bible translation in minority languages around the world. For twenty years, Buth worked in Bible translation projects with the Summer Institute of Linguistics and the United Bible Societies (1977–1996), until he began working on communicative language pedagogies for Hebrew and Greek, and in 2001 he founded the Biblical Language Center. His publications appear in the fields of Hebrew, Greek, Aramaic, Biblical Studies, Linguistics, and Language Pedagogy.

Cynthia L. Miller-Naudé (PhD, University of Chicago, 1992) is senior professor in the Department of Hebrew, University of the Free State (Bloemfontein, South Africa). Her research publications focus on pre-modern Hebrew linguistics, especially syntax and pragmatics, the syntactic structures of Shilluk (a Nilo-Saharan language of South Sudan), and Bible translation. She is a co-editor of the series Linguistic Studies in Ancient West Semitic published by Eisenbrauns/Penn State University Press. She also co-edited *Diachrony in Biblical Hebrew* (Eisenbrauns, 2012).

Jacobus A. Naudé (DLitt, University of the Free State, 1996) is senior professor in the Department of Hebrew, University of the Free State (Bloemfontein, South Africa). His research publications focus on pre-modern Hebrew linguistics, especially from generative and complexity theoretical perspectives, religious translation, and translation theory. He serves on the editorial boards of *Folia Orientalia* and *Journal of Northwest Semitic Languages*, among others, and is a co-editor of the series Linguistic Studies in Ancient West Semitic published by Eisenbrauns/Penn State University Press. He is a co-author of *A Biblical Hebrew Reference Grammar* (2nd ed., Bloomsbury, 2017).

Kaspars Ozoliņš (PhD, University of California, Los Angeles, 2016), is Assistant Professor of Old Testament at The Southern Baptist Theological Seminary. He was previously a research associate in Old Testament and the Ancient Near East at Tyndale House, Cambridge.

Sophia L. Pitcher (PhD, University of the Free State, 2020) is a Research Fellow at University of the Free State, an Adjunct Professor of Classical Hebrew at North Central University, and in her capacity with SIL International serves as an exegetical advisor to the South African Sign Language Bible Translation Project. Her doctoral thesis, 'A Prosodic Model for Tiberian Hebrew: A Complexity Approach to the Features, Structures, and Functions of the Masoretic Cantillation Accents', integrates the characteristic features of the *ṭaʿămē hammiqrā́* and presents an analysis of the orthography using the theoretical framework of prosodic phonology. Her publications include 'Towards a Prosodic Model for Tiberian Hebrew: An Intonation-based Analysis' (*Stellenbosch Papers in Linguistics Plus*, 2021) and 'The Medieval Prosodic Orthography of the Tiberian Masoretic Reading Tradition' (*Journal of Semitic Studies*, 2023).

Elizabeth Robar (PhD, University of Cambridge, 2013) is author of *The Verb and the Paragraph: A Cognitive Linguistic Approach*

(Brill, 2014), an adaptation of her doctoral dissertation. She founded Cambridge Digital Bible Research, a charity to make biblical scholarship available, accessible, and useful to interpreters of the Bible. Her research is philological, linguistic, and exegetical in nature, focusing on the Biblical Hebrew verbal system, syntax, linguistic change, and the ramifications of research in these areas for exegetical interpretation.

William A. Ross (PhD, University of Cambridge, 2018) is associate professor of Old Testament at Reformed Theological Seminary in Charlotte, North Carolina. His publications include *Postclassical Greek Prepositions and Conceptual Metaphor* (edited with Steven E. Runge; De Gruyter, 2022) and *Postclassical Greek and Septuagint Lexicography* (SBL Press, 2022). His research focuses on the Septuagint, linguistics and lexicography, and the history of biblical philology.

Willem Th. van Peursen (PhD, Leiden University, 1999) is Professor of Old Testament at the Faculty of Religion and Theology, Vrije Universiteit Amsterdam. His publications include *The Verbal System in the Hebrew Text of Ben Sira* (Brill, 2004), *Language and Interpretation in the Syriac Text of Ben Sira* (Brill, 2007), and *The Two Syriac Versions of the Prayer of Manasseh* (with Ariel Gutman; Gorgias, 2011).

PREFACE

This volume came together as a result of the work of the Linguistics and the Biblical Text research group, which meets at the annual meeting of the Institute for Biblical Research. It was at the 2021 session that the initial versions of four chapters included here were presented (Naudé and Miller-Naudé, Buth, Ross, and Pitcher). To round out the content of those chapters into the contents of this volume, we subsequently invited two further contributions (van Peursen and Ozoliņš). As the editors of this volume and co-chairs of the research group, we are entirely grateful to the contributors for their dedication to this project. We are very pleased to publish these essays in such a distinguished series in open-access format. We would especially like to express our sincere gratitude to the blind peer-reviewers for their time and expertise. Our thanks goes also to Ethan Greb for his capable assistance in helping to copy-edit the manuscript in its final stages, and to Ken McMullen for his labour preparing the indexes.

William A. Ross and Elizabeth Robar
March MMXXIII

ABSTRACTS AND KEYWORDS

Jacobus A. Naudé and Cynthia L. Miller-Naudé, Generative Linguistics as a Theoretical Framework for the Explanation of Problematic Constructions in Biblical Hebrew

This article provides a brief, historical overview of seven decades of generative linguistic theory, from its inception by Chomsky in 1957 to the present day, with special emphasis on its emerging concepts. The major contributions of the application of generative linguistic theory to the identification and explication of problematic constructions in Biblical Hebrew are illustrated. Finally, the article describes the prospects for further research in Biblical Hebrew using linguistics in general and generative linguistics in particular through a programmatic approach to the meaning-making processes of the languages of the biblical text.

Keywords: Pronominalisation, topicalisation, left dislocation, extraposition, quantification, negation

Randall Buth, Functional Grammar and the Pragmatics of Information Structure for Biblical Languages

Functional grammars include pragmatic information within formal grammar. Information structure refers to how languages keep track of the topics and introductory material of a text, and how they present the salient main points of a text. There are differences between normal handling of topical material and special marking of topical material. Likewise, there are default ways of presenting the main points and specially marked ways. The Functional Grammar of Simon Dik is helpful in pointing out constituents that carry pragmatic marking through word order. This facilitates reading for meaning in the biblical languages so that readers may recognise special presentations of material in text. The linking of sentences together in a text with marked Topics, recognising Focus constituents, some unit discontinuities in a text, and some rhetorical features in a text, can be described. Functional Grammar describes how audiences may perceive these features in various languages and process them rapidly. This adds both to the accuracy and enjoyment of listening to a text or reading it. Extensive application and illustration are provided in Hebrew with additional application to Greek. Modern readers of ancient languages, where normal processes of language internalisation may not have taken place, may receive a special benefit from considering the interactions of Functional Grammar and information structure.

Keywords: Topic, Focus, Functional Grammar, word order, Hebrew, Greek

William A. Ross, Cognitive Linguistic Theory and the Biblical Languages

This chapter introduces Cognitive Linguistic theory with special attention to its application to the study of the ancient languages of the Bible. Beginning with a brief survey of the historical background and origins of Cognitive Linguistics, this chapter then identifies four key theoretical commitments that unify an otherwise diverse approach. Subsequently, this chapter identifies six major concepts within Cognitive Linguistics—image schemas, frame semantics, domains and conceptual metaphor, mental spaces and conceptual blending, prototypes and semantic extension, and cognitive approaches to grammar—explaining them in some detail and demonstrating their application to biblical texts in either Greek or Hebrew. The chapter concludes with a discussion of the use of Cognitive Linguistics within biblical studies over the past few decades, highlighting recent applications and identifying potential for future research.

Keywords: Cognitive Linguistics, Greek, Hebrew, biblical languages, biblical studies

Kaspars Ozoliņš, Historical Linguistics and the Biblical Languages

Historical linguistics enjoys a venerable history among the many subfields of linguistic study. Many of the tools employed in historical linguistics, as well as some of its theoretical concepts, are well-suited for biblical studies which engage in the ancient languages of the Bible. Knowledge about the kinds of language change common to many of the world's languages can be useful as one type of evidence for the periodisation of biblical books. Additionally, knowledge about the external linguistic influences that shaped the biblical languages, as well as their prior histories (both Semitic and Indo-European), provides a helpful context for studying many synchronic aspects of the texts of Scripture. Furthermore, text-critical judgments about the biblical text can be

strengthened when informed by knowledge of language change across the manuscript tradition. In short, historical linguistics offers a number of unique insights for biblical scholars engaging in the study of the biblical languages.
Keywords: Historical linguistics, diachronic, sound change, analogy, Indo-European, Semitic

Willem Th. van Peursen, Computational Linguistic Analysis of the Biblical Text

This chapter discusses the various ways in which computational linguistics has been applied to biblical languages. It describes the development that started in the 1970s and 1980s with the first attempts in text representation and that continued with the creation of morphological and syntactic databases. Until the early twenty-first century, most computational linguistic approaches concerned rule-based linguistic analysis, which allowed for a systematic and distributional analysis of biblical corpora. Since the beginning of the twenty-first century, statistical approaches and machine learning have entered the field of biblical studies, although most of their applications to the Bible still have an experimental character. Because of the various computational approaches that have emerged in the last decades, computational linguistics is not one single theory, but rather an amalgam of approaches in a rapidly changing field. The relation with other linguistic theories is complex, because the databases that are used in the computational analysis of the Bible are each rooted in different linguistic theories. However, the various computational approaches have developed further in ways that are typical of computational corpus linguistics and that go beyond the linguistic theories underlying the annotations in the respective databases. Because of the large amount of data it can handle, computational linguistics provides valuable contributions to well-established fields in the study of the biblical languages, such as orthography or syntax. In addition, more advanced computational techniques, such as author clustering and text-classification, provide new ways to approach long-standing problems such as source-critical questions and genre distinctions. The application of computational linguistics to the biblical languages also touches upon fundamental questions about the interpretation of the Bible, because it blurs the traditional distinction between the sciences, conceived of as a mode of scholarship involving calculation and pattern recognition, and the humanities, understood as a hermeneutic and critical mode of scholarship.

Keywords: Computational linguistics, databases, syntax, transparency and reproducibility

Sophia L. Pitcher, Emerging from Silos of Analysis: A Complexity Theory Approach to the Study of Biblical Texts

This chapter surveys a Complexity Theory (CT) approach applied in five areas of biblical scholarship: diachrony, language pedagogy, translation theory, syntax, and the Masoretic accents of the Hebrew Bible. A complexity approach to linguistic theory foremostly recognises that language is a complex system and accordingly aims to situate a particular subject of study within a context that more closely resembles the complex interactions of various dimensions of the system. CT is different from the other linguistic theories presented in this volume in that it functions as a metatheory. An understanding of the general principles of CT can mitigate an inclination towards reductionist analysis and enable researchers to perceive fundamental properties and interactions of language phenomena that remain opaque to traditional theoretical frameworks. As a metatheory, CT can provide a helpful perspective for the scholar or practitioner, transforming an analysis via the questions it raises, the manner in which answers to these questions are pursued, and the conclusions ultimately drawn. A brief overview of CT is provided with particular attention to its application in the field of linguistics.

Keywords: Complexity Theory, complex systems, linguistics, biblical studies

INTRODUCTION

Elizabeth Robar

Scholarship on biblical languages is rooted in Classical Philology, but Classical Philology has all but disappeared after birthing the full range of humanities. The linguistics portion of philology has developed several separate schools of linguistic thought, each of which offers a different perspective on how to analyse and explain language. These different perspectives heavily influence how we interpret the biblical text, which places a burden on the student and scholar not to remain ignorant about formative influences behind their own interpretations.

This edited volume presents the most important linguistic theories in use today for interpreting the biblical languages, with the intent of educating the student and scholar about what lies behind many of their favourite language tools and resources. All too often, both student and scholar are unaware of the prior theoretical commitments that drive many of the conclusions in these resources.

All work is, of necessity, done within a theoretical framework of some kind. When that framework remains unexamined and unarticulated, it becomes a liability for interpretations based on it. Ignorance of theoretical frameworks has become pervasive and problematic enough, even in academic circles, that one response is to require that linguistic proposals submitted for conferences express 'a well-articulated linguistic method' in order to even be considered for acceptance (Society of Biblical Literature, Linguistics and Biblical Hebrew section).

This volume is a response to the need for students and scholars first to understand the various theories on offer, in order to be able to decide which theoretical framework is most suitable for their own work. The chapters fall into three *categories*:

1. Distinct linguistic *theories*, each with their own presuppositions, purpose and methods. Scholars with a strong theoretical background will often identify with one of these in particular.
    a. Generative linguistics (Chapter 2)
    b. Functional Grammar (Chapter 3)
    c. Cognitive Linguistics (Chapter 4)
    d. Historical linguistics (Chapter 5)
2. Practical *implementation* of a theory, which has been applied to each of the above theories.
    a. Computational linguistic analysis (Chapter 6)
3. *Umbrella theory* that seeks to enable interaction between theories, as a practical form of interdisciplinarity.
    a. Complexity Theory (Chapter 7)

Significant areas of linguistic theory not covered in this volume include structuralism and typological linguistics. The influence of these theories on biblical studies has either been indirect or very localised. Chapter 3 (Ross) provides an overview of structuralism as it bears on generative linguistics and Cognitive Linguistics. Typological linguistics, in connection to Biblical

Hebrew, is best known from John Cook's application of Bybee, Perkins, and Pagliuca (1994) in his *Time and the Hebrew Verb* (2012).

It should be noted that Chapter 4 is entitled *Computational Linguistic Analysis* rather than *Computational Linguistics*, because, as van Peursen writes, application of computational linguistics has been largely restricted to syntactic databases of the biblical text, along with a few dissertations on machine learning. The term computational linguistics now tends to refer to Natural Language Processing (NLP) and machine learning, which are only in their infancy within biblical studies.

These linguistic theories differ in specific areas. One such area is how the nature of language itself is understood. Ferdinand de Saussure famously distinguished between *la parole* (spoken language, with all the messiness of everyday interaction) and *la langue* (the abstract system of language, as found in edited writing). Spoken language may be broadened to communication, whether largely linguistic (Functional Grammar) or embodied and extending far beyond language (Cognitive Linguistics). Formal (written) language is understood as grammatical (following the rules) or ungrammatical (generative linguistics).

The nature of grammar flows from the understanding of language: it can be inherently meaningful, a key to interpreting communication; or it can be a formal system explicating the abstract linguistic system. Theories approaching language as an abstract system have different purposes for their grammatical analysis: the diachronic (historical) development of language (historical linguistics), the synchronic reality (e.g., structuralism), or the delimitation of acceptable ('grammatical') constructions (e.g., generative linguistics).

While not a focus of this volume, the extent of language analysed has also been a significant distinguishing factor between theories: whether a theory addresses grammar of linguistic levels at the sentence and below (e.g., structuralism, generative linguistics), or linguistic levels above the sentence (e.g., discourse analysis), or conceptual representations beyond language itself (e.g., Cognitive Linguistics).

A final distinction between these theories is the priority they accord to various linguistic levels: morphology (e.g., structuralism and historical linguistics), semantics (e.g., Cognitive Linguistics), syntax (e.g., generative linguistics), and pragmatics (e.g., Functional Grammar).

Complexity Theory stands out for not taking an explicit stance on any of these questions, precisely because its purpose is to enable different systems to interact while preserving their own internal composition. For perhaps each of the theories, theoretical clarity, in the form of dogmatic claims, has often come at the cost of explanatory adequacy, when confronted with the complexity of real language and texts. No one theory can explain everything. Complexity Theory aims to create space for each separate theory both to operate on its own and to interact with other theories.

Each chapter follows the same format: history and development of the theory; key theoretical commitments and major concepts; use and contributions in biblical studies to date; and prospects for further study, application, and collaboration. Each chapter concludes with both a handful of suggestions for next reading (handbooks, introductions, and foundational texts) as well as a full bibliography for fuller research. Each chapter is therefore self-contained and may be read on its own, but the parallel structure should facilitate comparison and contrast between theories, as the reader seeks to evaluate each theory.

The biblical text has come to us as written language, a reduced form of the original communication. The various linguistic theories have done much to illuminate that text and that communication. May this volume be one more step in furthering the pursuit of studying the text for the sake of understanding.

References

Bybee, Joan, Revere Perkins, and William Pagliuca. 1994. *The Evolution of Grammar: Tense, Aspect and Modality in the Languages of the World*. Chicago: University of Chicago Press.

Cook, John A. 2012. *Time and the Biblical Hebrew Verb: The Expression of Tense, Aspect, and Modality in Biblical Hebrew*. Winona Lake, IN: Eisenbrauns.

GENERATIVE LINGUISTICS AS A THEORETICAL FRAMEWORK FOR THE EXPLANATION OF PROBLEMATIC CONSTRUCTIONS IN BIBLICAL HEBREW[1]

Jacobus A. Naudé and Cynthia L. Miller-Naudé

1.0. Introduction

Do linguistic theories, in general, and generative linguistics, in particular, benefit the interpretation of a biblical text in any way and, if so, how? This is the question addressed in this chapter.

In the meaning-making process of textual interpretation, linguistic knowledge provides interpreters of the text with knowledge of language structure, metalanguage, and methodology through which they can describe and explain problematic instances of language use in the text under consideration. The

---

[1] This work is based on research supported in part by the National Research Foundation of South Africa (Jacobus A. Naudé UID 85902 and Cynthia L. Miller-Naudé UID 95926). The grantholders acknowledge that opinions, findings, and conclusions or recommendations expressed in any publication generated by the NRF-supported research are those of the authors, and that the NRF accepts no liability whatsoever in this regard.

process of linguistic inquiry proceeds by observation, description, and explanation of language use. Explanation of language use is the stage at which linguists endeavour to establish the underlying rules that speakers internalise to construct and use sounds, words, and sentences, as well as the ways in which meanings are assigned to these units of language in order to communicate (Naudé and Miller-Naudé 2020, 15). By developing a consistent analysis of the systematic regularities in the language of a text, linguistics contributes to interpretation (Traugott and Pratt 1980, 20). A linguistic reading that is sensitive to the grammatical, sociological, and psychological aspects of language (such as choices of words and sentence types) possesses conventional reverberations and associations for readers (Fowler 1977, 4). We will argue that the linguistic knowledge contributed by linguistic theories, in particular generative linguistics, is indispensable for the text interpretation process.

2.0. Historical Development and Concepts of Generative Linguistics

2.1. Goal of the Generative Enterprise

Noam Chomsky (1928–), Institute Professor Emeritus in the Department of Linguistics and Philosophy at the Massachusetts Institute of Technology, introduced generative grammar with his book *Syntactic Structures* (1957). The main purpose of the generative enterprise is to suggest an explanatory hypothesis concerning the nature of language and ultimately human thought (Chomsky 1982a, 5–58; 2019, 265–66). Accordingly, the object of linguistic study from a generative point of view is the knowledge that native speakers possess that enables them to produce and understand sentences. A generative grammar is thus an analysis of the mental mechanisms that enumerate all the grammatical sentences of a language—and only those that are grammatical—and assign to each an appropriate structural description (Chomsky 1965, 4–5). Chomsky (1986a, 3; 1991a, 6) formulated three basic questions that frame this inquiry: (1) what constitutes knowledge of language, (2) how is such knowledge acquired, and (3) how is such knowledge put to use?

Concerning the first question, the internalised knowledge of speakers is called 'language competence' (Chomsky 1965, 3–9). It refers to the knowledge of finite sounds and rules of phonology, finite words and rules for the formation of meaningful words, as well as finite rules for the production of an infinite number of sentences and their meanings. The notion of language as generative (i.e., language as a system that provides for infinite use of finite means) lies at the heart of generative linguistics and provides a solution to Von Humboldt's problem of what constitutes knowledge of language (Chomsky 1991a, 6–14).

The second problem is known as 'Plato's problem': how is it possible that children acquire language so early, effortlessly, and with so little experience with language data, in comparison to the acquisition of number systems and writing systems, which take many years to learn? Furthermore, how is this rich system of language knowledge shared (Chomsky 1986a, 51–220; 1991a, 15–17)? Chomsky proposed that the innate component of the language faculty as represented in the mind/brain makes early child language acquisition effortless. This biologically innate language faculty (or Universal Grammar, UG) helps children to make sense of the language data to which they are exposed and to build an internal grammar (I[nternal]-language; Chomsky 1986a, 21–24), which is used to produce the sentences the children utter (E[xternal]-language; Chomsky 1986a, 19–21).

The third question concerns the individual's use of language knowledge in acts of communication—namely speech production and speech perception—which Chomsky (1965, 10–15) called 'language performance'. In this regard, Descartes and his followers made three observations (Chomsky 1972a, 5–14). Firstly, normal use of language is innovative; utterances are mostly new and not a repetition or even similar in pattern to previous utterances. This is similar to Chomsky's (1957, 15) view that a speaker is able to understand/interpret and produce an infinite number of new, previously unheard utterances. Secondly, humans do not have to communicate in response to stimuli or instinct; humans are free to think and express themselves at will. This is similar to Chomsky's (2002 [1966], 52–62) view that normal use of language is free from stimulus control and can therefore serve as an instrument of thought and self-expression. Thirdly, the normal use of language is coherent and appropriate to the situation. This creative aspect of language use provides an answer to Descartes's problem of how knowledge of language is put to use (Chomsky 2002 [1966], 51–71; 1991a, 15–19). One can explain the complex creative linguistic behaviour of humans only by concluding that it is determined by intrinsic properties of mental organisation. This happens as an internal grammar

(I-language) generates structural descriptions or representations that specify the linguistic elements for each expression (E-language; Chomsky 1964c, 7–9; 2002 [1966], 72–93; 1991a, 17–20).

The goal of generative linguistics is therefore "to construct a formalized general theory of linguistic structure" to account for these states of affairs and provide solutions for many other related problems for which the theory was not actually designed (Chomsky 1957, 5). To achieve this goal, focus is specifically on "syntactic structure, both in the broad sense (as opposed to semantics) and the narrow sense (as opposed to phonemics and morphology)" (Chomsky 1957, 5). Although generative linguists use deduction and intuition to construct theories of language structure, they test them against actual language data.

2.2. Autonomy of Syntax

Chomsky's *Syntactic Structures* (1957) introduced the theoretical study of syntax. To derive sentences, Chomsky (1957, 45–46) formalised a tripartite arrangement of grammar, consisting of phrase structure, transformational structure, and morphophonemics. The output of phrase structure is a sequence of morphemes, though not necessarily in the correct order. The rules of the transformational structure may rearrange, add, or delete morphemes to yield a string of words. The morphophonemic rules convert this string of words into a string of phonemes. In short, to encode dependencies between sentence parts (word order), a system of phrase structure rules produces basic sentences, while transformational rules derive all other sentences from these basic sentences. For example, active sentences are considered basic, whereas passive sentences are derived from active sentences by means of transformational rules (Chomsky 1957, 42–43). Accordingly, transformations must involve important semantic consequences.

Although Chomsky (1957, 13–17, 92–105) considered the question of how the meaning of a sentence is related to its syntactic form, his conclusion was that grammar is "best formulated as a self-contained study independent of semantics" (106). To avoid misunderstanding of the nature of the relationship between syntax and semantics, this conclusion must be understood in light of the following statement by Chomsky (1957, 102):

> We can judge formal theories in terms of their ability to explain and clarify a variety of facts about the way in which sentences are used and understood. In other words, we should like the syntactic framework of the language that is isolated and exhibited by the grammar to be able to support semantic description, and we shall naturally rate more highly a theory of formal structure that leads to grammars that meet this requirement more fully.

Instead of viewing the emergence of the theory of linguistic structure as a succession of different models with numerous modifications, it must rather be viewed as a single model that is continually subject to critical assessments in terms of new questions and insights, and that is accordingly modified (Van Riemsdijk and Williams 1986, 171). The various terms used to designate the model are used to refer to the respective periods in the history of generative linguistics over nearly seven decades. The following sections provide an overview of these respective periods.

2.3. Standard Theory Model

The success of a linguistic theory is tested for adequacy by the degree to which the structures generated by the syntactic rules form a suitable basis for semantic interpretation. In 1962, Chomsky (1964a, 936; 1964b, 77; 1964c, 51) considered the incorporation of semantics into generative grammar:

> In general, as syntactic description becomes deeper, what appear to be semantic questions fall increasingly within its scope; and it is not entirely obvious whether or where one can draw a natural bound between grammar and 'logical grammar', in the sense of Wittgenstein and the Oxford philosophers. Nevertheless, it seems clear that explanatory adequacy for descriptive semantics requires, beyond this, the development of an independent semantic theory (analogous, perhaps, to the theory of universal phonetics as mentioned below) that deals with questions of a kind that can scarcely be coherently formulated today, in particular, with the question: what are the substantive and formal constraints on systems of concepts that are constructed by humans on the basis of presented data?

This role of semantics was addressed by Katz and Fodor (1963) and Katz and Postal (1964; see Chomsky 1964c, 14). In the same way that Chomsky (1957) wanted to make explicit what the speaker knows of *syntactic* structure, they wanted to make explicit what the speaker knows of the *meanings* of words and sentences. These proposals led to the incorporation of semantics into the model known as the Standard Theory (ST; Chomsky 1969, 5), which was described by Chomsky (1965, 132–36).

The ST exhibits a triangular organisation containing a syntactic component and two interpretive components, one phonological and one semantic (Chomsky 1964c, 9–10; 1965, 15–18; Katz and Postal 1964, 161). Chomsky (1965, 135) puts forward the hypothesis that semantic interpretation is made only in the underlying or deep structure. Specifically, the syntactic component consists of a base sub-component and a transformational sub-component (Chomsky 1965, 106–11, 141). The former generates a deep structure where words from the lexicon are inserted into a preterminal string of dummy elements of the categorial part (Chomsky 1965, 120), which is submitted to the semantic component for semantic interpretation. Without changing meaning, the transformational sub-component maps deep structure into surface structure by reordering elements (Chomsky 1965, 123–24), which enter the phonological component for phonetic interpretation by the rules for pronunciation (Chomsky 1965, 135).

The interpretive components play no part in the recursive generation of sentence structures (Chomsky 1965, 141). Syntax is self-contained (see Chomsky 1965, 226 n. 15). For the interpretation of a sentence, the syntactic component of the grammar relates a semantic interpretation of the underlying structure to a phonetic representation on surface level (Chomsky 1965, 136). Chomsky (1965, v–vi) clearly states that this hypothesis is merely tentative and emerging.

2.4. Generative Semantics

Katz and Postal (1964, 71) argued that semantic interpretations are uniquely assigned to deep structures, a viewpoint also reflected in the ST. This requirement means that the transformational sub-component of the syntactic component does not contribute in any way to semantic interpretation. "Transformations do not affect meaning" became known as the Katz-Postal Hypothesis (Chomsky 1965, 132, 135; 1977a, 140–43). Katz and Postal (1964, 72–156) defend their hypothesis by re-examining apparent counterexamples, for example, the derivations of active/passive, negatives, imperatives, questions, etc., and claim that "their present formulation is not entirely adequate" (71). Unsurprisingly, this model, known as 'interpretive semantics' (Chomsky 1977a, 145), was soon challenged, especially because of the exclusive link it postulated between semantics and deep structure.

In his exposition of the ST, Chomsky (1965, 224 n. 9) already expressed his doubts about the Katz-Postal Hypothesis. Chomsky (1977a, 151) mentioned the critique of Ray Jackendoff as the first to show that surface structure plays a role in semantic interpretation. Chomsky (1972a, 100–14) argued that this restriction on the nature of transformations is too strong; there are cases where transformations have semantic effects. Both deep and surface structure enter into the determination of meaning: deep structure *inter alia* for predication and modification, and surface structure for focus, presupposition, topic and comment, the scope of logical elements (including quantifiers), and pronominal reference, a view that eventually led to the Extended Standard Theory model (see §2.5).

George Lakoff laid the foundations for the development of Generative Semantics in his dissertation published in 1970. Lakoff and others argued that, if the deep component were of a semantic rather than a syntactic nature, and if the difference between the semantic component and the deep syntactic component were erased, meaning differences could all be expressed as an underlying semantic representation. Consequently, the independent deep syntactic component of the ST would cease to exist as an independent level of description and become indistinguishable from the semantic level. From 1966 until the early 1970s, the theory of Generative Semantics was developed, which replaced the base of the ST with an abstract semantic level from which meanings were mapped into surface structures by transformations according to a unilinear structure of input-output relations (Lakoff 1968, 1–84; 1971, 232–96). This approach is known as the transformationalist position (Chomsky 1972b, 17).

Chomsky argued that transformational derivation in Generative Semantics cannot naturally capture structures that exhibit significant syntactic differences, when they are assigned identical underlying structures (Chomsky 1966, 48–49; 1972b, 11–61). Jackendoff (1972, xi) opted for the formulation of proper rules of semantic interpretation to account for semantic phenomena and to leave the syntactic component as free of semantic intervention as it was in *Syntactic Structures*. Katz (1972; 1977) continued to pursue the basic approach to semantics as exposed in Katz and Fodor (1963).

Although Generative Semantics was eventually unsuccessful because of the failure to distinguish between syntactic and non-syntactic properties of sentence structure, it served as a catalyst for the further study of semantics (Van Riemsdijk and Williams 1986, 88).

2.5. Extended Standard Theory Model

In 1972, Chomsky published a more refined theory of semantic interpretation. Chomsky (1972b, 11–202) described in three essays the shortcomings that arose within the ST, resulting in the emergence of the Extended Standard Theory (EST; Chomsky 1970, 10). In EST, the semantic component does not operate solely on the output of the deep syntactic component, but also on the output of the transformational component (Chomsky 1972b, 5). This constitutes the Chomskyan departure from the ST set out in Katz and Postal (1964) and Chomsky (1965). In EST, semantic representation is shared between the underlying structure (for thematic and case structure) and the surface structure (for rules of anaphora and quantification; Chomsky 1972b, 62–119). In other words, the semantic component relates both the deep structure and the surface structure to a semantic representation. However, the grammatical relations expressed in a sentence are inherent in the syntactic deep structure. A separate semantic component with a purely interpretive role is still assumed (Chomsky 1972b, 120–202).

Chomsky (1972b, 11–61) also extends grammatical theory to incorporate syntactic features, thus formulating the 'lexicalist position'. He also presents evidence that EST is to be preferred over Generative Semantics on methodological as well as empirical grounds (62–202).

2.6. Revised Extended Standard Theory Model

Chomsky (1975a) proposed further theoretical refinements, in particular the Revised Extended Standard Theory (REST), where semantic representation appears only in the surface structure. The syntactic and semantic properties of the deep structures of the ST and the EST are dissociated (Chomsky 1975a, 81–82). Chomsky (1975a, 82) also dropped the term 'deep structure', utilising instead 'initial phrase marker', but retaining the term 'surface structure' (see also Chomsky 1977a, 169–79). This theoretical change was made possible by the introduction of 'traces' (called 'copies' since 1995), which mark the original positions of moved elements in the underlying structure (Chomsky 1975a, 86–103; 1977a, 165). As a result, the rules of thematic and case structure were applied to surface structure, thereby simplifying the semantic component (Chomsky 1975a, 116–18).

Accordingly, derivations within the REST model are as follows (Chomsky 1975a, 103–5; 1977a, 165). The rules of the categorial component (i.e., the lexical categories) and the lexicon provide initial phrase markers. The rules of the transformational component convert the initial phrase markers to surface structures (including traces), which undergo semantic interpretation (involving bound anaphora, scope, thematic relations, etc.) to convert the surface structures into logical forms (Chomsky 1977a, 165–66). For fuller representation of meaning, the generated logical forms are subject to further interpretation by other semantic rules that interact with other cognitive structures.

The picture which emerged with the REST model suggests that the grammar consists of various autonomous components (syntax, phonology, semantics), which have their own rules and interact with each other only at the relevant interface (Van Riemsdijk and Williams 1986, 174). In the description and explanation of a particular language, each of these components and their interrelations must come into its own.

Enriched with idiosyncratic transformational rules, the model at this stage faced the problem of how to characterise the initial state of the language faculty (to have explanatory adequacy) and show how it maps language experience to the final state attained (to have descriptive adequacy). To achieve explanatory adequacy, a theory of the initial state can allow only limited variation. This insight led to a refinement of generative grammar with the shift towards the Principles-and-Parameters approach (Chomsky 1981a; 1991b, 417), discussed below, where the initial state of language is represented as a system of innate formal principles with associated open parameters, the values of which are fixed by linguistic experience for each specific language.

2.7. Principles-and-Parameters Approach

So far the emphasis was on the *similarities* between languages. The question was how to account for the *differences* between languages. Chomsky realised that the apparent complexity and variety of languages can be viewed as superficial, the result of minor changes in a fixed and invariant system. Accordingly, it is possible to attribute only limited variation to the innate language faculty (or UG) so that explanatory adequacy can be achieved.

In a series of publications, Chomsky (1977b; 1977c; 1978; 1980; Chomsky and Lasnik 1977) dismantled the rich idiosyncratic transformational rules of the previous models. The rethinking of many problematic aspects of the theory of grammar during this period is discussed in Chomsky (1982a, 61–120). The process resulted in the Pisa Lectures (Chomsky 1981b), which are an exposition of the Principles-and-Parameters approach (Chomsky 1991b, 417) or so-called Government-Binding theory—the principle of 'government' relates items to one another; the principle of 'binding' determines which nominals in a sentence are co-referential. Chomsky (1991b, 448 n. 1) depicted the name Government-Binding theory as "a misleading term that should be abandoned." The model consists of a subsystem of rules and a subsystem of parameterised principles. Chomsky (1982b, 7) remarked:

> In the course of this work, there has been a gradual shift of focus from the study of rule systems, which have increasingly been regarded as impoverished (as we would hope to be the case) to the study of systems of principles, which appear to occupy a much more central position in determining the character and variety of possible human languages.

According to Chomsky (1991b, 417), "a language is not, then, a system of rules, but a set of specifications for parameters in an invariant system of principles of Universal Grammar (UG)."

The subsystem of rules is reduced as follows: the notions of deep- and surface-structures have been renamed D-structure and S-structure, respectively, since their roles are similar but not identical. The levels of D-structure and S-structure are mapped by the transformational operation of Move α ('move alpha'), where α is a variable, meaning that a structure may be altered by movement of one or more elements; independent principles determine what can move and where it can move (Chomsky 1981b, 5). Semantic representation is replaced by the notion

Logical Form (LF) as a level of representation, which is a partial representation of the structural meaning of a sentence. Quantifier scope, the scope of question-words, and reflexive interpretation are examples that are dealt with on this level. Similarly, the phonetic representation is replaced by Phonetic Form (PF; Chomsky 1981b, 18).

The subsystem of universal principles consists of bounding theory (subjacency), government theory, theta-theory (assignment of thematic roles), binding theory (co-referentiality of nominals), Case theory (assignment of abstract Case), and control theory (reference of abstract pronominals; Chomsky 1981b, 5–6). Each of these theories comprises a principle or set of principles. Each of the principles has a parameter which has to be set as plus/minus on the basis of language-specific evidence. Parametric settings account for variation across languages, as well as for language acquisition (Hyams 1986). The rules of a specific language are the principles of UG as parameterised for that specific language (Chomsky 1991b, 417).

The setting of parameters provides the opportunity for a new comparative syntax to explain language variation historically and cross-linguistically. An example is the null subject or pro-drop parameter, which distinguishes languages that do not allow a subject pronoun to be omitted (e.g., English) and those that do (e.g., Italian; Rizzi 1982, 117–84). Certain properties systematically correlate with the null subject property, for example that an overt subject can occupy a postverbal position (Chomsky 1981b, 240–48). In §3.2, the null subject or pro-drop parameter is used to explain the syntactic distribution of independent personal pronouns in Biblical Hebrew.

Generative grammar, and specifically the Principles-and-Parameters approach, is couched in traditional grammatical terminology. Lexical categories include N(oun), V(erb), A (adjective/adverb), and P(reposition); functional/grammatical categories include D(eterminer), T(ense), Asp(ect), M(ood), and C (complementiser/coordinator). Whereas lexical categories are acquired, can be translated, borrowed, and have meaning, functional grammatical categories do not have lexical meaning, are rarely borrowed, and may be contracted or lack stress. All of these categories project into phrases (i.e., groups of words that belong together), which are named after their most important part, the head. Phrases may be formed from lexical categories (verb phrase, noun phrase, etc.) and functional/grammatical categories (determiner phrase, tense phrase, etc.).

From 1982 to 1991, Chomsky proposed numerous refinements to the Principles-and-Parameters approach (see 1982b; 1986a; 1986b; 1988; Chomsky and Lasnik 1993). The most important of these refinements (which directly influenced existing syntactic analyses of Biblical Hebrew syntax and have implications for further analyses) concerns functional projections (Pollock 1989; Abney 1987; Rizzi 1997). These include the VP-Internal Subject Hypothesis, which proposes that the thematic position of the subject is internal to the VP (verb phrase), as well as the Split INFL (Inflection) Hypothesis, which proposes that Inflection be decomposed into two separate functional heads, AGR (Agreement) and T (Tense; Pollock 1989). These two functional projections have implications for the analysis of the infinitive in Biblical Hebrew as well as for verb agreement and pro-drop (see §§3.2, 3.4, 3.5, and 3.8). A third functional projection is the DP (determiner phrase) Hypothesis, which proposes that noun phrases are in fact projections of a functional head, the determiner (D; Abney 1987). This functional projection has implications for the analysis of the quantifier כל, which may occur inside or outside of the DP to produce different meanings (see §3.6). A fourth innovation is the Split CP (complementiser phrase) Hypothesis, which concerns "the fine structure of the left periphery" (Rizzi 1997, 281). A central point of departure is that the discourse-pragmatic orientation of sentences is expressed within the CP domain. Accordingly, the C (complementiser) head is divided into four heads, each with its own projection, namely, Topic, Focus, Force (overt morphological encoding for declaratives, questions, relatives, etc.), and Finiteness (expresses a distinction related to tense and other inflectional specifications). This refinement accounts for at least the distribution of the *wayyiqtol/waw* consecutive construction as well as for left dislocation and topicalisation in Biblical Hebrew (see §3.3).

2.8. Minimalist Programme

Considerations of conceptual naturalness that have some independent plausibility, which the human language faculty should be expected to satisfy—such as simplicity, economy, symmetry, and nonredundancy (see Chomsky 1975b, 113–28; 1991b, 417–54; 2019, 264–65)—led to further refinements in the 1990s with the Minimalist Programme, the most recent instantiation of generative syntax. Despite some differences, many of the concepts developed in the Principles-and-Parameters approach carry over to the Minimalist Programme and the challenge is how to integrate them (e.g., V[erb]-movement).

Chomsky introduced the Minimalist Programme in three publications (1992; 1994; 1995). In the main source (Chomsky 1995), the computational system of language (i.e., the syntactic component) is assumed to contain only what is necessary to build representations that connect meaning to sound (or signs or writing); these representations are the same for all languages. In other words, the computational system of language serves as input to the semantic component, which maps (or converts) the syntactic structure into a corresponding semantic representation (i.e., a representation of linguistic aspects of its meaning). The semantic representation interfaces with systems of thought, namely, the Conceptual-Intentional system (responsible for interpretation and non-linguistic knowledge). The computational system of language serves also as input to the Phonetic Form (PF) component, which maps the syntactic structure into a PF representation (i.e., a representation that provides a phonetic 'spellout', or pronunciation, of sentences). The PF representation interfaces with the Sensory-Motor system (responsible for externalising the derivation in speech systems, i.e., providing spoken, but also signed or written, representations). The Minimalist model for deriving a sentence involves making a selection from the lexicon (which contains all the lexical items in a language as well as their linguistic properties) and then using the computational operation 'Merge' to bring these items together from bottom to top. Merge includes what was previously referred to as 'move' (e.g., when the merging element is taken from inside the derivation and copied). Refinements of the Minimalist Programme followed (Chomsky 1998; 1999).

Derivations and structural representations have become extremely bare in the Minimalist Programme. In recent years, the focus has shifted from a rich UG to innate mechanisms that are part of more general cognitive principles of organic systems (Chomsky 2004; 2005; 2007; 2013; 2015; 2019):

a) Chomsky (2004; 2005) identifies the factors that are crucial in the development of language, namely, the previous two factors—UG and experience (the input of a specific language)—and a new factor, principles of efficient computation (not specific to the language faculty), which include the Economy Principles.

b) Chomsky (2007) follows Borer (1984), where parameters are seen as choices of feature specifications as the child acquires a lexicon, the so-called Borer-Chomsky Conjecture (see Baker 2008, 156). The computational system of every language is identical, but the parametric choices are lexical and account for the variety of languages, as well as, for example, the determination of linear order.

c) Representation by means of trees is common in generative grammar, but they are no longer used in the Problems-of-Projection approach to phrase/clause structure, according to Chomsky (2013; 2015). A derivation is not labelled when it is built. The labelling is done when the syntax hands over its combined sets to the interfaces, the interaction between components of grammar.

d) Chomsky (2019) reviews some foundational aspects of the theory of structure building—essentially, Merge and Label—while still accounting for recursive structure, displacement, and reconstruction (as the main empirical goals of the Minimalist Programme).

To summarise, Chomsky's vision of a fixed syntactic component with cross-linguistic variation triggered by differences in the lexicon continues as the most productive avenue of research in the Minimalist Programme, whose core assumption is that grammars are minimally complex systems of optimal design with parameters set by features of lexical items. The main innate mechanism of UG is seen as Merge, an operation by which two constituents are combined to form a single larger constituent (e.g., a complement merges first with its head and then the specifier of the head is merged to this complex). In other words, a derivation starts with a selection from the lexicon and then merges these elements from bottom to top. The derivation proceeds as follows: a verb phrase (VP), which includes the verb with its aspectual information and the arguments with their thematic roles; a tense phrase (TP), which connects the VP to information on finiteness, tense, agreement, and case; a complementiser phrase (CP), which connects the TP to pragmatic information (mood, topic, focus) or to another clause. Movement of constituents may include movement of topic, focus, and wh-elements (that is, a question/interrogative word or relative item, such as *what, who, which, when, why, how*) as well as head-movement of the verb (V) and tense (T).

The most productive work using generative grammar to explain syntactic constructions in Biblical Hebrew has been done in terms of the Principles-and-Parameters approach and the refinements in the Minimalist Programme. An overview of these contributions will be provided in the following section.

3.0. Contributions of Generative Linguistics to Biblical Hebrew

3.1. Introduction

As is clear from the overview of the development of Chomskyan generative linguistics in the preceding section, the focus has been on the syntactic structure of language. For this reason, the examples selected for discussion in this section relate primarily to syntax. The focus on syntax, however, should not detract from the fact that generative linguistics has developed and contributed to other linguistic subdisciplines (e.g., phonology, morphology, semantics, pragmatics), which have also benefitted Biblical Hebrew.[2]

---

[2] These linguistic subdisciplines include: phonology and morphology (e.g., Prince 1975; Rappaport 1984; McCarthy 1985 [1979]; Malone 1993; Dresher 1994; Churchyard 1999; Coetzee 1999; DeCaen 2003; Dresher 2009a; 2009b; Himmelreich and Bat-El Foux 2021); phonological aspects of the Masoretic accentual system (e.g., Dresher 1994; DeCaen and Dresher 2021; Pitcher 2021); and the morphology, syntax, and semantics/pragmatics of the Biblical Hebrew verbal system and verb phrase (e.g., DeCaen 1995; Hatav 1997; DeCaen 1999; Harbour 1999; Pereltsvaig 2002; Hatav 2004; 2006; Holmstedt 2009;

3.2. Null Subjects, Constituent Order, and the Meaning-Making of Independent Pronouns

An important typological classification based on the Principles-and-Parameters approach concerns the observation that languages can be divided into those with grammatically *optional* subjects (i.e., null subject languages or pro-drop languages) like Hebrew and those with *obligatory* subjects (i.e., non-null subject languages or non-pro-drop languages) like English. In this regard, Chomsky (1981b, 65) introduced the 'Avoid Pronoun Principle', which imposes the choice of a null subject over an overt subject pronoun where possible. The availability of null subjects in Hebrew correlates with the inflectional richness of agreement on the finite verb form (Borer 1989). Naudé (1991a; 1993b; 1994a; 1994b) demonstrates the specific aspects of null subjects for BH and Qumran Hebrew, where the *qaṭal*/perfect, *yiqṭol*/imperfect, *wayyiqṭol*, and *wəqaṭal* verb forms allow null subjects. Subject pronouns that are used with null subject verb forms can be utilised only as subject topics (see §3.3 below on topicalisation and the differences between Biblical Hebrew and Qumran Hebrew in this regard). By contrast, participles functioning as the predicate in clauses do not allow null subjects. As a result, an overt subject with a participial predicate, as in (1), is not 'marked' for topic or focus; it is neutral because an overt subject is grammatically required:

Hatav 2011; 2017; 2020; Boulet 2021; Cowper and DeCaen 2021; Doron 2021; Grasso 2021; Hatav 2021).

(1) כַּחֲצֹת הַלַּיְלָה אֲנִי יוֹצֵא בְּתוֹךְ מִצְרָיִם

'Towards midnight I will go out in the midst of the Egyptians.' (Exod. 11.4)

The 'Avoid Pronoun Principle' of the Principles-and-Parameters approach and the Economy Principles of the Minimalist Programme explain the distribution of independent subject pronouns as opposed to null subjects in BH in a principled syntactic way for the first time. With the *qaṭal*/perfect and *yiqṭol*/imperfect, the subject pronouns as topics appear only in preverbal position, but with *wayyiqṭol* and *wəqaṭal* verb forms they occur only in postverbal position. In the following section, we demonstrate that there are syntactic mechanisms that explain this asymmetry.

Government and Binding also provides insight into the syntax of BH participial forms. For example, the structure of BH allows the use of participles in attributive constructions while maintaining the verbal characteristics of the verbal form (i.e., its verbal valency; e.g., Num. 13.32, הָאָרֶץ אֲשֶׁר עָבַרְנוּ בָהּ לָתוּר אֹתָהּ אֶרֶץ אֹכֶלֶת יוֹשְׁבֶיהָ הִוא 'the land which we crossed into it to explore it is a land *eating* its inhabitants'). English, in contrast, does not allow attributive participial constructions, but requires that a relative clause be used.

3.3. Non-Canonical Constituent Order and Meaning-Making at Sentence Edges

From its conception, one of the central concerns of generative linguistics has been to characterise the positions in which nominal elements can appear in a specific language, that is, word order (both canonical and non-canonical positions). In early forms of generative linguistics, this was achieved by a transformation (see §2.7) in Principles-and-Parameters and by 'Merge' in the Minimalist Programme, which also entails movement. These theoretical advances made it possible to formally identify and differentiate the constituents that occur at the edges of sentences, a necessary prerequisite for determining what each construction contributes to meaning.[3]

A syntactic construction involving constituents moved to non-canonical positions at the initial sentence periphery is topicalisation. This construction was described in Naudé (1994a) as involving movement to the preverbal topic position:

(2) הַכְזוֹנָה יַעֲשֶׂה אֶת־אֲחוֹתֵנוּ

'<u>Like a whore</u> should he treat our sister $_{\text{like a whore}}$?' (Gen. 34.31)

In this example, the topicalised constituent (underlined) is a prepositional phrase that has been moved to the very beginning of the sentence from its normal position at the end of the sentence. A zero trace (or copy) marks the location where the constituent originally occurred in the sentence (indicated by subscripted type; see §2.6 and §3.8). As indicated in the previous section, the *qaṭal*/perfect and *yiqṭol*/imperfect verbal forms in BH and Qumran Hebrew allow an independent subject pronoun as a subject topic before these verbal forms, but not after them (Naudé 2001).

Naudé (1996a, 181) demonstrates that when the verb is one of the so-called consecutive verb forms in BH, this topic

---

[3] Five of these six edge-constructions in BH were treated together for the first time from a generative perspective in Holmstedt (2014).

position is not preverbal but postverbal. Independent pronouns that occur with consecutive verbs in BH sentences are still subject topics, even though they occur postverbally:

(3) לָק֗וֹחַ מֵאֵ֣ת הַגּוֹלָ֗ה מֵחֶלְדַּ֤י וּמֵאֵ֣ת טוֹבִיָּה֙ וּמֵאֵ֣ת יְדַֽעְיָ֔ה וּבָאתָ֤ אַתָּה֙ בַּיּ֣וֹם הַה֔וּא וּבָאתָ֗ בֵּ֚ית יֹאשִׁיָּ֣ה בֶן־צְפַנְיָ֔ה אֲשֶׁר־בָּ֖אוּ מִבָּבֶֽל

'Take from the exiled community, from Heldai, Tobijah, and Jedaiah, who have come from Babylon—and (you) will go, you, proceed on that day—you will go to the house of Josiah son of Zephaniah.' (Zech. 6.10)

Naudé (1996a) argues that the sentence-initial position of the consecutive verb forms is the result of obligatory verb movement ('verb raising' in generative grammar). This parameter occurs in BH, but not in later forms of Hebrew (e.g., Qumran Hebrew and Mishnaic Hebrew) or Biblical Aramaic. As a result, consecutive verb forms in Qumran Hebrew, for example, are not attested with the independent subject pronoun following the verb. Generative grammar thus provides a principled means to distinguish the appearance and absence of independent subject pronouns with finite, pro-drop verbs. It also assists in identifying the locus of both language difference and language change (see further §3.9 below).

The second construction, left dislocation (identified in Naudé 1990), involves a constituent that occurs outside of the sentence (indicated by double underlining) and has a resumptive element that occurs within the sentence (indicated by underlining and bold type):

(4) וּלְמִיכַ֣ל בַּת־שָׁא֗וּל לֹֽא־הָ֥יָה לָ֛הּ יָ֖לֶד עַ֥ד י֥וֹם מוֹתָֽהּ

'To Michal daughter of Saul, there was **to her** no child (i.e., she had no child) until the day of her death.' (2 Sam. 6.23)

In this example, the resumptive element occurs *in situ*, that is, in the normal position of the constituent in the sentence. It is also possible for the resumptive element itself to be in a preverbal topic position so that it occurs at the beginning of the sentence proper:

(5) וְעִם־הָאֲמָהוֹת אֲשֶׁר אָמַרְתָּ עִמָּם אִכָּבֵדָה

'…and <u>among the slave girls that you speak of</u>, **among them** I will be honoured _{among them}.' (2 Sam. 6.22)

In other words, the example exhibits both left dislocation of a constituent and its resumption in the matrix sentence, and also topicalisation of the resumptive element within the matrix sentence. Because topicalisation and left dislocation may occur in the same sentence, they must be distinct constructions. Analyses that indiscriminately merge the two constructions into 'fronting' (or *casus pendens*) obscure the distinctive features and thus the meanings of the constructions.

A third construction is like topicalisation in having no resumptive element within the sentence, although a constituent apparently occurs outside of the left edge of the sentence. Naudé (1990, 124; see also 1999), who first identified this construction, referred to it as a variety of topicalisation. Holmstedt (2014) refers to it as 'heavy topic fronting'. We use the term 'heavy topicalisation' (Miller-Naudé and Naudé 2019; 2021):

(6) וַאדֹנִי הַמֶּלֶךְ לָמָּה חָפֵץ בַּדָּבָר הַזֶּה

'…but (as for) <u>my lord the king</u>, why does he delight _{my lord the king} in this thing?' (2 Sam. 24.3)

In this example, the initial boundary of the matrix sentence is indicated by the interrogative particle, but the constituent outside of the left edge of the sentence is not resumed within the sentence proper.

The fourth construction is extraposition. In the same way that topicalisation moves a constituent out of its canonical position to the preverbal topic position at the beginning of a sentence, extraposition involves a constituent that is moved to the end of the sentence outside of its canonical position:

(7) יִהְיוּ כְאַיִן וּכְאֶפֶס אַנְשֵׁי מִלְחַמְתֶּךָ

'_{…the men who battle against you} will be as nothing and non-existent <u>the men who battle against you</u>.' (Isa. 41.12)

Like topicalisation, extraposition does not involve resumption within the matrix sentence.[4]

The fifth construction is right dislocation. In many ways this construction is the mirror image of left dislocation in that a constituent occurs outside of the end-periphery of the sentence and a co-referential element occurs within the sentence proper:

(8) וַיֵּצֵא מֶלֶךְ־סְדֹם וּמֶלֶךְ עֲמֹרָה וּמֶלֶךְ אַדְמָה וּמֶלֶךְ צְבֹיִים וּמֶלֶךְ בֶּלַע הִוא־צֹעַר וַיַּעַרְכוּ אִתָּם מִלְחָמָה בְּעֵמֶק הַשִּׂדִּים אֵת כְּדָרְלָעֹמֶר מֶלֶךְ עֵילָם וְתִדְעָל מֶלֶךְ גּוֹיִם וְאַמְרָפֶל מֶלֶךְ שִׁנְעָר וְאַרְיוֹךְ מֶלֶךְ אֶלָּסָר אַרְבָּעָה מְלָכִים אֶת־הַחֲמִשָּׁה

'The king of Sodom and the king of Gomorrah and the king of Admah and the king of Zeboiim and the king of Bela, which is Zoar, went forth and engaged **them** in battle in the Valley of Siddim—<u>Chedorlaomer king of Elam and</u>

---

[4] For an approach to the differentiation of extraposition from extraposed apposition, see Holmstedt and Jones (2017, 42–47).

<u>Tidal king of Goiim and Amraphel king of Shinar and Arioch king of Ellasar</u>—four kings against five.' (Gen. 14.8-9)

The sixth construction is heavy extraposition, which is the counterpart of heavy topicalisation in having a constituent that is moved beyond the end-periphery of the sentence without resumption inside the sentence. It was identified for the first time in Miller-Naudé and Naudé (2019):

(9) וּבְיָמִים אֲחָדִים יִשָּׁבֵר וְלֹא בְאַפַּיִם וְלֹא בְמִלְחָמָה׃

'And in a few days he will be broken _{not by anger and not in battle} and <u>not by anger and not in battle</u>.' (Dan. 11.20)

If the *waw* is understood as indicating a sentence boundary, then the negated prepositional phrases occur outside of the sentence boundary. Another possible example of heavy extraposition occurs in the following example, where a *waw* introduces a prepositional phrase:

(10) וְאַעֲלֶה בְאֹשׁ מַחֲנֵיכֶם וּבְאַפְּכֶם וְלֹא־שַׁבְתֶּם עָדַי נְאֻם־יְהוָה

'...and I made the stench of your armies rise _{in your nostrils} and <u>in your nostrils</u>. But you did not turn back to me—declares the LORD.' (Amos 4.10)

Furthermore, generative linguistics allows for the differentiation of various kinds of left dislocation on the basis of the nature of agreement features between the dislocated element and the resumptive element. In addition to the heavy topicalisation construction discussed above, Miller-Naudé and Naudé (2021) identify five kinds of left dislocations, namely: clitic left dislocation, where a dislocated constituent exhibits case agreement with its resumptive (11); hanging topic, where the dislocated constituent is always a noun phrase, but the resumptive within the matrix sentence may bear any grammatical relation to the predication (12); left dislocation with deictic resumptive which is coreferential with the dislocated constituent (13); left dislocation with independent pronoun resumptive (14); and left dislocation with a noun phrase resumptive (15).

(11) אֶת־זִמָּתֵךְ וְאֶת־תּוֹעֲבוֹתַיִךְ אַתְּ נְשָׂאתִים
'<u>Your wickedness and your abominations</u>, you bear **them**' (Ezek. 16.58)

(12) צָפוֹן וְיָמִין אַתָּה בְרָאתָם
'<u>North and south</u>, you created **them**' (Ps. 89.13)

(13) וְלִבְנֹתַי מָה־אֶעֱשֶׂה לָאֵלֶּה הַיּוֹם אוֹ לִבְנֵיהֶן אֲשֶׁר יָלָדוּ
'...and <u>for my daughters</u>, what should I do **for these** today or for their sons which they have borne?' (Gen. 31.43)

(14) יְהוָה אֱלֹהֵיכֶם הַהֹלֵךְ לִפְנֵיכֶם הוּא יִלָּחֵם לָכֶם
'<u>The LORD your God who goes before you</u>, **he** will fight for you.' (Deut. 1.30)

(15) וְהַנֶּפֶשׁ אֲשֶׁר־תֹּאכַל בָּשָׂר מִזֶּבַח הַשְּׁלָמִים אֲשֶׁר לַיהוָה וְטֻמְאָתוֹ עָלָיו וְנִכְרְתָה הַנֶּפֶשׁ הַהִוא מֵעַמֶּיהָ
'But <u>the person who eats flesh from the sacrifices of wellbeing which belong to the LORD and his uncleanness is upon him</u>, **that person** shall be cut off from his relatives.' (Lev. 7.20)

A further insight was the discovery of the 'frame of reference' construction, which is neither left dislocation nor topicalisation, but rather a detached noun phrase, which provides the frame of reference for the discourse that follows (Miller-Naudé and Naudé 2021):

(16) וְהַדָּבָר אֲשֶׁר דִּבַּרְנוּ אֲנִי וָאָתָּה הִנֵּה יְהוָה בֵּינִי וּבֵינְךָ עַד־עוֹלָם

'And <u>the word which we spoke, I and you</u>—behold the LORD is between me and between you forever.' (1 Sam. 20.23)

3.4. Pronominal Syntax and the Meaning-Making of Pronominal Reference

The so-called tripartite verbless clause in BH consists of two nominal phrases and a 3ms pronominal element. In the differentiation of the pronominal element, it is either a resumptive element of a left dislocation construction or it is a 'last resort' syntactic strategy in which the pronominal element is a pronominal clitic, providing agreement features for the subject in order to prevent ambiguity in the assignment of subject and predicate (Naudé 1990; 1993b; 1994c; 1999; 2002a; 2002b). Disjunctive and conjunctive accents provide important evidence for prosodic phrasing, which can be utilised for differentiating the role of the pronoun in these two types of sentences, which are otherwise structurally identical (Naudé and Miller-Naudé 2017). Cross-linguistically, left dislocation involves a 'gap' at the boundary between the dislocated constituent and the matrix sentence. In spoken language, this gap may be realised by a small pause or an interjection (Berman and Grosu 1976); in the MT it is marked by a disjunctive accent. In this case the pronominal element is a resumptive of a left dislocation construction:

(17) וְדָוִד הוּא הַקָּטָן

'And (as for) <u>David</u>, **he** was the youngest.' (1 Sam. 17.14)

Where it is marked by a conjunctive accent, there is no gap and the pronominal element is utilised as a 'last resort' syntactic strategy. The pronominal element is a pronominal clitic, which is used to prevent ambiguity in the assignment of subject and predicate (see Doron 1986):

(18) צַדִּיק הוּא יְהוָה

'A righteous one (he) is the LORD.' (Lam. 1.18)

The pronominal clitic is used to indicate that the adjectival constituent should be understood as the subject, rather than the predicate. The conjunctive accent on the first constituent and the pronominal clitic that follows it indicates that the sentence should be interpreted as 'A righteous one is the LORD', not as 'The LORD is righteous' (with the adjective as the predicate).

Generative linguistics has also been used to provide new and insightful analysis of several syntactic constructions involving pronouns. First, the so-called ethical dative with the preposition *lamed* is not a sentence constituent but a reflexive anaphor that is translated in English as *x-self* (e.g., Gen. 22.2 וְלֶךְ־לְךָ אֶל־ אֶרֶץ הַמֹּרִיָּה 'and take *yourself* to the land of Moriah'; Naudé 1995, 1997).

Second, all of the dative constructions in BH can be differentiated with attention to their syntactic features as identified by generative grammar (Naudé 2013); these are summarised in Table 1.

Table 1: Summary of Dative Constructions in Biblical Hebrew

	Ethical	Possessive	Indirect object	Commodi	Experiential
Subcategorised	–	–	+	–	–
Compulsory clitic	+	–	–	+	+
Reflexive anaphor	+	–	–	–	–
Bound to external argument	+	–	–	+	–
Bound to internal argument	–	+	+	–	+

Third, coordinate subjects consisting of an independent personal pronoun and a noun phrase should be understood as an adjunct to the null subject of the finite verb rather than as its subject (Naudé 1999; cf. Holmstedt 2009; Scheumann 2020). In light of the characteristics of null subject languages generally, it is preferable to identify so-called coordinate subjects with independent personal pronouns in BH as adjuncts rather than sentence subjects (e.g., Judg. 11.37 וְאֵלְכָה וְיָרַדְתִּי עַל־הֶהָרִים וְאֶבְכֶּה עַל־בְּתוּלַי אָנֹכִי וְרֵעוֹתָי 'and I will go up and down on the mountains and mourn for my virginity, *I and my companions*'). The structural position of an independent pronoun as a coordinate subject coincides with that of a dislocated constituent in a left/right dislocation, namely, a constituent that is base generated in an adjunct position (Naudé 1999, 75–99).

Finally, generative syntax provides a means to distinguish between pronouns and anaphora (i.e., linguistic units deriving their interpretation from a previously expressed unit of meaning, viz., an antecedent, such as reflexive pronouns and reciprocal pronouns). Because pronouns and anaphora in BH have identical morphological forms (contrast English pronouns *I, me, my* as distinct from the reflexive anaphor *myself* and the reciprocal anaphor *ourselves*), one can only distinguish pronouns and anaphora in BH on the basis of the theoretical syntactic principles of generative grammar; contrast the translation of the pronominal suffix on לוֹ with the pronoun ('him') in Neh. 13.5 as opposed to the anaphor ('himself') in 1 Chron. 15.1. The syntax of the two sentences *appears* to be identical unless one appropriates the insights afforded by generative linguistic theory (see Miller-Naudé and Naudé 2019). Identifying whether a Hebrew form is an anaphor as opposed to a pronoun is critical for translating and interpreting these biblical sentences.

3.5. Lexical Categories and the Meaning-Making of Lexical Morphology

Lexical categorisation or word classes (traditionally called 'parts of speech') in generative grammar is part of Universal Grammar.[5] As indicated above in §2.7, each lexical item in the mental lexicon is identified as a member of a particular category. For lexical categories (as opposed to functional/grammatical categories—see §3.6), generative grammar employs the traditional philological terms N(oun), V(erb), A (adjective/adverb), and P(reposition).

A generative approach to lexical categories provides a heuristic method for lemmatisation within lexica as well as a

---

[5] See Miller-Naudé and Naudé (2017a, 276–88) for a description of categorisation in generative grammar and a comparison of categorisation in Functional Grammar, Cognitive Linguistics, and linguistic typology.

framework for differentiating morphosyntactic characteristics of lexical items as a basis for determining their semantic and pragmatic value(s). As an example of a generative approach to lexical categories, an analysis of טוֹב demonstrates that it must be categorised as an adjective and not a noun on the basis of morphological as well as internal and external syntactic features (Miller-Naudé and Naudé 2017a, 288–303; see also §3.8).

3.6. Quantification and the Meaning-Making of Quantifiers

Quantifiers are a functional category in generative linguistics. Quantifiers specify the amount or quantity of the referents of a noun. In this section, two kinds of quantification are considered: negation and the quantifier כֹל.

3.6.1. Negation

Generative linguistics has contributed to a nuanced understanding of the semantics of negation in BH through the concept of negative scope, which allows interpreters to distinguish between a negative marker that has scope over the entire predication (sentential negation) as opposed to scope over only a constituent (constituent negation; see Snyman and Naudé 2003; Snyman 2004; Naudé and Rendsburg 2013; Miller-Naudé and Naudé 2015; 2017b).

Sentential negation requires the negative marker to immediately precede the verb (e.g., Jer. 23.21 לֹא־שָׁלַחְתִּי אֶת־הַנְּבִאִים 'I did not send the prophets'). By contrast, constituent negation immediately precedes a non-verbal constituent (e.g.,

Gen. 45.8 וְעַתָּ֕ה לֹֽא־אַתֶּ֞ם שְׁלַחְתֶּ֤ם אֹתִי֙ הֵ֔נָּה כִּ֖י הָאֱלֹהִ֑ים 'And now *you* did not send me here, but rather God'). For the negative cycle in BH, see §3.9.

3.6.2. Quantifier כל

Generative linguistics allows interpreters to distinguish four syntactic constructions involving the quantifier כל, differentiated by specific features of the noun phrase (NP) modified by כל (see Table 2).[6] The most important features are definiteness and number, but countability (count nouns, mass nouns, collectives), nominal status, and specificity are also relevant. Each construction conveys various semantic nuances: singular definite (e.g., כָּל־הַיּ֥וֹם הַה֖וּא 'all that day' Exod. 10.13), plural definite (e.g., כָּל־יְמֵ֣י חַיֶּ֑יךָ 'all the days [totality of the specific group] of your life' Gen. 3.14), singular indefinite (e.g., כָּל־י֑וֹם 'every day' Ps. 140.3), plural indefinite (e.g., כָּל־יְמֵ֗י הֱי֛וֹת בֵּית־הָאֱלֹהִ֖ים בְּשִׁלֹֽה 'all [each and every one of] the days the house of God was in Shiloh' Judg. 18.31). When the noun refers to a unique entity or a collective, the singular definite quantified phrase means 'the whole' (e.g., כָּל־הָאָ֑רֶץ 'the whole earth' Gen. 1.29; כָּל־הַקָּהָ֖ל 'the whole assembly' Ezra 2.64).

---

[6] See Naudé (2011a; 2011b) for BH and Naudé and Miller-Naudé (2015; 2022) and Miller-Naudé and Naudé (2020b) for Qumran Hebrew.

Table 2: Syntax and Semantics of כל

		Definite collective, inclusive, specific		Indefinite distributive, implicitly inclusive, non-specific
Singular NP	Meaning	Totality of the individual members of the single entity—each individual entity	Totality of the entity—the whole	Each, every
	Individuation	[+individuation]	—	[+individuation]
	Countability	count noun, mass noun	count noun referring to unique entity / collective noun	count noun
	Nominal status	nominal or pronominal	nominal	nominal
Plural NP	Meaning	Totality of the specific group		Each and every one of the members of the group
	Individuation	[–individuation]	—	[–individuation]
	Countability	count noun, mass noun		count noun
	Nominal status	nominal or pronominal		nominal

Grey highlighting indicates a distinctive class of singular definite nouns that are either count nouns referring to a unique entity or mass nouns. The semantics of כל with this class of nouns differs from other singular definite nouns.

Because BH has additional constructions with כל that are not attested in English or in Modern Hebrew, determining the precise nuance of each construction requires careful attention to the constellation of features—morphological, syntactic, and semantic—that differentiate them.

3.7. Relative Clauses and the Meaning-Making of Relative Nominal Modification

The fact that relative clauses in BH may be either restrictive (identifying the precise referent of the head noun) or non-restrictive (qualifying but not identifying the head noun) in their semantics went unnoticed by philologically-orientated Hebrew grammars, but it is an important linguistic distinction with exegetical ramifications.

Holmstedt (2016, 194–215) provides the linguistic analysis of the two types of relative clauses and the linguistic indicators for differentiating them.[7] For example, in 2 Chron. 15.11 (וַיִּזְבְּחוּ לַיהוָה בַּיּוֹם הַהוּא מִן־הַשָּׁלָל הֵבִיאוּ), the relative clause is syntactically marked as restrictive because of the zero marked relative with a definite head (by contrast, zero marked relative clauses with an indefinite head are non-restrictive). The translation must be 'and they sacrificed to the LORD on that day from the booty that they had brought' (restrictive), rather than 'and they sacrificed to the LORD on that day from the booty, which they had brought' (non-restrictive; see Holmstedt 2016, 210).

---

[7] For the restrictions on the resumptive element in Biblical Aramaic clauses, see Naudé (1991b; 1996).

3.8. Empty Categories, Null Constituents, and the Meaning-Making of Invisible Structure

Generative grammar employs a number of null (or, zero) items. Null items are present in the underlying structure of language but not in the surface structure. Nonetheless, null items affect both the surface realisation of language and its semantic interpretation. A few of these null items are mentioned briefly in this section.

In §3.2, null subjects of finite verbs were discussed. These subjects are not expressed in the surface structure, but they can nonetheless serve as an antecedent (see also §3.4).

In §3.3, the edge constructions that involve movement of a constituent to the left (beginning) of the sentence (viz. topicalisation) or to the right (end) of the sentence (viz. extraposition) contain a null constituent. Moved constructions leave a trace in their original position, which may affect the structure of the sentence.

Relative clauses may optionally have two types of null constituents. Null heads are used frequently in BH (Holmstedt 2016, 113–28) instead of a NP as head (contrast Gen. 27.45 with a null head and Gen. 24.66 with an overt NP as head; see Holmstedt 2016, 114). Interpretation of the semantics of the null head depends upon both "the position of the gap (or trace) or resumptive within the relative clause and the discourse context" (Holmstedt 2016, 115). Zero relatives also occur in BH, alongside a range of overt relative markers (Holmstedt 2016, 81–83). As indicated in §3.7, zero marked relative clauses have a restrictive semantic interpretation when the head of the relative is definite, whereas overtly marked relative clauses may have a restrictive or non-restrictive semantic interpretation.

Recognising that adjectives in BH may modify a null noun provides a principled way to handle the identification of the 'adjective' lexical category. For example, in Gen. 29.16 (וּלְלָבָן שְׁתֵּי בָנוֹת שֵׁם הַגְּדֹלָה לֵאָה וְשֵׁם הַקְּטַנָּה רָחֵל), the determined adjectives הַגְּדֹלָה 'the big' and הַקְּטַנָּה 'the small' must be understood as morphologically agreeing with and modifying the null noun בַּת, so that the adjectives refer to 'the elder [daughter]' and 'the younger [daughter]' (see Miller-Naudé and Naudé 2016). Recognition that an adjective may modify a null noun provides a principled linguistic argument against so-called 'substantival adjectives' in BH.

Another advance has been made in recognising that so-called 'verbless sentences' should be understood as sentences in which the copular verb היה is a null constituent (see, e.g. Naudé 1993a; DeCaen 1999; Sinclair 1999; Cowper and DeCaen 2017; Wilson 2020). Recognition that all predications in Biblical Hebrew have the same underlying structure provides a simplified and unified analysis.

Finally, ellipsis comprises a number of distinct syntactic constructions in which one or more required constituents are present in the underlying representation but are absent in the surface structure (see Miller-Naudé 2005; 2007a; 2007b; 2007c; 2008; 2011; 2013; Holmstedt 2021). Ellipsis therefore requires the hearer/reader to be able to reconstruct appropriate semantic interpretations of sentences with apparently incomplete structures.

3.9. Historical Linguistics and Meaning-Making through Language Change and Variation

Generative linguistics provides a way to identify language change and variation through the change of feature parameters. In examining the change of feature parameter settings between BH and Qumran Hebrew, Naudé (2000; see also 1996a) identifies the following types of changes: change in syntactic category description (viz. grammaticalisation); change in subcategorisation frame of some lexical verbs (e.g., the use of the preposition בְּ to mark the accusative; contrast Jer. 7.26 with 4Q506 131–132.IV.13) and lexical nouns (contrast Isa. 48.17 and 1QIsa^a XL:23); and changes in lexical features of both nouns and verbs.

Another important development in historical linguistics relates to cyclic change, the observation that change often occurs in stages, with later stages of the language resembling earlier stages (Van Gelderen 2011). One important cycle that has been identified in many languages involves the negative existential (see Veselinova 2016), which is also operative in pre-modern Hebrew (see Naudé and Miller-Naudé 2016; Naudé, Miller-Naudé, and Wilson 2019; 2022). One of the most important insights for Biblical Hebrew is the fact that the stages of a cycle are usually overlapping, resulting in synchronic variation alongside diachronic change.

4.0. Prospects for Further Study

The survey of the study of BH in Van der Merwe, Naudé, and Kroeze (2017, 6–12) reveals that comparatively little work has been conducted from the theoretical standpoint of generative linguistics, in spite of its rich and insightful contributions to the study of language in general and to the study of languages in particular. As a point of comparison, Radford's (1997a; 1997b; 2004; 2009) analyses of the structure of English from a Minimalist perspective demonstrate how generative linguistics can be applied to the study of a specific language to produce comprehensive grammatical analyses. There is, unfortunately, nothing even remotely comparable for BH from a generative perspective. The research described in the previous sections only begins to scratch the surface of some of the numerous important, unsolved problems in the structure of BH, which have direct implications for the meaning-making enterprise of textual interpretation.

To conclude, we return to our initial questions. Is linguistics necessary for the interpretation of the languages of the biblical texts? Is it not better—and easier—just to read the texts without theory? In our view, the reading of the biblical texts in the light of linguistic analysis can be compared to the work of meteorologists. Meteorologists study weather patterns scientifically, employing relevant theories for the observation, description, and prediction of weather patterns. The results of meteorological inquiry feed into weather reports, which are delivered in simple, accessible terms for ordinary people to understand. Although sustained observation of the weather by laypersons (e.g., in farming almanacs) may *sometimes* prove to produce accurate forecasts, it is not theoretically informed and does not rest upon scientifically proven methodology. It is therefore vastly inferior to the analysis of weather produced by meteorologists.

If linguistics is necessary for insightful understanding of the biblical text, then which linguistic theory should be used? We need to break with the tradition of viewing linguistics through the reductive lenses of schools, theories, or interdisciplinary exchanges. Instead of the fragmentation of knowledge, the focus must be on the progress of knowledge by its growth or accumulation (see D'hulst and Gambier 2018). Furthermore, the search for knowledge must be a purposeful, meaning-making activity that is functionalist in orientation (Nord 2018). In other words, the search for knowledge within a discipline must be nuanced and it must be typified by the purpose for which it is intended.

In applying the discipline of linguistics to the study of the biblical text, instead of competition between linguistic theories, the move should be to a search for a complex viewpoint, seeing the study of BH as a complex whole (Miller-Naudé and Naudé 2020a; Naudé and Miller-Naudé 2020). However, within a complex approach, the significant and insightful generative linguistic contributions to understanding BH language structure cannot be minimised or ignored.

5.0. Further Reading

5.1. Handbooks, Companions, Glossaries

1. Den Dikken (2013)
2. England (1978)
3. Everaert and Van Riemsdijk (2006)
4. Sells (1985)
5. Webelhuth (1995)

5.2. General Introductions

1. Bach (1964)
2. Carnie (2007)
3. Haegeman (1994)
4. Hornstein, Nunes, and Grohmann (2005)
5. Radford (2004; 2009)
6. Van Gelderen (2017)
7. Van Riemsdijk and Williams (1986)

5.3. Foundational Texts

1. Borer (1984)
2. Chomsky (1957; 1965; 1969; 1975b; 1980; 1981b; 1986b; 1992; 1995; 1998; 2013)
3. Jackendoff (1972)
4. Katz and Postal (1964)

References

Abney, Steven P. 1987. *The English Noun Phrase in Its Sentential Aspect*. Cambridge, MA: Department of Linguistics and Philosophy, MIT.

Bach, Emmon. 1964. *An Introduction to Transformational Grammars*. New York: Holt, Rinehart and Winston.

Baker, Mark. 2008. *The Syntax of Agreement and Concord*. Cambridge: Cambridge University Press.

Berman, Ruth, and Alexander Grosu. 1976. 'Aspects of the Copula in Modern Hebrew'. In *Studies in Modern Hebrew Syntax and Semantics*, edited by Peter Cole, 265–85. Amsterdam: North-Holland.

Borer, Hagit. 1984. *Parametric Syntax: Case Studies in Semitic and Romance Languages*. Dordrecht: Foris.

———. 1989. 'Anaphoric AGR'. In *The Null Subject Parameter*, edited by Osvaldo Jaeggli and Kenneth J. Safir, 69–110. Dordrecht: Kluwer.

Boulet, Jacques E. J. 2021. 'Argument Sharing Secondary Predicates in Biblical Hebrew'. In *Linguistic Studies on Biblical Hebrew*, edited by Robert D. Holmstedt, 191–208. Studies in Semitic Languages and Linguistics 102. Leiden: Brill.

Carnie, Andrew. 2007. *Syntax: A Generative Introduction*. 2nd ed. Oxford: Blackwell.

Chomsky, Noam. 1957. *Syntactic Structures*. The Hague: Mouton.

———. 1964a. 'The Logical Basis of Linguistic Theory'. In *Proceedings of the Ninth International Congress of Linguists, Cambridge, Mass., August 27–31, 1962*, edited by Horace G. Lunt, 914–1008. The Hague: Mouton.

———. 1964b. 'Current Issues in Linguistic Theory'. In *The Structure of Language: Readings in the Philosophy of Language*, edited by Jerry A. Fodor and Jerold J. Katz, 50–118. Englewood Cliffs, NJ: Prentice-Hall.

———. 1964c. *Current Issues in Linguistic Theory*. The Hague: Mouton.

———. 1965. *Aspects of the Theory of Syntax*. Cambridge, MA: The MIT Press.

———. 1966. *Topics in the Theory of Generative Grammar*. The Hague: Mouton.

———. 1969. *Deep Structure, Surface Structure, and Semantic Interpretation*. Bloomington, IN: Indiana University Linguistics Club.

———. 1970. *Some Empirical Issues in the Theory of Transformational Grammar*. Bloomington, IN: Indiana University Linguistics Club.

———. 1972a. *Language and Mind*. New York: Harcourt.

———. 1972b. *Studies on Semantics in Generative Grammar*. The Hague: Mouton.

———. 1975a. *Reflections on Language*. Glasgow: Fontana.

———. 1975b. *The Logical Structure of Linguistic Theory*. New York: Plenum.

———. 1977a. *Language and Responsibility: Based on Conversations with Mitsou Ronat*. New York: Pantheon.

———. 1977b. 'On Wh-Movement'. In *Formal Syntax*, edited by Peter W. Culicover, Thomas Wasow, and Adrian Akmajian, 71–132. New York: Academic Press.

———. 1977c. 'Conditions on Rules of Grammar'. In *Current Issues in Linguistic Theory*, edited by Roger W. Cole, 3–50. Bloomington, IN: Indiana University Press.

———. 1978. 'A Theory of Core Grammar'. *GLOT* 1: 7–26.

———. 1980. 'On Binding'. *Linguistic Inquiry* 11 (1): 1–46.

———. 1981a. 'Principles and Parameters in Syntactic Theory'. In *Explanations in Linguistics: The Logical Problem of Language Acquisition*, edited by Norbert Hornstein and David Lightfoot, 32–75. London: Longman.

———. 1981b. *Lectures on Government and Binding: The Pisa Lectures*. Dordrecht: Foris.

———. 1982a. *The Generative Enterprise: A Discussion with Riny Huybregts and Henk van Riemsdijk*. Dordrecht: Foris.

———. 1982b. *Some Concepts and Consequences of the Theory of Government and Binding*. Cambridge, MA: The MIT Press.

———. 1986a. *Knowledge of Language: Its Nature, Origin and Use*. New York: Praeger.

———. 1986b. *Barriers*. Cambridge, MA: The MIT Press.

———. 1988. *Language and Problems of Knowledge: The Managua Lectures*. Cambridge, MA: The MIT Press.

———. 1991a. 'Linguistics and Adjacent Fields: A Personal View'. In *The Chomskyan Turn*, edited by Asa Kasher, 3–25. Cambridge, MA: Basil Blackwell.

———. 1991b. 'Some Notes on Economy of Derivation and Representation'. In *Principles and Parameters in Comparative Grammar*, edited by R. Freidin, 417–54. Cambridge, MA: The MIT Press.

———. 1992. *A Minimalist Program for Linguistic Theory*. MIT Occasional Papers in Linguistics 1. Cambridge, MA: Department of Linguistics and Philosophy, MIT.

———. 1994. *Bare Phrase Structure*. MIT Occasional Papers in Linguistics 5. Cambridge, MA: Department of Linguistics and Philosophy, MIT.

———. 1995. *The Minimalist Program*. Cambridge, MA: The MIT Press.

———. 1998. *Minimalist Inquiries: The Framework*. MIT Occasional Papers in Linguistics 15. Cambridge, MA: Department of Linguistics and Philosophy, MIT.

———. 1999. *Derivation by Phase*. MIT Occasional Papers in Linguistics 18. Cambridge, MA: Department of Linguistics and Philosophy, MIT.

———. 2002 [1966]. *Cartesian Linguistics: A Chapter in the History of Rationalist Thought*. 2nd ed. Edited with an Introduction by James McGilvray. Christchurch, New Zealand: Cyber-editions.

———. 2004. 'Beyond Explanatory Adequacy'. In *Structures and Beyond: The Cartography of Syntactic Structure*, edited by Adriana Belleti, 104–31. Vol. 3. Oxford: Oxford University Press.

———. 2005. 'Three Factors in Language Design'. *Linguistic Inquiry* 36 (1): 1–22.

———. 2007. 'Approaching UG from below'. In *Interfaces + Recursion = Language? Chomsky's Minimalism and the View from Syntax-Semantics*, edited by Uli Sauerland and Hans-Martin Gärtner, 1–29. Studies in Generative Grammar 89. Berlin: De Gruyter Mouton.

———. 2013. 'Problems of Projection'. *Lingua* 130: 33–49.

———. 2015. 'Problems of Projection: Extensions'. In *Structures, Strategies and Beyond: Studies in Honour of Adriana Belletti*, edited by Elisa Di Domenico, Cornelius Hamann, and Simona Matteini, 1–16. Amsterdam: Benjamins.

———. 2019. 'Some Puzzling Foundational Issues: The Reading Program'. *Catalan Journal of Linguistics Special Issue*, 263–85.

Chomsky, Noam, and Howard Lasnik. 1977. 'Filters and Control'. *Linguistic Inquiry* 8 (3): 425–504.

———. 1993. 'The Theory of Principles and Parameters'. In *Syntax: An International Handbook of Contemporary Research*, edited by Joachim Jacobs, Armin von Stechow, Wolfgang Sternefeld, and Theo Vennemann, 506–69. Berlin: Walter de Gruyter.

Churchyard, Henry. 1999. 'Topics in Tiberian Biblical Hebrew Metrical Phonology and Phonetics'. PhD dissertation, University of Texas at Austin.

Coetzee, Andries W. 1999. *Tiberian Hebrew Phonology: Focussing on Consonant Clusters*. Assen: Van Gorcum.

Cowper, Elizabeth, and Vincent DeCaen. 2017. 'Biblical Hebrew: A Formal Perspective on the Left Periphery'. *Toronto Working Papers in Linguistics* 38: 1–33.

———. 2021. 'A Unified Account of the Infinitive Absolute in Biblical Hebrew'. In *Linguistic Studies on Biblical Hebrew*, edited by Robert D. Holmstedt, 103–24. Studies in Semitic Languages and Linguistics 102. Leiden: Brill.

DeCaen, Vincent. 1995. 'On the Placement and Interpretation of the Verb in Standard Biblical Hebrew Prose'. PhD dissertation, University of Toronto.

———. 1999. 'Verbal and Verbless Clauses within Government-Binding Theory'. In *The Verbless Clause in Biblical Hebrew: Linguistic Approaches*, edited by Cynthia L. Miller, 109–31. Linguistic Studies in Ancient West Semitic 1. Winona Lake, IN: Eisenbrauns.

———. 2003. 'Hebrew Sonority and Tiberian Contact Anaptyxis: The Case of Verbs *Primae Gutturalis*'. *Journal of Semitic Studies* 48: 35–46.

DeCaen, Vincent, and Bezalel Elan Dresher. 2021. 'Prosodic Dependency in Tiberian Hebrew'. In *Linguistic Studies on Biblical Hebrew*, edited by Robert D. Holmstedt, 39–59. Studies in Semitic Languages and Linguistics 102. Leiden: Brill.

Den Dikken, Marcel (ed.). 2013. *The Cambridge Handbook of Generative Syntax*. Cambridge Handbooks in Language and Linguistics. Cambridge: Cambridge University Press.

Dresher, Bezalel Elan. 1994. 'The Prosodic Basis of the Tiberian Hebrew System of Accent'. *Language* 70: 1–52.

———. 2009a. 'Stress Assignment in Tiberian Hebrew'. In *Contemporary Views on Architecture and Representations in Phonology*, edited by Charles Cairns and Eric Raimy, 213–24. Cambridge, MA: The MIT Press.

———. 2009b. 'The Word in Tiberian Hebrew'. In *The Nature of the Word: Essays in Honor of Paul Kiparsky*, edited by Kristin Hanson and Sharon Inkelas, 95–111. Cambridge, MA: The MIT Press.

D'Hulst, Lieven, and Yves Gambier. 2018. 'General Introduction'. In *A History of Modern Translation Knowledge: Sources, Concepts, Effects*, edited by Lieven D'Hulst and Yves Gambier, 1–14. Amsterdam: Benjamins.

Doron, Edit. 1986. 'The Pronominal "Copula" as Agreement Clitic'. In *The Syntax of Pronominal Clitics,* edited by Hagit Borer, 313–32. Syntax and Semantics 19. New York: Academic Press.

———. 2021. 'The Infinitive in Biblical Hebrew'. In *Linguistic Studies on Biblical Hebrew*, edited by Robert D. Holmstedt,

144–68. Studies in Semitic Languages and Linguistics 102. Leiden: Brill.

England, Barbara R. 1978. *Glossarized Charts of Noam Chomsky's Grammar.* Bloomington, IN: Maccallum House.

Everaert, Martin, and Henk van Riemsdijk. 2006. *The Blackwell Companion to Syntax.* 5 vols. Oxford: Blackwell.

Fowler, Roger. 1977. *Linguistics and the Novel.* London and New York: Methuen.

Grasso, Kevin. 2021. 'The Causative-Inchoative Alternation and the Semantics of Hiphil'. In *Linguistic Studies on Biblical Hebrew,* edited by Robert D. Holmstedt, 209–30. Studies in Semitic Languages and Linguistics 102. Leiden: Brill.

Haegeman, Liliane. 1994. *Introduction to Government & Binding Theory.* 2nd ed. Oxford: Blackwell.

Harbour, Daniel. 1999. 'The Two Types of Predicate Clefts: Classical Hebrew and Beyond'. In *Papers on Morphology and Syntax, Cycle Two,* edited by Vivian Lin, Cornelia Krause, Benjamin Bruening, and Karlos Arregi, 159–75. Cambridge, MA: MIT Working Papers in Linguistics.

Hatav, Galia. 1997. *The Semantics of Aspect and Modality: Evidence from English and Biblical Hebrew.* Studies in Language Companion Series 34. Amsterdam: John Benjamins.

———. 2004. 'Anchoring World and Time in Biblical Hebrew'. *Journal of Linguistics* 40 (3): 491–526.

———. 2006. 'The Deictic Nature of the Directives in Biblical Hebrew'. *Studies in Language* 30 (4): 733–75.

———. 2011. 'Past and Future Interpretation of *Wayyiqtol*'. *Journal of Semitic Studies* 56 (1): 85–109.

———. 2017. 'The Infinitive Absolute and Topicalization of Events in Biblical Hebrew'. In *Advances in Biblical Hebrew Linguistics: Data, Method, and Analyses*, edited by Adina Moshavi and Tania Notarius, 185–207. Linguistic Studies in Ancient West Semitic 12. Winona Lake, IN: Eisenbrauns.

———. 2020. 'Verb Phrase Secondary Predication: Biblical Hebrew as a Case Study'. *Linguistics* 58 (2): 363–78.

———. 2021. 'The Nature of the Infinitive Absolute'. In *Linguistic Studies on Biblical Hebrew*, edited by Robert D. Holmstedt, 125–43. Studies in Semitic Languages and Linguistics 102. Leiden: Brill.

Himmelreich, Roman, and Outi Bat-El Foux. 2021. 'Pausal vs. Context Forms in Tiberian Hebrew: A Multi-Planar Analysis of Vowel Reduction and Stress'. In *Linguistic Studies on Biblical Hebrew*, edited by Robert D. Holmstedt, 9–38. Studies in Semitic Languages and Linguistics 102. Leiden: Brill.

Holmstedt, Robert D. 2009. 'So-Called "First Conjunct" Agreement in Biblical Hebrew'. In *Afroasiatic Studies in Memory of Robert Hetzron: Proceedings of the 35th Annual Meeting of the North American Conference on Afroasiatic Linguistics (NACAL 35)*, edited by Charles Häberl, 105–29. Newcastle upon Tyne, UK: Cambridge Scholars Press.

———. 2014. 'Constituents at the Edge in Biblical Hebrew'. *KUSATU: Kleine Untersuchungen zur Sprache des Alten Testaments und seiner Umwelt* 17: 110–58.

———. 2016. *The Relative Clause in Biblical Hebrew*. Linguistic Studies in Ancient West Semitic 10. Winona Lake, IN: Eisenbrauns.

———. 2021. 'Investigating Ellipsis in Biblical Hebrew'. In *Linguistic Studies on Biblical Hebrew*, edited by Robert D. Holmstedt, 84–102. Studies in Semitic Languages and Linguistics 102. Leiden: Brill.

Holmstedt, Robert D., and Andrew R. Jones. 2017. 'Apposition in Biblical Hebrew: Structure and Function'. *KUSATU: Kleine Untersuchungen zur Sprache des Alten Testaments und seiner Umwelt* 22 (1): 21–51.

Hornstein, Norbert, Jairo Nunes, and Kleanthes K. Grohmann. 2005. *Understanding Minimalism*. Cambridge Textbooks in Linguistics. Cambridge: Cambridge University Press.

Hyams, Nina H. 1986. *Language Acquisition and the Theory of Parameters*. Dordrecht: Reidel.

Jackendoff, Ray. 1972. *Semantic Interpretation in Generative Grammar*. Cambridge, MA: The MIT Press.

Katz, Jerrold J. 1972. *Semantic Theory*. New York: Harper & Row.

———. 1977. *Propositional Structure and Illocutionary Force: A Study of the Contribution of Sentence Meaning to Speech Acts*. Hassocks, Sussex: The Harvester Press.

Katz, Jerrold J., and Jerry A. Fodor. 1963. 'The Structure of a Semantic Theory'. *Language* 39 (2): 170–210.

Katz, Jerrold J., and Paul M. Postal. 1964. *An Integrated Theory of Linguistic Descriptions*. Cambridge, MA: The MIT Press.

Lakoff, George. 1968. *Deep and Surface Grammar*. Bloomington, IN: Indiana University Linguistics Club.

———. 1970. *Irregularity in Syntax*. New York: Holt, Rinehart and Winston.

———. 1971. 'On Generative Semantics'. In *Semantics: An Interdisciplinary Reader in Philosophy, Linguistics, and Psychology*, edited by Danny D. Steinberg and Leon A. Jakobovits, 232–96. Cambridge: Cambridge University Press.

Malone, Joseph L. 1993. *Tiberian Hebrew Phonology*. Winona Lake, IN: Eisenbrauns.

McCarthy, John J. 1985 [1979]. *Formal Problems in Semitic Phonology and Morphology*. [PhD dissertation, MIT.] New York: Garland Press.

Miller-Naudé, Cynthia L. 2005. 'Ellipsis Involving Negation in Biblical Poetry'. In *Seeking Out the Wisdom of the Ancients: Essays Offered to Honor Michael V. Fox on the Occasion of His Sixty-Fifth Birthday*, edited by R. L. Troxel, K. G. Friebel, and D. R. Magary, 37–52. Winona Lake, IN: Eisenbrauns.

———. 2007a. 'Constraints on Ellipsis in Biblical Hebrew'. In *Studies in Comparative Semitic and Afroasiatic Linguistics Presented to Gene B. Gragg*, edited by Cynthia L. Miller, 165–80. Chicago: The Oriental Institute of the University of Chicago.

———. 2007b. 'The Relation of Coordination to Verb Gapping in Biblical Poetry'. *Journal for the Study of the Old Testament* 32 (1): 41–60.

———. 2007c. 'The Syntax of Elliptical Comparative Constructions'. *Zeitschrift für Althebraistik* 18: 136–49.

———. 2008. 'A Reconsideration of "Double-Duty" Prepositions in Biblical Poetry'. *Journal of the Ancient Near Eastern Society* 31: 99–110.

———. 2011. 'Exploring the Limits of Ambiguity in Biblical Poetry: Interpreting Elliptical Structures'. *Journal for Semitics* 22: 323–52.

———. 2013. 'Ellipsis: Biblical Hebrew'. In *Encyclopedia of Hebrew Language and Linguistics,* edited by Geoffrey Khan, I: 807–12. Leiden: Brill.

Miller-Naudé, Cynthia L., and Jacobus A. Naudé. 2015. 'The Participle and Negation in Biblical Hebrew'. *KUSATU: Kleine Untersuchungen zur Sprache des Alten Testaments und seiner Umwelt* 19: 165–99.

———. 2016. 'Is the Adjective Distinct from the Noun as a Grammatical Category in Biblical Hebrew?'. *In die Skriflig / In Luce Verbi* 50 (4), a2005. doi.org/10.4102/ids.v50i4.2005.

———. 2017a. 'A Re-Examination of Grammatical Categorization in Biblical Hebrew'. In *From Ancient Manuscripts to Modern Dictionaries: Select Studies in Aramaic, Hebrew, and Greek*, edited by Tarsee Li and Keith Dyer, 331–76. Perspectives on Linguistics and Ancient Languages 9. Piscataway, NJ: Gorgias Press.

———. 2017b. 'The Scope of Negation Inside and Outside of the Biblical Hebrew Prepositional Phrase'. In *Advances in Biblical Hebrew Linguistics: Data, Methods, and Analyses*, edited by Adina Moshavi and Tania Notarius, 297–319. Linguistic Studies in Ancient West Semitic 12. Winona Lake, IN: Eisenbrauns.

———. 2019. 'Differentiating Dislocations, Topicalisation, and Extraposition: Evidence from Negation'. *Stellenbosch Papers in Linguistics Plus* 56: 177–99.

———. 2020a. 'A Programmatic Proposal for the Study of Biblical Hebrew as a Language'. *Journal for Semitics* 29 (2) [29 pages]. doi.org/10.25159/2663-6573/9103

———. 2020b. 'Negative Polarity in כל Constructions in Qumran Hebrew'. *Dead Sea Discoveries* 27: 351–71.

———. 2021. 'Differentiating Left Dislocation Constructions in Biblical Hebrew'. In *New Perspectives in Biblical and Rabbinic Hebrew*, edited by Aaron D. Hornkohl and Geoffrey Khan, 617–40. Cambridge Semitic Languages and Cultures 7. Cambridge: University of Cambridge / Open Book Publishers. doi.org/10.11647/OBP.0250

Naudé, Jacobus A. 1990. 'A Syntactic Analysis of Dislocations in Biblical Hebrew'. *Journal of Northwest Semitic Languages* 16: 115–30.

———. 1991a. 'Qumran Hebrew as a Null Subject Language'. *South African Journal of Linguistics* 9 (4): 119–25.

———. 1991b. 'On the Syntax of *dy*-Phrases in the Aramaic of 11QtgJob'. *Journal of Northwest Semitic Languages* 17: 45–67.

———. 1993a. 'Aspects of the Verbless Clause in Biblical Aramaic'. *South African Journal of Linguistics Supplement* 18: 49–63.

———. 1993b. 'On Subject Pronoun and Subject Noun Asymmetry: A Preliminary Survey of Northwest Semitic'. *South African Journal of Linguistics* 11 (1): 17–28.

———. 1994a. 'The Asymmetry of Subject Pronouns and Subject Nouns in Qumran Hebrew and Cognates'. *Journal of Northwest Semitic Languages* 20 (1): 139–64.

———. 1994b. 'Towards a Typology of Qumran Hebrew'. *Journal of Northwest Semitic Languages* 20 (2): 65–83.

———. 1994c. 'The Verbless Clause with Pleonastic Pronoun in Biblical Aramaic'. *Journal for Semitics* 6: 74–93.

———. 1995. 'Die Nut van Teoretiese Linguistiek vir Taalstudie: die "Etiese Datief" in Bybelhebreeus'. *South African Journal of Linguistics* 13 (3): 119–27.

———. 1996a. *Independent Personal Pronouns in Qumran Hebrew Syntax*. DLitt thesis, University of the Free State.

———. 1996b. 'Resumptive Pronouns in Biblical Aramaic Relatives'. *South African Journal of Linguistics Supplement* 29: 117–38.

———. 1997. 'The Syntactic Status of the Ethical Dative in Biblical Hebrew'. *Journal for Semitics* 9: 129–65.

———. 1999. 'Syntactic Aspects of Co-ordinate Subjects with Independent Personal Pronouns'. *Journal of Northwest Semitic Languages* 25 (2): 75–99.

———. 2000. 'Diachronic Syntax and Language Change: The Case of Qumran Hebrew'. *Southern African Linguistics and Applied Language Studies* 18: 1–14.

———. 2001. 'The Distribution of Independent Personal Pronouns in Qumran Hebrew'. *Journal of Northwest Semitic Languages* 27: 91–112.

———. 2002a. 'The Third Person Pronoun in Tripartite Verbless Clauses of Qumran Hebrew'. In *Pronouns: Representation and Grammar*, edited by H.J. Simon and H. Wiese, 161–82. Amsterdam: Benjamins.

———. 2002b. 'Verbless Clauses Containing a Personal Pronoun as Subject in Qumran Hebrew'. *Journal for Semitics* 11: 126–68.

———. 2011a. 'The Interpretation and Translation of the Biblical Hebrew Quantifier *kol*'. *Journal for Semitics* 20 (2): 408–21.

———. 2011b. 'Syntactic Patterns of Quantifier Float in Biblical Hebrew'. *Hebrew Studies* 52: 351–66.

———. 2013. 'Dative: Biblical Hebrew'. In *Encyclopedia of Hebrew Language and Linguistics*, edited by Geoffrey Khan, vol. 1: 655–58. Leiden: Brill.

Naudé, Jacobus A., and Cynthia L. Miller-Naudé. 2015. 'Syntactic Features of כל in Qumran Hebrew'. In *Hebrew of the Late Second Temple Period: Proceedings of a Sixth International Symposium on the Hebrew of the Dead Sea Scrolls and Ben Sira*, edited by Eibert Tigchelaar and Pierre van Hecke, 88–111. Studies on the Texts of the Desert of Judah 114. Leiden: Brill.

———. 2016. 'Historical Linguistics, Editorial Theory and Biblical Hebrew: The Current Stage of the Debate'. *Journal for Semitics* 25: 501–31.

———. 2017. 'At the Interface of Syntax and Prosody: Differentiating Left Dislocated and Tripartite Verbless Clauses in Biblical Hebrew'. *Stellenbosch Papers in Linguistics Plus* 48: 223–38.

———. 2020. 'Linguistics and Philology: Separate, Overlapping or Subordinate/Super-ordinate Disciplines?'. *Journal for*

Semitics 29 (2) [28 pages]. doi.org/10.25159/2663-6573/857

———. 2022. 'Unity and Diversity in Qumran Hebrew: Evidence from Quantification'. In *Emerging Sectarianism in the Dead Sea Scrolls: Continuity, Separation, and Conflict,* edited by John J. Collins and Ananda Geyser-Fouché, 78–118. Discoveries in the Judean Desert 141. Leiden: Brill.

Naudé, Jacobus A., Cynthia L. Miller-Naudé, and Daniel J. Wilson. 2019. 'Trajectories of Diachronic Change in Qumran Hebrew: Evidence from the Negative Existential in Post-Predicate Position'. In *Scribal Practice, Text and Canon in the Dead Sea Scrolls: Essays in Memory of Peter Flint*, edited by John Collins and Ananda Geyser-Fouché, 273–96. Studies in the Texts of the Desert of Judah. Leiden: Brill.

———. 2022. 'The Negative Existential Cycle in Ancient Hebrew'. In *The Negative Existential Cycle from a Historical Comparative Perspective,* edited by Ljuba Veselinova and Arja Hamari, 181–96. Berlin: Language Science Press.

Naudé, Jacobus A. and Rendsburg, Gary A. 2013. 'Negation: Pre-Modern Hebrew'. In *Encyclopedia of Hebrew Language and Linguistics*, edited by Geoffrey Khan, II: 801–11. Leiden: Brill.

Nord, Christiane. 2018. *Translating as a Purposeful Activity: Functionalist Approaches Explained.* 2nd ed. London: Routledge.

Pereltsvaig, Asya. 2002. 'Cognate Objects in Modern and Biblical Hebrew'. In *Themes in Arabic and Hebrew Syntax*, edited by Jamal Ouhalla and Ur Shlonsky, 107–36. Dordrecht: Kluwer Academic / Springer.

Pitcher, Sophia L. 2021. 'Towards a Prosodic Model for Tiberian Hebrew: An Intonation-based Analysis'. *Stellenbosch Papers in Linguistics Plus* 63: 1–27.

Pollock, J.-Y. 1989. 'Verb Movement, Universal Grammar, and the Structure of IP'. *Linguistic Inquiry* 20 (3): 365–424.

Prince, Alan. 1975. 'The Phonology and Morphology of Tiberian Hebrew'. PhD dissertation, MIT.

Radford, Andrew. 1997a. *Syntactic Theory and the Structure of English: A Minimalist Approach*. Cambridge Textbooks in Linguistics. Cambridge: Cambridge University Press.

———. 1997b. *Syntax: A Minimalist Introduction*. Cambridge: Cambridge University Press.

———. 2004. *Minimalist Syntax: Exploring the Structure of English*. Cambridge Textbooks in Linguistics. Cambridge: Cambridge University Press.

———. 2009. *Analysing English Sentences: A Minimalist Approach*. Cambridge Textbooks in Linguistics. Cambridge: Cambridge University Press.

Rappaport, Malka. 1984. 'Issues in the Phonology of Tiberian Hebrew'. PhD dissertation, MIT.

Rizzi, Luigi. 1982. *Issues in Italian Syntax*. Dordrecht: Foris.

———. 1997. 'The Fine Structure of the Left Periphery'. In *Elements of Grammar: Handbook in Generative Syntax*, edited by Liliane Haegeman, 281–337. Dordrecht: Kluwer.

Scheumann, Jesse Roy. 2020. 'A Syntactic Analysis of Phrasal Coordination in Biblical Hebrew'. PhD thesis, University of the Free State.

Sells, Peter. 1985. *Lectures on Contemporary Syntactic Theories.* Stanford: Stanford University.

Sinclair, Cameron. 1999. 'Are Nominal Clauses a Distinct Clause Type?'. In *The Verbless Clause in Biblical Hebrew: Linguistic Approaches,* edited by Cynthia L. Miller, 51–75. Linguistic Studies in Ancient West Semitic 1. Winona Lake, IN: Eisenbrauns.

Snyman, F. P. J. 2004. *The Scope of the Negative lō' in Biblical Hebrew.* Acta Academica Supplementum 3. Bloemfontein: UFS-SASOL Library.

Snyman, F. P. J., and Naudé, Jacobus A. 2003. 'Sentence and Constituent-Negation in Biblical Hebrew'. *Journal for Semitics* 12: 237–67.

Traugott, Elizabeth Closs, and Mary Louise Pratt. 1980. *Linguistics for Students of Literature.* New York: Harcourt Brace Javanovich.

Van der Merwe, Christo H. J., Jacobus A. Naudé, and Jan H. Kroeze. 2017. *A Biblical Hebrew Reference Grammar.* 2nd ed. London: Bloomsbury.

Van Gelderen, Elly. 2011. *The Linguistic Cycle: Language Change and the Language Facility.* Oxford: Oxford University Press.

———. 2017. *Syntax: An Introduction to Minimalism.* Amsterdam: Benjamins.

Van Riemsdijk, Henk, and Edwin Williams. 1986. *Introduction to the Theory of Grammar.* Cambridge, MA: The MIT Press.

Veselinova, Ljuba. 2016. 'The Negative Existential Cycle Viewed through the Lens of Comparative Data'. In *Cyclical Change*

Continued, edited by Elly van Gelderen, 138–87. Amsterdam: Benjamins.

Webelhuth, Gert (ed.). 1995. *Government and Binding Theory and the Minimalist Program: Principles and Parameters in Syntactic Theory*. Oxford: Blackwell.

Wilson, Daniel J. 2019. '*Wayhî* and Theticity in Biblical Hebrew'. *Journal of Northwest Semitic Languages* 45 (1): 89–118.

———. 2020. *Syntactic and Semantic Variation in Copular Sentences: Insights from Classical Hebrew*. Linguistics Today 261. Amsterdam: Benjamins.

FUNCTIONAL GRAMMAR AND THE PRAGMATICS OF INFORMATION STRUCTURE FOR BIBLICAL LANGUAGES

Randall Buth

The pragmatics of information structure, and Functional Grammar in particular, encourage and provide a framework for students and scholars of the biblical languages to read with increased nuance and precision.

1.0. Historical Development

Functional grammatical approaches include semantic and pragmatic information in a grammatical description. Pragmatics refers to the effects that are made within communication and will be discussed below. This inclusion of pragmatic information within a formal grammatical description can be contrasted to transformational-generative approaches that adopt a policy of autonomous syntax. The Functional Grammar (FG) developed by Simon Dik in particular reflects the confluence of two developments in linguistics: (1) the pragmatics of information structure as extrapolated, for example, from Functional Sentence

Perspective (FSP)[1] and (2) generative-transformational grammars that stem from Noam Chomsky, especially 1957–1980. The primary pragmatic functions that were incorporated in the early sentence grammar of FG were Topic and Focus, discussed below.

Generative and transformational grammar were a major impetus for FG. A generative grammar wants to know the rules that will produce all acceptable, grammatical sentences of a language and restrict the production of unacceptable, ungrammatical sentences. The primary difference between a strictly generative approach and functional approaches can be summarised in the notion 'autonomous syntax', which is the restricted domain of formal grammar without including semantic or pragmatic information in the rules. Functional approaches to grammar, on the other hand, reject such a restriction and recognise that pragmatic functions like Topic and Focus exert direct influence on the rules. In addition to including pragmatics in formal grammatical description, FG eschews the idea of transformations and filtering devices in formal grammar as psychologically problematic, as discussed below.

Dik published the basis of this approach in two volumes (1978; 1980). From the beginning, he embraced a principle of

---

[1] For examples, see Daneš (1974) and Firbas (1992). The roots of FSP precede World War II. FSP broadly analyses communication as comprising known or assumed information as a base that is called the Theme. New or salient information is then added to the Theme as the intended communication. This salient meaning is termed the Rheme. In English, these two perspectives are often called Topic and Comment, respectively.

rigorous formalism in his theory. The various systems of syntax (like predicates, subjects, and objects), semantic roles (like agent, experiencer, and patient), and pragmatics (like Topic and Focus) are assumed to influence the final output of a sentence and should be included within formal grammar. However, as these ideas were applied in studies on various languages, the complexities inherent in these notions have led to increasingly complex notation. Dik (1989) expanded many kinds of Topics and Foci. Some ideas from discourse analysis and greater attention to pragmatics led to positing multiple layers of underlying representation before the surface level sentences would be generated or interpreted within a grammar.

A former student and colleague, Kees Hengeveld, edited and published Dik's work posthumously in 1997. Hengeveld and J. Lachlan McKenzie then went on to include a formal discourse framework within that theory, ideas that developed out of a concern to include syntax, semantics, and pragmatics within formal grammatical theory. Hengeveld and McKenzie forged these into a comprehensive theory with four abstract layers. They published their collaborative effort in 2008, *Functional Discourse Grammar* (FDG; for a brief description of FDG, see Hengeveld and McKenzie 2005, 668–76). Since then, FDG has been considered the successor of FG and current studies tend to use the 2008 volume as a starting point. However, the complex metalanguage of later developments presents a barrier for those primarily interested in biblical languages, while the initial pragmatic functions in FG are more accessible. Concepts from information structure are widely used within other functional grammars (see, e.g.,

Givón 1984, who downplays rigorous formalism, and then Givón 2001, where he reincorporates some formalism; see also Foley and Van Valin 1984). The pragmatic functions of information structure within FG will therefore be the primary focus here.

2.0. Key Theoretical Commitments and Major Concepts

People communicate with language, prototypically with sound, but also in written media and in sign languages. A signal is intended to communicate meaning. In 'The girl walked to the market', the speaker wants the hearer to think about a particular girl, a particular market, and communicates that the girl walked there. Grammatical theories attempt to explain how that sentence is produced.

With this in mind, FG aims at several goals.[2] These include, first, typological adequacy, meaning the theory should be formulated in terms of rules and principles that apply to any natural language. Second, pragmatic adequacy, meaning the theory should explain how linguistic expressions may be used in communication. Third, psychological adequacy, meaning that what the theory says about a language should be compatible with what is known about the psychological mechanisms involved in natural language processing.

To these ends, FG has identified certain functions that affect the output of a predication into sentences. These include:[3]

---

[2] See Dik (1980, 2).
[3] See Dik (1980, 3).

SEMANTIC FUNCTIONS (Agent, Patient, Recipient, etc.), which define the roles that participants play in states of affairs, as designated by predications.

SYNTACTIC FUNCTIONS (Subject and Object), which define different perspectives through which states of affairs are presented in linguistic expressions.

PRAGMATIC FUNCTIONS (Theme and Tail, Topic and Focus), which define the informational status of constituents of linguistic expressions. These relate to the embedding of the expression in ongoing discourse and are determined by the status of the pragmatic information of Speaker and Addressee as it develops in verbal interaction.

Using these functions, FG posits that an underlying abstract predication frame could produce the following sentences:

(1) The girl walked to the market in the morning.

(2) In the morning the girl walked to the market.

(3) As for the girl, she walked to the market in the morning.

The predication frame comes from the abstract lexicon of a language and would join three arguments (sentence constituents) to that predication, 'to walk': *the girl, to the market,* and *in the morning*. These arguments receive different taggings for syntax, semantic roles, and optionally pragmatics. In (1), *the girl* $_{[Subject, Agent]}$ is a syntactic Subject and semantic Agent, while *to the market* $_{[Goal]}$ is a semantic Goal and *in the morning* $_{[Time]}$ is a semantic Time. The semantic taggings are the same for (2), however *in the morning* $_{[Time, Topic]}$ is both semantic Time and pragmatic Topic. In (3), *as for the girl* $_{[Theme]}$ is a pragmatic Theme, a framework for the sentence similar to Topic but outside the sentence syntax. *She* [Subject, Agent] is a syntactic Subject and semantic Agent, while *to the market* [Goal] is a semantic Goal. Notice the difference between (1) and (2). The predication frame and the semantics are the same, but the pragmatics differ. In (1) the Time *in the morning* is part of the new, salient, rhemic/comment information, but in (2) *in the morning* has been placed at the beginning according to pragmatic placement rules. There the argument is tagged a Topic to provide a pragmatic setting or situational orientation for the communication that follows.[4]

FG assumes that predications use the functions explained above to generate sentences, a process which occurs with abstract templates specific to a particular language. The template specifies where certain functions may appear, and positions in the templates can be filled by individual words, phrases, and clauses. So discussions about word order are actually about constituents or 'pieces' of a sentence that are positioned to fulfil one of the syntactic, semantic, or pragmatic functions. A sentence is able to organise and output the functions as follows:[5]

(4)   Theme; Pragmatic positions, Syntactic positions; Tail

Within this template, syntactic positions might involve numerous variations, such as S–O–X; S–V–O–X; V–S–O–X, etc. But

---

[4] A Topic is pragmatically marked material that orientates a sentence to its context. It does not have Focus intonation and is not necessarily the broader subject matter of the sentence.

[5] The templates in (4) are also simplified and without the algebraic notation of much of FG and FDG.

pragmatic positions appear before syntactic positions, which is fundamentally important for FG and for human communication in general.[6] Such a pragmatic position allows FG to explain a phenomenon in V–S–O languages, namely the possibility of S–V–O as an/the alternative order (see Dik 1980, 155).

While syntactic, semantic, and pragmatic functions are all necessary for FG as a theory, understanding pragmatic functions may help readers of biblical languages most. Pragmatic functions are part of all natural language and must be internalised to communicate in any given language. Two of the pragmatic functions noted in (4) operate outside sentence syntax and are separated by semicolons in the templates. First, the Tail is an afterthought, prototypically at the end of a sentence, whether as a side comment or reinforcement. Also, a phrase like an appositive or parenthetical comment can be treated as a Tail that may be placed inside a syntactical sentence. Second, the Theme is any introductory, setting, or topical material that is prototypically at the beginning of a sentence, traditionally treated as a *casus pendans* and called left dislocation in linguistics.

The FSP distinction between Topic and Comment has led to a foundational distinction of marked information structure in FG: Topic and Focus. A Topic constituent is specially marked

---

[6] As part of typological adequacy, FG theorises that a potential pragmatic position exists at the beginning of a main clause of whatever the basic order may be. FG does not claim that devices like intonation, morphology, or special vocabulary do not also play roles in informational pragmatics. But placement rules and positions before the main syntactic components are stipulated as universal.

information that is presupposed or already established. It is a starting point for the rest of the sentence and potentially linked to the larger context. A sentence constituent that functions as Topic is eligible for placement in a pragmatic position before the main, default sentence order. But a Topic is not necessarily the syntactic Subject, which often creates confusion. In English, the word 'topic' is a synonym of 'subject'. But in FG a marked Topic is specifically a constituent that provides a framework and link to the larger context in which a sentence occurs. It may be a Subject, but it may also be some other constituent. Given this potential confusion, I use the term Topic in this article when trying to relate primarily to FG and broader linguistic literature. But I use the term Contextualising Constituent (CC) when including the multivalent nature of pragmatic Topics that goes beyond marked constituents as subjects and settings.

A Focus constituent is a specially marked part of the Comment, which contains the new or most important information of a sentence. Focus may be marked by word order, particles, and often intonation. It can include many kinds of Comment information, including new, supplemental, reinforced old, contrastive, or contra-expected information.[7]

FG thus helps identify pragmatic placements in word order and the resulting nuances of understanding. But because FG aims at both psychological and pragmatic adequacy, it does not allow unmotivated, *ad hoc* rules to correct mis-predictions of hypothesised rules. This can be stated in four principles:

---

[7] Lambrecht (1994) adds 'sentence focus' to the Topic and Focus of information structure, as discussed below.

1. Avoid transformations in the sense of structure-changing operations;
2. Avoid empty elements in underlying structure that are unexpressed;
3. Disallow filter devices;
4. Disallow abstract lexical decomposition (instead, account for meaning with definitions).

So if a constituent is pragmatically placed at the beginning of the clause, and the language regularly follows with V–S, then that language shows a basic order of V–S. FG does not unnecessarily multiply rules. FG would not suggest an abstract S–V order, place a pragmatic function in front, and then add a filter to flip the S–V order to match the data. An additional rule that would switch the placement of S and V after a pragmatic placement would be *ad hoc*. Instead, FG asks simple questions: Would such rules be psychologically real? Is there any pragmatic motivation for the rule? Are such rules necessary? If the not, then Occam's Razor and the minimal abstractness principle of FG declare such a rule to be contra-indicated and *ad hoc*.

These principles have been particularly helpful in describing word order patterns in Germanic languages, but may also be applied to the biblical languages.[8] For illustration, FG can demonstrate a continuum between various V–S languages to the point where one may develop into an S–V language. Four categories of these languages are described:

---

[8] Dik (1980, 152–77) devotes a whole chapter to this question.

> V1 (verb first), where the statistical majority of sentences show V–S at the beginning of the clause.

There do not appear to be any V–S languages that do not also allow S–V word order. This fact supports the typological adequacy of FG, which assumes a pragmatic position before a main clause of whatever the basic order may be.

> V2 (verb second), where the majority of sentences show some non-verb element first in a pragmatic position.

In these languages, a pragmatic position rule is activated fairly commonly.

> V2s (verb strongly second), where all sentences, allowing for some pragmatic exceptions, show the verb in a second position.

A V2s language might look like an S–V language at first glance. A pragmatic positioning rule becomes mandatory, thereby diluting the strength of the pragmatic marking. The only choice is whether the Subject or some other constituent fills the pragmatic position. "A V2s language will only have the following constituent orderings: a. SVO, b. XVS(O)" (Dik 1980, 158). In terms of pragmatics, the S–V orders in a V2s language will function similarly to the way that Subjects function in real S–V languages.

> V3 (verb third), where the verb comes third whenever a constituent is pragmatically placed at the beginning, before the syntactic S–V.

In V3 languages, the Subject follows the pragmatic position, so that the Verb comes third. Without a pragmatically positioned constituent, the Verb may appear second, after the Subject. In other words, a V3 language is a true S–V language, as is English.⁹

Not only can FG meaningfully describe the various categories of word order, but FG also predicts historical development with increasing optional use of pragmatic placement rules through time. Eventually, a V2s language can become a V3 language. Dik (1980, 169–75) lists Celtic languages and Welsh as examples of V1. Then, within Germanic languages, Old Icelandic, Old High German, and Middle Dutch are V2; Icelandic, Norse, Danish, and others are V2s; and finally English is V3 (SVO).

The importance of these basic concepts of FG is best appreciated when looking at the data of real languages. The next section shows how an FG approach can aid the reading and understanding of biblical texts.¹⁰

---

⁹ This does not mean that additional patterns do not exist. For example, English has a vestigial question order 'When did the girl return?' The order 'did the girl' is V–S and reflects an archaic word order pattern in the history of Germanic languages.

¹⁰ FG also deals with highly presupposed information that is attracted to Verbs in what is called Language Independent Preferred Order of Constituents (LIPOC), as well as secondary clines of post-verbal saliency. These ideas are not discussed in this essay, as they are less important for the general reader of biblical languages.

3.0. Use and Contributions of FG in Biblical Studies

3.1. Application to Hebrew

Some scholars of Biblical Hebrew have claimed that the language is based on S–V order, while a majority counter that it has a V–S order. Even claims that there is *no* basic order must still explain the examples of both S–V and V–S order.[11] Recognising constituents in communication that have special pragmatic marking can be a powerful tool for readers and for an audience. Pragmatic signals add information and perspective beyond the basic referential semantics of a communication.

3.1.1. A Test for V–S–O in Hebrew

Dik (1980, 154) provides a simple test that has explanatory power for Biblical Hebrew:

> If, whenever some constituent other than the Subject is brought to P1, the Subject itself appears in preverbal position, then the language is a 'real' SVO language with basic pattern P1SVO.

---

[11] See Hornkohl (2018), who has provided a review of word order studies and found the arguments for a S–V word order unpersuasive. He also recognises that this means that all S–V orders would need pragmatic explanations, both by those positing a V–S default order and by those who might claim that all orders are pragmatically motivated in BH.

If on the other hand, the Subject appears in postverbal position in that condition, then the basic pattern must have been P1VSO.

This is so because FG provides no other means for explaining the occurrence of postverbal Subjects than the assumption that the basic position of the Subject is postverbal in such cases. In particular, purported rules of Subject Postposing of Subject Verb Inversion simply cannot be formulated within the framework of FG. Part of the aim of this chapter is to demonstrate that this is an advantage rather than a weakness.

According to the criterion formulated above, English is a real P1SVO language. On the other hand, Dutch, German, and in fact all the other living Germanic languages come out as P1VSO languages according to this criterion.

Generally speaking, in BH, when some item other than a conjunction and a Subject is pre-verbal, the remaining order is V–S, which is what FG predicts for a V–S–O language, as in (5a):

(5) (a) אֶת־הָאֱלֹהִים הִתְהַלֶּךְ־נֹחַ
'With God Noah walked' [X_{Focus}–V–S] (Gen. 6.9)

(b) *אֶת־הָאֱלֹהִים נֹחַ הִתְהַלֵּךְ [X_{Focus}–S–V][12]

An S–V model with the same contextual pragmatics would have incorrectly predicted (5b).[13] The texts in (6) and (7) provide

---

[12] In linguistics, an asterisk marks either an incorrect/ungrammatical or an unattested form. Here it signals that this is not the attested form in the passage under discussion. An X–S–V order would have been a poor fit here, but it can occur in a different context with different pragmatics.

[13] Holmstedt (2009; 2011) invokes a special rule here to switch S–V to V–S to avoid the mis-prediction, but this is unmotivated and *ad hoc* from a FG perspective.

similar examples, in which (6b) and (7b) show what an S–V language would have produced:

(6) (a) וּבְיוֹם הָקִים אֶת־הַמִּשְׁכָּן כִּסָּה הֶעָנָן אֶת־הַמִּשְׁכָּן

'And on the day of raising the tabernacle the cloud covered the tabernacle' [X–V–S–O] (Num. 9.15)

(b) *וּבְיוֹם הָקִים אֶת־הַמִּשְׁכָּן הֶעָנָן כִּסָּה אֶת־הַמִּשְׁכָּן [X–S–V–O]

(7) (a) וּבְאַרְבַּע עֶשְׂרֵה שָׁנָה בָּא כְדָרְלָעֹמֶר וְהַמְּלָכִים אֲשֶׁר אִתּוֹ

'And in the 14th year Kadorlaʿomer came, and the kings that were with him' [V–S] (Gen. 14.5)

(b) *וּבְאַרְבַּע עֶשְׂרֵה שָׁנָה כְדָרְלָעֹמֶר בָּא וְהַמְּלָכִים אֲשֶׁר אִתּוֹ [S–V]

These examples illustrate that BH is a V–S language, whose basic template can be listed in simple form as

P–V–S–O–X

where P is a pragmatically placed constituent. If this is correct, then every case of some non-verb item preceding the verb is a pragmatic signal to the audience. That is a strong claim and a helpful guideline for readers.

3.1.2. Topic and Focus in a VSO Framework

Several examples in Hebrew can illustrate how Topic and Focus function in a V–S–O framework before looking at greater sentence-level effects.

Looking first at examples of Focus, consider (8):

(8) בְּתָם־לְבָבִי וּבְנִקְיֹן כַּפַּי עָשִׂיתִי זֹאת

'with an innocent heart and clean hands$_{[Focus]}$ I did this' (Gen. 20.5)

In this example, the pre-verbal material is the main point, part of the Comment and a marked Focus construction. Something similar occurs in (9):

(9) כִּי־מֵרֹב שִׂיחִי וְכַעְסִי דִּבַּרְתִּי

'because from much thought and anger[Focus] I was speaking' (1 Sam. 1.16)

In the context, Hanna is explaining her own behaviour, so the words 'much thought and anger' are the salient, main part of the Comment of the sentence. They are placed in front of the verb as a marked Focus. As a final example, answers to questions frequently use fronting for the most meaningful part of an answer, as in (10):

(10) וּמֵאַיִן תָּבֹאוּ וַיֹּאמְרוּ אֵלָיו מֵאֶרֶץ רְחוֹקָה מְאֹד בָּאוּ עֲבָדֶיךָ

'"…and from where would you be coming?" And they said to him, "From a very far country[Focus] have come your servants"' (Josh. 9.8–9)

Turning now to consider pragmatic Topics, the text in (11) provides a good example:

(11) בְּגִבְעוֹן נִרְאָה יְהֹוָה אֶל־שְׁלֹמֹה בַּחֲלוֹם הַלָּיְלָה וַיֹּאמֶר אֱלֹהִים

'In Gibeon[Topic] appeared the LORD to Solomon in a night dream, and God said…' (1 Kgs 3.5)

This is classic syntax of V–S where the MT has a pragmatic Topic (CC) that provides a locational setting to the sentence and the greater context.[14] Something similar occurs in (12):

(12) (a) וַיֵּצֵא יִשְׂרָאֵל לִקְרַאת פְּלִשְׁתִּים לַמִּלְחָמָה

'and Israel went out[VS] to the Philistines for war'

(b) וַיַּחֲנוּ עַל־הָאֶבֶן הָעֵזֶר

'and they camped at Even-Ezer[VX]'

---

[14] The place Gibeon provides a Setting for the scene rather than a subject of a sentence, which is why the term Topic can be misleading and why I prefer Contextualising Constituent.

(c) וּפְלִשְׁתִּים חָנוּ בַאֲפֵק

'and the Philistines[S, Topic] camped at Afeq' (1 Sam. 4.1)

In this example, the Philistines are marked as a Topic that provides comparison and contrast with Israel.

3.1.3. Subordinating Clause with Focus

Most subordinating conjunctions in BH introduce a V–S clause. However, pragmatic frontings may occur. The following two examples have subordinating conjunctions, one with a fronted Subject and one with a fronted Object. Both fronted constituents are pragmatically marked as Focus.

(13) וְלֹא־יָדַע יַעֲקֹב כִּי רָחֵל גְּנָבָתַם

'And Jacob did not know[V-S] that Rachel[S, Focus] stole them [the household gods]' (Gen. 31.32)

The Subject comes before the Verb inside this כִּי-clause. 'Rachel' can be read as a Focus and as exclusive and contra-expected information from Jacob's perspective. He already knew that a theft had occurred. Consider also (14):

(14) כְּגוֹי אֲשֶׁר־צְדָקָה עָשָׂה

'as a nation that righteousness[Focus, Obj] it did' (Isa. 58.2)

Again, placing the Object before the Verb can be explained here as Focus, because צְדָקָה 'righteousness, justice' is a contra-expected point for irony: 'as if they were a nation that did what would be, in fact, right'.

In general, subordinating conjunctions provide a link to a context themselves, so they do not regularly need a pragmatic Topic to link to the context. Thus, if the subordinate clause marks a pragmatic position, it is most often Focus, with the most salient part of a sentence placed before the Verb. This, too, helps the audience and readers, who would add a Focal intonation to differentiate Focus from Topic.

3.1.4. Template for Participles in Hebrew

The advantage of a rule-based approach to word orders can be illustrated with participles as well. Most grammarians recognise that the Hebrew participle fits a pattern that is more congruent to a Verbless clause than to a clause with a finite verb (for more details, see Buth 1999). In FG, the template for Biblical Hebrew participles is thus

(+/- Topic) (+/- Focus) S–Predicate

where the '+/-' notation makes explicit that the use of either a Topic or a Focus is optional. In the case of participles, the predicate would be Participle + Complements. Consider the following example:

(15) (a) מָה־אַתָּה רֹאֶה יִרְמְיָהוּ

'What$_{[O, Focus]}$ do you see, Jeremiah?'

(b) מַקֵּל שָׁקֵד אֲנִי רֹאֶה

'An almond stick$_{[O, Focus]}$ I see.' [S–V$_{Participle}$]

(c) הֵיטַבְתָּ לִרְאוֹת

'You've done well to see'

(d) כִּי־שֹׁקֵד אֲנִי עַל־דְּבָרִי לַעֲשֹׂתוֹ

'for diligent$_{[Focus]}$ am I on my word to do it' (Jer. 1.11–12)

In (15), a question word 'what?' in (15a) is positioned as Focus and helps us recognise the salient, new information in the following answer. Jeremiah's answer in (15b), 'an almond stick', has been placed ahead of the Subject–Participle, in the pragmatic position as Focus, as the pragmatically marked new information. The main sentence in (15b), 'I see', is known, pre-supposed information and follows the Focal Object. The Subject immediately ahead of the participle is not pragmatically marked.

Participial clauses and verbless clauses have a default, Subject–Predicate word order, different from finite verbal clauses with V–S order. When a word order of Participle–Subject occurs, then, as in (15d) and (16) below, there is pragmatic marking of the Participle, most often Focus:

(16) וְגַם אֶת־הַגּוֹי אֲשֶׁר יַעֲבֹדוּ דָּן אָנֹכִי

    'and in addition, the nation that they serve (as slaves)[Topic]

    I am going to judge[Focus]' (Gen. 15.14)

In (16), the long Object 'the nation that they serve' is positioned as a Topic to provide the starting point and contextual link for the sentence 'I am going to judge the nation'. However, contrary to the basic Subject–Participle word order, the participle comes before the Subject so that the participle is a second, pragmatically positioned constituent. The immediate and most natural reading is that the 'judging' is Focus, contra-expected, and specially marked.

We should also note the pattern of Topic–Focus order in all of the above examples that have more than one pragmatically positioned constituent. This Topic–Focus order is normal in BH and fits with a universal tendency seen in languages around the world. Consider the text in (17):

(17) (a)   דּוֹר הֹלֵךְ

    'A generation goes,'

(b) וְדוֹר בָּא

'a generation comes,'

(c) וְהָאָרֶץ לְעוֹלָם עֹמָדֶת

'and as for the earth[Topic] it remains forever[Focus]'
(Eccl. 1.4)

In (17c), 'the earth' is not first because it is a grammatical Subject, but because it is pragmatically marked. In this verse, the rules of pragmatic placement help the reader to interpret the functions of the sentence pieces. The adverbial complement לְעוֹלָם 'forever' in (17c) has been pragmatically placed before the main sentence, most transparently as a Focus, since it is specific, new information that also contrasts with the notion of temporality in the previous clauses. Note that the word order is not *וּלְעוֹלָם הָאָרֶץ עֹמָדֶת 'and forever the earth remains', which has only a pragmatically marked Focus. In (17c), the Subject is also placed before the pragmatically marked Focus, such that it, too, is pragmatically marked as a Topic. The earth is marked as a Topic because it is being compared to and contrasted with passing generations. Then the main point is brought out with a Focus structure, לְעוֹלָם '(remain) forever', which is pragmatically marked salient information.

It is this mix of interpreting pragmatically positioned information with the need to account for all of the results through rule identification that makes the recognition of pragmatic functions a powerful tool for practised readers of the biblical text.

3.1.5. Sentence Marking and Discourse Pragmatics

The above examples have illustrated pragmatic functions of Focus and Topic (CC) within a V–S perspective. However, scholars agree that there are many examples of seemingly insipid Topics.[15] Many sentences have a fronted constituent that is not the most salient point of a sentence and thus is not a candidate for Focus intonation as a Focus function. Likewise, the constituent does not provide a contextual comparison or set up a new Topic chain. Instead, the Topic introduces an isolated sentence on its own with interesting Semantics and discourse Pragmatics. Hornkohl (2018, 44) has summarised the problem:

> Frequently in BH, elements are fronted for purposes of marking something special about the entire clause. Though some formulations of information structure include the possibility of whole-clause marking by means of a fronted constituent—for example, Lambrecht's sentence focus, which may usefully explain certain cases of preverbal positioning in BH—this is inappropriate for the vast majority of XV instances in BH in which X is neither topic nor focus.

We need to define and identify the 'signal' and then discuss proposed meanings or function. A fronted constituent is only part of the signal. We can assume that intonation would have distinguished a Focus from a Topic.[16] So we may call a fronted

---

[15] Moshavi (2010, 119) lists over 43% of her examples in Genesis as not clearly either Topic or Focus. Atkinson (2021, 227–30) lists between 281 and 451 out of 1,029 examples in Samuel–Kings as being not clearly Topic or Focus, which would be 27%–44%. He lists 281 examples as 'thetic' and 170 as unclear.

[16] Khan and van der Merwe (2020, 361) point out that it is reasonable to assume that an intonational distinction existed even if we do not have access to it.

constituent for Focus a different signal from a fronted constituent for Topic.

But these signals are not alone. They come with an entailment in BH: placing a constituent in front of the verb means that a *wayyiqtol* verb cannot be used. It means that the functions signalled by a *wayyiqtol* verb are blocked. This consideration is vital in a small, closed system. Bickerton (1981, 90) points out the constraints of meaning in a closed system, and although his comments are about tense, mood, and aspect, they equally apply to any closed system, like *wayyiqtol* V–X order versus X–V orders:

> We must note a particular characteristic of TMA [tense-mood-aspect] systems which, though seemingly obvious, has been ignored by virtually all work up to and including Comrie's (1976) influential study of aspect. ... What each marker of modality, tense, or aspect means will be largely determined by how many markers of these things there are in the system and by what each of the others mean.

The restrictions of a closed system affect meaning, not just for the structure itself but against the other structures with which it is in contrast. The functions of fronted constituents in Hebrew are morpho-syntactically restricted to being non-*wayyiqtol* or non-*weqatal*. These X–V sentences become a signal that expands the Topic signal—structurally, a fronted constituent without a Focus intonation—into a sentence-level structural signal, rather than simply being a signal for the fronted constituent. The fronted constituent blocks and breaks any continuation of a *wayyiqtol* or *weqatal*. Although a single constituent, it affects the whole sentence and becomes a signal for discourse functions of various kinds of discontinuities: temporal non-sequentiality, backgrounding, and discourse discontinuity (see Hornkohl 2018, 45–51, for examples and discussion).

Khan and van der Merwe (2020, 349–50) agree that discourse pragmatics are the primary motivation for these kinds of non-focus, non-topic structures, stating: "We shall argue that subjective choices concerning discourse structure and organization are the ultimate motivations for using thetic sentences."[17] They analyse such X–V sentences as 'thetic', a concept discussed further in the next section. But they also define thetic sentences notionally and not uniquely as a structure, saying that "thetic sentences may be expressed by constructions other than constituent fronting and have different contours" (2020, 361).

3.1.6. Fronting and Thetic Sentences

The discussion of thetic sentences is a contribution to Hebrew studies that is congruent to the concept of Background in discourse studies, although it comes from a different analysis of information structure and is broader.[18] A thetic sentence 'posits' the whole predication without assuming a clear Theme–Rheme structure (also called Topic–Comment, meaning pre-supposed/established versus salient/non-established information). Prototypically, a thetic sentence answers a question like 'What happened?', where the whole predication that follows is new

---

[17] Both Khan and van der Merwe (2020) and Atkinson (2021) link fronted non-focal fronted constituents to "thetic sentences."

[18] The idea of thetic sentences was first proposed in Linguistics by Sige-Yuki Kuroda (1972) and Hans-Jürgen Sasse (1987).

information and thus there is little expectation of Theme–Rheme information structure.

One may ask whether thetic sentences are driving the Hebrew word order or if, within Hebrew, the word order is signalling something else that happens to be broadly congruent with what one might call thetic. A point to remember is that the fronted Contextualisation (Topicalisation) breaks any chain of *wayyiqtol* clauses or *weqatal* clauses. In doing that, it is an iconic structure where the fronted constituent provides a discourse-level function of breaking some continuity that would otherwise have been implied by a *wayyiqtol* structure. This function of signalling discontinuity is acknowledged by Atkinson (2021, 119), who says that "the notion *discontinuity* correlates well with theticity, in that a new entity is introduced into the CG [i.e., common ground of shared understanding], or an inaccessible event which closes, transitions, or opens discourse units."

We can start to answer our questions from §3.1.5 about what is driving X–V sentence orders and what the structure is signalling by looking at a few of the prototypical situations that would produce a fully salient thetic information structure. Consider (18) and (19):

(18) (a) מַה־נִּהְיָתָה
         'What happened?'

     (b) הֹבִישׁ מוֹאָב
         'Moab is in shame' [V–S] (Jer. 48.19–20)

(19) (a) וַיֹּאמֶר מֶה־הָיָה הַדָּבָר בְּנִי
         'And he said, "What happened, my son?"'

     (b) וַיַּעַן הַמְבַשֵּׂר וַיֹּאמֶר
         'And the herald answered and said,'

(c) נָס יִשְׂרָאֵל לִפְנֵי פְלִשְׁתִּים
"'Israel fled from the Philistines;' [V–S]

(d) וְגַם מַגֵּפָה גְדוֹלָה הָיְתָה בָעָם
'additionally, there was a great blow upon the people;' [S–V][19]

(e) וְגַם־שְׁנֵי בָנֶיךָ מֵתוּ חָפְנִי וּפִינְחָס
'additionally, your two sons died, Hophni and Phineas,' [S–V]

(f) וַאֲרוֹן הָאֱלֹהִים נִלְקָחָה
'and the ark of the Lord was taken.'" [S–V] (1 Sam. 4.16–17)

In the two examples above, an answer is given to a 'What happened?' question. Both answers could be called thetic from an information structure perspective, but structurally they use a V–S order.

These answers could also be called 'event-central thetic sentences' (Khan and van der Merwe 2020, 361; Sasse 1987, 554) as opposed to 'entity-central'. Khan and van der Merwe (2020, 361) propose such an example after הִנֵּה in (20), but the context is problematic:

(20) (a) מֶה עָשִׂיתָה
'What did you do?'

(b) הִנֵּה־בָא אַבְנֵר אֵלֶיךָ
'Look, Abner came to you.' [V–S]

---

[19] The first clause answered 'what happened' with V–S order. The following three clauses all avoid thematic ('sequential') verbs by using X–V order. This becomes a list of unordered events rather than a BH narrative. See below for discussion on potential rhetorical effects.

(c) לָמָה זֶּה שִׁלַּחְתּוֹ וַיֵּלֶךְ הָלוֹךְ

'Why is this that you sent him away and he went off?'

(d) יָדַעְתָּ אֶת־אַבְנֵר בֶּן־נֵר

'You [well] know[qatal] Abner, son of Ner,'

(e) כִּי לְפַתֹּתְךָ בָּא

'that to deceive you[Goal,Focus] he came!' (2 Sam. 3.24–25)

The context in (20) revolves around Abner. More importantly, the time of the הִנֵּה clause is past and we are seeing the most unmarked word order for a past/*qatal* reading, just like examples (18) and (19). An S–V order *אבנר בא in (20b) would have been normal for a participle and a present tense, but the morphologically ambiguous בא is clearly past *qatal*. In other words, it is likely the time of *qatal* versus *qotel* that is affecting the word order in (20b), and not the kind of theticity.

It appears that, elsewhere, fronted constituents are doing something other than, or in addition to, marking theticity.[20] If theticity were semantically defined according to information structure, then it would already be the signal. Consider (21):

(21) (a) וַיֵּלְכוּ אֶל־הָעִיר אֲשֶׁר־שָׁם אִישׁ הָאֱלֹהִים

'And they went to the city where the man of God was'

(b) הֵמָּה עֹלִים בְּמַעֲלֵה הָעִיר

'and they were going up to the city' [S–V_Participle]

(c) וְהֵמָּה מָצְאוּ נְעָרוֹת יֹצְאוֹת לִשְׁאֹב מָיִם

'and they[S,Topic] found girls going out to draw water,'

---

[20] Despite the notional definition, Khan and van der Merwe (2020) focus on X–V structures, so that they are in broad agreement with this essay. Their thetic sentences + Topic sentences would equal sentences with a Contextualisation (Topicalisation) structure in my discussion.

(d) וַיֹּאמְרוּ לָהֶן

'and they said to them,'

(e) הֲיֵשׁ בָּזֶה הָרֹאֶה

'"Is there a seer in this place?"' (1 Sam. 9.10–11)

The description in (21b) and (21c) is normal BH for marking simultaneity.[21] Two 'unnecessary' pronouns were generated, apparently in order to block a *wayyiqtol* clause. Throughout the context, the same subject is being followed (Saul and his helper) without change or Focal saliency. As a follow-up sentence to what the participants were doing, it would normally be called a categorical sentence within the thetic/categorical dichotomy. But what is the 'artificial Topic' doing in (21b) and (21c)? It is not part of a sentence with equally presentative information structure. It actually has a fairly clear Topic and Comment differentiation that is associated with 'categorical sentences', so it is not a thetic sentence in that sense. One might argue that it is a special thetic by presenting a Background sentence that serves as a new setting for the following events. Khan and van der Merwe (2020, 379) call the sentence והמה מצאו 'and they found' in (21c) a "resultative situation."

But it is simpler to recognise the simultaneity in time signalled by the discontinuity of the CC and lack of *wayyiqtol*.[22] This

---

[21] Fassberg (2019, 85): במבנה נושא-פועל + נושא פועל 'with a structure "subject–verb" + "subject–verb"'. For additional examples, see Gen. 29.9; 38.25; Judg. 15.14; 1 Sam. 7.10; 1 Kgs 1.14; Isa. 25.24; Job 1.16.

[22] Contrast the participle + *wayyiqtol* in 1 Sam. 6.13: וּבֵית שֶׁמֶשׁ קֹצְרִים קְצִיר־חִטִּים בָּעֵמֶק וַיִּשְׂאוּ אֶת־עֵינֵיהֶם וַיִּרְאוּ אֶת־הָאָרוֹן 'and BetShemesh [were] harvesting wheat in the valley and they lifted their eyes and saw the ark'. The participle presents the setting and the *wayyiqtol* advances the

is true whether in a past narrative or future description, as in the following example.

(22) (a) הִנֵּה עוֹדָךְ מְדַבֶּרֶת שָׁם עִם־הַמֶּלֶךְ
'And then, you will be speaking there with the king'

(b) וַאֲנִי אָבוֹא אַחֲרַיִךְ
'and I will come after you'

(c) וּמִלֵּאתִי אֶת־דְּבָרָיִךְ
'and will confirm your words' (1 Kgs 1.14)

It would not be helpful to talk about the simultaneous entrance of the prophet as a resultative situation. The relationship between the participle clause and the finite verb clause is the same in (22) and (21). In (22), the participle is describing an ongoing progressive imperfective situation in the future, then the prophet will enter at that moment and complete the discussion with the king. The simultaneity is signalled by the CC, which prevents the use of the foregrounding *weqatal*.[23]

---

story with a foregrounded event. However, the *wayyiqtol* does not have the effect of 'just then' that comes with the discontinuity of the CC + *qatal*.

[23] This is described concisely by Fassberg (2019, 84, translation mine): "The storyline in the Bible advances through continuities of verbs that are connected by conversive-*waw*. The biblical story teller deviates from the continuity (*qatal*...) *wayyiqtol*... *wayyiqtol* and from the continuity (*yiqtol*...) *weqatal*... *weqatal* when he wishes to signal to the reader that this does not deal with a direct development in the story line. The sign for stopping the continuity is placing a word before the verb and the presentation of the verb without conversive-*waw*."

3.1.7. Pragmatic Effects of Contextualising Constituents

Practically, the processing for communication follows a simple order. If a constituent is placed before a finite Verb, the author has provided a signal for pragmatic effects.[24] The audience is led to recognise and interpret a special signal. If there is a Focus intonation, it is interpreted as specially marked salient information. Without Focus intonation, the fronted constituent is a Topic/Contextualisation structure that simultaneously breaks any *wayyiqtol* chain. The signal would be easy to perceive, although its application would be multivalent.

There are many examples where a Focus interpretation is ruled out and yet an analysis as a prototypical Topic may not be readily apparent:

(23) (a) וְהָאָדָם יָדַע אֶת־חַוָּה אִשְׁתּוֹ
'And the man knew Eve his wife$_{[S-V]}$'

(b) וַתַּהַר וַתֵּלֶד אֶת־קַיִן
'and she conceived and gave birth to Cain'

(c) וַתֹּאמֶר קָנִיתִי אִישׁ אֶת־יְהוָה
'and said, "I have acquired a man with the Lord."'
(Gen. 4.1)

The Subject הָאָדָם 'the man' is not an extended topic of this verse or the following verses, nor does this Subject provide any natural framework for these immediate verses. In terms of information structure, the whole sentence posits a new situation.[25] The

---

[24] Conjunctions are not included in this statement, as they precede the clause in their own special position.

[25] It would probably rightly be classed as thetic by Khan and van der Merwe (2020) and Atkinson (2021).

Subject and Object are equally re-established in this sentence, which serves as a setting or starting point for the story that follows. The Subject is not marked, salient information, so it is not a Focus in FG terms. But in what sense should הָאָדָם be called Topic? Why didn't the author use *וַיֵּדַע הָאָדָם אֶת חַוָּה אִשְׁתּוֹ, which would be more of a default for Hebrew narrative?

This appears to be an example where a Topic/CC is used to set off the whole clause, and where the pre-verbal Topic/CC prevents the thematic verb structure (*wayyiqtol*). Within BH, the marked constituent simultaneously breaks the continuity of the thematic verb system (sometimes called sequential or consecutive verbs).[26] The Topic/CC sets off the whole sentence with pragmatic marking, and iconically signals some sense of a break in continuity. Consider (24):

(24) (a) וַיהוָה הֵטִיל רוּחַ־גְּדוֹלָה אֶל־הַיָּם
'And the Lord threw down$_{[S-V]}$ a big wind to the sea'

(b) וַיְהִי סַעַר־גָּדוֹל בַּיָּם
'and there was a big storm in the sea'

(c) וְהָאֳנִיָּה חִשְּׁבָה לְהִשָּׁבֵר
'and the boat planned $_{[S-V]}$ to break apart' (Jon. 1.4)

The text in (24) shows a similar problem to (23). The Subject comes before the Verb, but it does not make a transparent Topic for the following verses. It is not a Focus, either, since 'throwing

---

[26] These verb categories of *wayyiqtol* in the past/realis/perfective and *weqatal* in the future/irrealis/imperfective are often called sequential verbs. However, they do not uniquely entail strict temporal sequentiality, nor do they induce their Tense-Mood-Aspect from a previous verb, so a more abstract term like *thematic* may be preferable as providing a term for unit structure and for foregrounding.

down a wind' is really the newest and most salient information in the story at this point. The sentence is not answering an implied question ('who threw down a wind?'), but is presenting the wind as a new development, a new setting or scene, but without using the normal *wayyiqtol* syntax (... וַיָּטֵל יהוה *).

These examples, as well as hundreds more, lead to a recognition that a non-Focal pragmatic positioning can also mark the whole clause as a pragmatic signal for the larger discourse and not just for the constituent itself. For example, Rashi, one of the outstanding medieval commentators, suggested that the word order at Gen. 4.1 was used to mark a break in the timeline of the story and the conception (and maybe the birth) took place while the couple was still in Eden (see Rashi 1986, 68). Such a suggestion is possible because choosing a pragmatic function that uses fronting prevents the use of the most common narrative structure, *wayyiqtol* (the thematic past-tense verb). Thus, the pragmatic positioning of pieces of a Hebrew clause is directly linked to the verb system.

Hebrew is a language with an interesting information packaging strategy. For over 1,000 years, the language used two binary, finite verb systems: *qatal* (past-realis-perfective) versus *yiqtol* (future-irrealis-habitual) on the one hand and *wayyiqtol* (past-realis-perfective) versus *weqatal* (future-irrealis-imperfective) on the other hand, the latter being a 'thematic finite verb' system. The *wayyiqtol* thematic verb system provided a packaging structure in narrative and past contexts, and the *weqatal* provided a similar structural packaging in future contexts, volitional contexts, and as continuing habitual sentences in the past.[27] The thematic verb system requires a V–S order. By contrast, the non-thematic system has an X–V order. This means that if an author wants to use a non-thematic verb and break a thematic sequence, he must use a pragmatic constituent between a conjunction and the verb. In other words, a Topic (CC) may be used to create a non-thematic sentence, as well as to mark a Topic constituent.

Such sentences may be used in multiple ways. In their most basic sense, they break the flow of the thematic sentences (*wayyiqtol* and *weqatal*). This structure is chosen to signal a break, and the break may be (a) a break in time (whether simultaneously or as a flashback); or (b) a break in structure (whether a unit boundary with a transitional setting or a parenthetical comment); or simply (c) a break for rhetorical-literary effect. Both (23) and (24) can be interpreted as unit boundaries in the discourse, as the story time advanced forward in each. Similar situations occur in the following exmaples.

(25) (a) וַיְהִי אַחַר הַדְּבָרִים הָאֵלֶּה וְהָאֱלֹהִים נִסָּה אֶת־אַבְרָהָם

'And it happened after these events and God tested Abraham$_{[S-V]}$' (Gen. 22.1)

(b) *וַיְהִי אַחַר הַדְּבָרִים הָאֵלֶּה וַיְנַס הָאֱלֹהִים אֶת־אַבְרָהָם

The word order in (25a) is S–V, where the Subject does not appear to be a Focus as the most salient information, nor is it

---

[27] With a binary verbal system, it should be assumed that the description here is necessarily simplified. A binary tense-mood-aspect finite verb system must describe most of the distinctions in the world of communication, including time, modality, and aspect, with only two verb forms.

readily explained as a Topic. Rather, the whole sentence is set apart, and here it appears to be like a section heading that summarises the following story in 22:2–16. The V–S word order in (25b) would make use of the thematic verb system and would imply that this is the first foregrounded event that develops the story proper after the time setting 'and it happened after these events'. But by using S–V order with a Topic/CC, the author was able to signal a discontinuity, setting the whole first sentence apart and presenting a summary of the whole story.

Such a summary sentence can be understood as one of many kinds of literary settings before the development of the story, as in (26):

(26) (a) וְהָאָרֶץ הָיְתָה תֹהוּ וָבֹהוּ
'And the earth was empty chaos'

(b) וְחֹשֶׁךְ עַל־פְּנֵי תְהוֹם
'and darkness [was] on the surface of the deep water'

(c) וְרוּחַ אֱלֹהִים מְרַחֶפֶת עַל־פְּנֵי הַמָּיִם
'and God's spirit was hovering over the water surface'

(d) וַיֹּאמֶר אֱלֹהִים יְהִי אוֹר
'and God said "Let there be light,"'

(e) וַיְהִי־אוֹר
'and there was light.' (Gen. 1.2–3)

In (26), lines (a) through (c) set the stage for the main event in (d) and (e). The S–V order in (26a) avoids a thematic verb and avoids implying that this is the first main event of the narrative. The whole sentence becomes a setting for the story that follows. Likewise, the verbless clause and the participial clause in (b) and (c) continue a description of the background setting. They do not advance the events of the story, so they do not use the *wayyiqtol* structure. We thus find a satisfying reading of the authorial choice of S–V order in (26a).

The example in (27) provides a similar case:

(27) וְיוֹסֵף הוּרַד מִצְרָיְמָה

'And Joseph had been taken$_{[S-V]}$ to Egypt' (Gen. 39.1)

This verse returns the story in Genesis to Joseph and Egypt after a long, multi-generational hiatus in chapter 38. The S–V order might be called a Topic in order to return to discussing Joseph. However, it also blocks the thematic, *wayyiqtol* verb system and repeats the action that had already been narrated at Gen. 37.28 and 36. Therefore, the sentence as a whole marks a chronological reordering in the story, conveying a pluperfect sense to the audience.

In (28), we might try to explain the S–V word order as a Topic/CC in order to compare the sailors' action and Jonah's action.

(28) וְיוֹנָה יָרַד אֶל־יַרְכְּתֵי הַסְּפִינָה וַיִּשְׁכַּב וַיֵּרָדַם

'And Jonah went down$_{[S-V]}$ to the back of the ship and lay down and went into a deep sleep' (Jon. 1.5b)

However, one should consider that Jonah went below and went to sleep before the storm and the actions of the sailors. The choice of Topic/CC structure, instead of *וַיֵּרֶד יוֹנָה, forces a non-thematic, non-*wayyiqtol* sentence structure and the whole sentence becomes a potential break in the timeline of the story. Here, the time most probably goes back to an earlier point in the story.

From the context around (29), we know that Jacob left with the livestock, along with Rachel, at a time while Laban was already away (Gen. 31.17, 20).

(29) (a) וַיִּנְהַג אֶת־כָּל־מִקְנֵהוּ ... לָבוֹא אֶל־יִצְחָק אָבִיו אַרְצָה כְּנָעַן
'And he [Jacob] led all his livestock ... to Isaac his father in Canaan.'

(b) וְלָבָן הָלַךְ לִגְזֹז אֶת־צֹאנוֹ
'And Laban had gone₍S–V₎ to shear his sheep'

(c) וַתִּגְנֹב רָחֵל אֶת־הַתְּרָפִים
'and Rachel stole₍V–S₎ the house-gods.' (Gen. 31.18–19)

It appears, then, that the Subject–Verb order וְלָבָן הָלַךְ in (29b) is not used as a Focus or Topic for 'Laban', but to avoid the implications of *וַיֵּלֶךְ לָבָן 'and Laban went'. That thematic verb would normally have sounded as if Laban's visit to his sheep was after Jacob and Rachel started their journey. But then Rachel could not have stolen the idols afterwards (וַתִּגְנֹב), because she had already left the homestead with Jacob. The S–V order וְלָבָן הָלַךְ provides a signal to the reader that a break occurred and the reader can immediately apply this to a prior time for Laban's business trip.

3.1.8. Dramatic Pause as a Literary Effect

A remarkable string of S–V clauses appears in (30):

(30) (a) הַבֹּקֶר אוֹר
'The morning turned light₍S–V₎'

(b) וְהָאֲנָשִׁים שֻׁלְּחוּ הֵמָּה וַחֲמֹרֵיהֶם
'and the men were sent off₍S–V₎, they[28] and their donkeys.'

---

[28] In FG, such an afterthought is called a Tail function.

(c) הֵם יָצְאוּ אֶת־הָעִיר
'They left the city[S-V],'

(d) לֹא הִרְחִיקוּ
'they didn't go far,'

(e) וְיוֹסֵף אָמַר לַאֲשֶׁר עַל־בֵּיתוֹ
'and Joseph said to his house-manager[S-V]' (Gen. 44.3–4)

The clause in (30a) has no conjunction and the pragmatically marked S-V sentence might be taken as a setting and a unit boundary. However, the second clause in (30b) is also S-V, a seemingly unnecessary word order since וַיְשַׁלְּחוּ הָאֲנָשִׁים* 'and the men were sent off' would have fit normal thematic verbs and would have been expected. The next clause in (30c) is also S-V, also without conjunction, and with the S-V order created by what might be seen as an unnecessary pronoun, since וַיֵּצְאוּ אֶת־הָעִיר* would have worked fine. The next clause in (30d) is a negative, ineligible for a thematic *wayyiqtol* verb, and without a conjunction. Finally, Joseph's speech is introduced in (30e) with S-V instead of the usual וַיֹּאמֶר*. The lack of conjunction in (30a) and (30c) gives a sense of a double beginning, while the negative clause becomes a parenthetical comment. In parallel with this, the avoidance of thematic verbs, despite an appropriate context for them, does not allow the story to progress normally. All of the verb forms here 'break' the obvious forward implications of the real-time events. The literary scene appears to have stalled in literary time with all of the actions piled on top of each other. If that is the intended effect of the author, we may call this a rhetorical use of the pragmatically marked sentences. The story has paused with a break extended literarily and syntactically, even though the real time has moved forward.[29] In literary terms, we could call this a kind of dramatic pause, perhaps leading to some kind of climax. If so, the suspense is held for considerable time, since it is thirty-two verses later, at Gen. 45.3, that Joseph dramatically reveals himself to his brothers.

The idea of a literary and syntactic pause can explain the example above in (24c). One would have expected the thematic form וַתְּחַשֵּׁב הָאֳנִיָּה לְהִשָּׁבֵר* 'and the boat planned to break apart'. However, the S–V order and the seemingly unnecessary CC (Topic) present a pragmatically marked sentence that breaks the forward movement of the unit and story, despite the real world advance in time. It rhetorically and syntactically pauses the story at a point of dramatic tension—a dramatic pause. The content, as well, leaves the outcome open-ended and on the verge of disaster.

3.1.9. Multiple Pragmatic Constituents in Hebrew

With multiple pragmatic constituents before the Verb, there is typically a scale from the more presupposed constituent(s), i.e., Topic/CC, to the most salient Focus. Consider (31).

(31) כִּי־פְשָׁעַי אֲנִי אֵדָע

'because my sins$_{[O,Topic]}$ I myself$_{[S,Focus]}$ would recognise' (Ps. 51.5 [7])

The syntactic Object of the sentence is פְּשָׁעַי 'my rebellious sins'. Its position in the sentence can be explained as linking to the sins mentioned in other verses, that is, as a Topic function that uses

---

[29] See, for example, Esth. 7.6–8 for a similar long string of non-thematic S–V sentences at a climax. Also, Gen. 19.23–25 in the description of the destruction of Sodom and Gomorrah.

established information to lead into the Comment and newer information of the sentence. Then, the explicit Subject 'I' is recognised as pragmatically fronted and as reinforced Focal information that is contra-expected by human nature.

To have both constituents before the Verb demands an explanation in an FG approach to a V–S language. In the example in (31), the first is a Topic/CC and the second a Focus.

(32) יְהוָה עֹז לְעַמּוֹ יִתֵּן

'the Lord[CC1] will give strength[CC2] TO HIS PEOPLE[Focus]' (Ps. 29.11)[30]

An FG approach provides for insightful reading. FG lets the audience know that there are three pragmatically marked constituents in (32), culminating in 'to his people'. The Psalmist wrote this text to exhort the audience to remain with the people of the covenant, since that is where the blessings of their incomparable God rest. That purpose is reflected in the word order choices.

3.2. Application to Greek

In Greek there are structural, frequency, and complexity differences from Hebrew. Nevertheless, the principles of FG and marked information structure pay dividends for those reading Greek texts. We can illustrate how pragmatics in FG are helpful for Greek in similar ways, although many of the issues go beyond the scope of a simple article.

---

[30] עֹז 'strength' is also a word of praise from v. 1. There is a crescendo of saliency, leading from the less salient to the more salient. The final, most salient item would receive Focus intonation.

Several obvious differences from Hebrew can be stated at the start. While Hebrew builds texts with finite verb sentences, Greek uses much more subordination. Participial phrases hang on finite-verb sentences seemingly everywhere. Greek has a more granular connective system and uses many more particles in shaping and presenting a text. The verbal system in Greek is highly aspectual, requiring users to encode aspect in imperatives, subjunctives, optatives, infinitives, and participles, as well as with finite indicatives in the past.[31] In word order, Greek has more flexibility, with words attracted phonologically to phrasal Heads (*enclitics*), phrases split and positioned differently (*hyperbaton*), flexible orders with Noun + Adjective, and more usage of pragmatic functions. However, those pragmatic functions of Topic and Focus provide much information to the practised audience.

3.2.1. Greek is V–S–O

Greek, like Hebrew, was a V–S language, as linguists working both within and outside of FG have concluded.[32] Here is a summary from Runge (2010, 189–90) in support:

---

[31] The binary verbal system in Hebrew was more time-mood orientated and had difficulty expressing aspect in comparison with Greek. See Hornkohl (2018); Buth (2019).

[32] Helma Dik (1995, 12) uses a template P1–PØ–V–X. The P1 is pragmatic Topic, the PØ is Focus, followed by the syntactic template V–X. Note that the numbers on the P position are different from those used by Runge (2010), although they are referring to the same concepts.

> Simon Dik has proposed that there are two different preverbal positions that may or may not be filled in any given clause, which he calls Position 1 (P1) and Position 2 (P2). ... The meaningful distinction between P1 and P2 is based largely upon whether the fronted information is presupposed or newly asserted, respectively.
>
> One or more established (i.e., topical) elements of the clause may be placed in position P1. These P1 elements establish a new *frame of reference*,[33] creating an explicit mental grounding point for the clause that follows. Position P2, on the other hand, is where newly asserted or focal information is placed.

Dik's preverbal template is given by Runge (2010, 191) as "(P1) (P2) Verb X." To this we may add another comment from Runge (2010, 207):

> Koiné Greek is a verb-prominent language, where the least-marked and most basic order of clause components is for the verb to be placed in the initial position. When other elements are placed in the initial position, such placement is motivated by some pragmatic reason.

3.2.2. Application to Greek Texts

The example in (33) provides a simple example to reinforce the claim that FG can help readers to recognise pragmatic signals and, thus, to enhance interpretation skills.

---

[33] Here Runge footnotes and acknowledges other terminology that covers the same kind of pragmatic function: 'topicalisation' (Lambrecht), 'point of departure' (Levinsohn), 'contextualising constituent' (Buth).

(33) Ἐν ἀρχῇ ἦν ὁ λόγος, καὶ ὁ λόγος ἦν πρὸς τὸν θεόν, καὶ θεὸς ἦν ὁ λόγος.

'In beginning$_{[\text{Topic,X}]}$ was the Word, and the Word$_{[\text{Topic,Sub}]}$ was with God, and the Word was God$_{[\text{Focus,Compl}]}$.' (John 1.1)

The whole sentence is technically new because it starts the book. However, the phrase ἐν ἀρχῇ 'in beginning' is clearly fronted before the Verb as a non-Focal constituent, and therefore as a Topic/CC. It turns out to be the most presupposed information in its clause and provides a framework for the rest of the sentence, even though it is not the larger topic of the sentence. The clause is a Setting, Background, and Thetic. That is why a name like 'Contextualising Constituent' for the fronted constituent is more transparent in English than 'Topic' (cf. Runge's 'Frame of reference' above). Syntactically, ἐν ἀρχῇ 'in beginning' is an adverbial complement to the Verb, something labelled 'X' in many of the templates above. This X has been chosen to function as a broadly defined Topic or CC. In addition, the Subject, ὁ λόγος 'the word', follows the Verb and suggests that Greek is a real Verb–Subject–Object language. (Obviously, a sample of three clauses can only be an illustration, not a substantive argument.)

In the second clause, the phrase ὁ λόγος 'the word' can be interpreted as a Topic/CC that marks and establishes the Subject as the primary topical link of the clause to the sentence. The 'word' is not the new or most salient information of the clause and it is not to be read as Focus or with Focal intonation.

Finally, the phrase θεός 'God' is the new, salient information of the clause and it comes before the default V–S order, so it is clearly marked as Focus. Again, the order of the Subject supports the idea that this is a V–S–O language and not S–V–O. We can try to paraphrase the pragmatic signals of the three clauses in English: 'In the beginning the Word existed. (Let's establish 'the Word' as our wider Topic): it was with God, and it was, in fact, God.' Presumably, the intonation of the Greek sentence would reinforce this reading and make the differences between the CC and the Focus transparent. All of this can be processed rapidly and subliminally by an accomplished reader or audience.

These verses in John are uncharacteristically simple for Greek, but that makes them good for illustrating how FG allows a speaker to encode word order and for an audience to interpret the text with the clues of the word order. The next example in (34) illustrates both the application of these functions and potential ambiguities.

(34) οὗτος ἦν ἐν ἀρχῇ πρὸς τὸν θεόν. πάντα δι' αὐτοῦ ἐγένετο, καὶ χωρὶς αὐτοῦ ἐγένετο οὐδὲ ἕν ὃ γέγονεν. ἐν αὐτῷ ζωὴ ἦν, καὶ ἡ ζωὴ ἦν τὸ φῶς τῶν ἀνθρώπων· καὶ τὸ φῶς ἐν τῇ σκοτίᾳ φαίνει, καὶ ἡ σκοτία αὐτὸ οὐ κατέλαβεν.

'This[Topic,Sub] was in the beginning with God. All things[Topic,Sub] through him[Focus,X] came to be, and outside of him[Topic,X] came to be nothing that came to be. In him[Topic,X] was life[Focus,Sub/Comp], and the life[Topic,Sub] was the light of people, and the light[Topic,Sub] shines in the darkness[Focus,X] and the darkness[Topic,Sub] did not comprehend it[Focus?,Obj].' (John 1.2–5)

Every clause makes use of pragmatic functions to help the audience follow the thoughts and grasp the points.

The first clause has a Topic οὗτος 'this' that restates items from the first verse, and the sentence re-establishes the starting base for the points that follow. The second clause may be read in two ways. As a Topic, πάντα 'all things' would introduce items that are assumed to be part of the beginning. The salient, important point in the clause would be that they came into being through the Word.[34] That salient point 'through him, the Word' was placed before the Verb and given prominence as Focus as being contra-expected. A reader/listener could distinguish these Topic and Focus placements through the use of a Focus intonation. On the other hand, πάντα 'all things' is technically newer information than the pronoun 'through it/him' and it could have been intended for Focus intonation with 'through it/him' remaining as a Topic. Such an order of Focus–Topic is rare.[35] In the next clause, the phrase 'outside of him' serves as a Topic that reiterates the idea of the previous clause with default word order.

The Word continues to serve as a pragmatic Topic 'in him', and the clause introduces marked (i.e., fronted), salient information, 'life', as Focus before the Verb. This begins a chain of

---

[34] I have translated the pronoun as 'him', even though it refers to an abstract noun. That noun isn't fully personalised until vv. 10–18.

[35] A fairly unambiguous example of Focus before marked Topic occurs at Gal. 3.2, ἐξ ἔργων νόμου τὸ πνεῦμα ἐλάβετε ἢ ἐξ ἀκοῆς πίστεως; 'Did you receive the spirit from works of law or from hearing of faith?' The phrases ἐξ ἔργων νόμου 'from works' and ἐξ ἀκοῆς πίστεως 'from hearing of faith' are the Focal question constituents. However, 'from works$_{[Focus]}$' comes before the Topical Object τὸ πνεῦμα 'Spirit$_{[Object,Topic]}$'. See also John 5.46, εἰ γὰρ ἐπιστεύετε Μωϋσεῖ, ἐπιστεύετε ἂν ἐμοί· περὶ γὰρ ἐμοῦ ἐκεῖνος ἔγραψεν 'for if you believed Moses, you would have believed me, because he$_{[Sub,Topic]}$ wrote about me$_{[X,Focus]}$'. So πάντα is functionally ambiguous and could have been read with two intonations.

clauses in which any salient information becomes a marked Topic in the following clause.

One tricky point of reading comes in the last clause. There may be two marked Topics in the clause 'and the darkness, it, did not comprehend'. Both 'darkness' and 'it [the light]' appear to be pre-supposed, established, topical constituents and may not receive any special reinforcement, therefore without focal intonation, leaving the negated Verb as most salient. So, although there are two pragmatic constituents before the Verb, there is no Focus constituent marked by word order. Alternatively, 'it' may be read with Focal intonation for a coming contrast with 'him' in verse 10.

4.0. Prospects for Further Application

Functional Grammar helps identify pragmatic markings in a language. Learning to identify pragmatic material in texts is a gateway to a wider world, whether in linguistic, literary, or biblical studies in particular.

Some researchers may want to work directly in the field of formalising grammar and knowledge about human language and the iterations that are found in Biblical Hebrew and ancient Greek. Many questions remain for formalising syntax. This is true for linguistics in general and for FG. Areas like the linguistic side of FG, word order, or discourse analysis and pragmatics in either Hebrew or Greek continue to develop. There is a continuum from studying how stories are constructed all the way down to the nuts and bolts of a language. Functional linguistics is poised to address that challenge. At the end of the day, these are tools that are used for describing and understanding messages in both their structure and their meaning. Research and understanding in both Hebrew and Greek literatures are enhanced as one develops a sensitivity to the pragmatic signals and language choices that are woven into every sentence in a text.

5.0. Further Reading

5.1. General Introductions

1. Dik (1980, 1–24)
2. Anstey (2004)
3. Kees and MacKenzie (2015)
4. Kees and MacKenzie (2008)

5.2. Foundational Texts (Greek-Orientated)

1. Dik (1995)
2. Runge (2010)

5.3. Foundational Texts (Hebrew-Orientated)

1. Moshavi (2010)
2. Hornkohl (2018)
3. Atkinson (2021)

References

Anstey, Matthew P. 2004. 'Functional Grammar from its Inception'. In *A New Architecture for Functional Grammar*, edited by J. Lachlan Mackenzie and María de los Ángeles Gómez-

González, 23–72. Functional Grammar Series 24. Berlin, New York: De Gruyter Mouton.

Atkinson, Ian T. 2021. 'In Pursuit of a More Comprehensive Framework for Fronting in Classical BH Prose'. PhD dissertation, University of Stellenbosch.

Bailey, Nicholas A., and Stephen H. Levinsohn. 1992. 'The Function of Preverbal Elements in Independent Clauses in the Hebrew Narrative of Genesis'. *Journal of Translation and Textlinguistics* 5 (3): 179–207.

Bickerton, Derek. 1981. *Roots of Language.* Ann Arbor: Karoma Publishers.

Buth, Randall. 1987. 'Word Order in Aramaic from the Perspectives of Discourse Analysis and Functional Grammar'. PhD dissertation, University of California, Los Angeles.

———. 1994a. 'Contextualizing Constituent as Topic, Nonsequential Background and Dramatic Pause: Hebrew and Aramaic Evidence'. In *Function and Expression in Functional Grammar*, edited by Elisabeth Engberg-Pedersen, Lisbeth Falster Jakobsen, and Lone Schack Rasmussen, 215–32. Functional Grammar Series 16. Berlin and New York: Mouton de Gruyter.

———. 1994b. 'Methodological Collision Between Source Criticism and Discourse Analysis: the Problem of "Unmarked Temporal Overlay" and the Pluperfect/Non-sequential *wayyiqṭol*'. In *Biblical Hebrew and Discourse Linguistics*, edited by Robert D. Bergen, 138–54. Dallas, TX: Summer Institute of Linguistics.

———. 1995. 'Functional Grammar, Hebrew and Aramaic: An Integrated, Textlinguistic Approach to Syntax'. In *Discourse Analysis of Biblical Literature: What It Is and What It Offers*, edited by Walter R. Bodine, 77–102. Atlanta: Scholars Press.

———. 1999. 'Word Order in the Verbless Clause: A Generative-Functional Approach'. In *The Verbless Clause in Biblical Hebrew: Linguistic Approaches,* edited by Cynthia Miller, 79–108. Linguistic Studies in Ancient West Semitic 1. Winona Lake, IN: Eisenbrauns.

———. 2019 [2007]. *Living Biblical Hebrew: Selected Readings with 500 Friends.* Jerusalem: Biblical Language Center. Including 'The Hebrew Verb: A Short Syntax', 137–64e.

Butler, Christopher C. 2005. 'Focusing on Focus: A Comparison of Functional Grammar, Role and Reference Grammar and Systemic Functional Grammar'. *Language Sciences* (27): 585–618.

Chomsky, Noam. 1957. *Syntactic Structures.* Janua Linguarum, Series Minor 4. The Hague: Mouton.

———. 1965. *Aspects of the Theory of Syntax.* Cambridge, MA: The MIT Press.

Daneš, Frantešek (ed.). 1974. *Papers on Functional Sentence Perspective.* Janua Linguarum, Series Minor 147. Prague: Academia; The Hague: Mouton.

Dik, Helma. 1995. *Word Order in Ancient Greek: A Pragmatic Account of Word Order Variation in Herodotus.* Amsterdam Studies in Classical Philology 5. Amsterdam: J. C. Gieben.

———. 2007. *Word Order in Greek Tragic Dialogue*. Oxford: Oxford University Press.

Dik, Simon C. 1978. *Functional Grammar*. Amsterdam: North Holland.

———. 1980. *Studies in Functional Grammar*. London: Academic Press.

———. 1989. *The Theory of Functional Grammar, Part 1: The Structure of the Clause*. Dordrecht: Foris Publications.

———. 1997. *The Theory of Functional Grammar, Part 1: The Structure of the Clause*. 2nd rev. ed. Edited by Kees Hengeveld. Functional Grammar Series 20. Berlin: Mouton de Gruyter.

———. 1997. *The Theory of Functional Grammar, Part 2: Complex and Derived Constructions*. Edited by Kees Hengeveld. Functional Grammar Series 21. Berlin: Mouton de Gruyter.

Fassberg, Stephen E. 2019. מבוא לתחביר לשון המקרא. Jerusalem: Bialik Institute.

Foley, William A., and Robert D. Van Valin Jr. 1984. *Functional Syntax and Universal Grammar*. Cambridge: Cambridge University Press.

Firbas, Jan. 1992. *Functional Sentence Perspective in Written and Spoken Communication*. Cambridge: Cambridge University Press.

Givón, Talmy. 1984. *Syntax: A Functional-Typological Introduction*. Vol. 1. Amsterdam: John Benjamins.

———. 2001. *Syntax: An Introduction.* Vol. 1. Rev. ed. Amsterdam: John Benjamins.

Greenberg, Joseph H. (ed.). 1966. *Universals of Language*. 2nd ed. Cambridge, MA: The MIT Press.

Gross, Walter. 2001. *Doppelt besetzes Vorfeld: Syntaktische, pragmatische und übersetzungstechnische Studien zum althebräischen Verbalsatz*. Beihefte zur Zeitschrift für die alttestamentliche Wissenschaft 305. Berlin and New York: Walter de Gruyter.

Heimerdinger, Jean-Marc. 1999. *Topic, Focus and Foreground in Ancient Hebrew Narratives*. Sheffield: Sheffield Academic Press.

Hengeveld, Kees, and J. Lachlan MacKenzie. 2005. 'Functional Discourse Grammar'. In *Encyclopedia of Language and Linguistics*, 2nd ed., edited by Keith Brown, 668–76. Amsterdam: Elsevier.

———. 2008. *Functional Discourse Grammar: A Typologically Based Theory of Language Structure*. Oxford: Oxford University Press.

———. 2015. 'Functional Discourse Grammar'. In *The Oxford Handbook of Linguistic Analysis*, 2nd ed., edited by Keith Brown, 311–44. Oxford: Oxford University Press.

Holmstedt, Robert. 2009. 'Word Order and Information Structure in Ruth and Jonah: A Generative-Typological Analysis'. *Journal of Semitic Studies* 54 (1): 111–39.

———. 2011. 'The Typological Classification of the Hebrew of Genesis: Subject-Verb or Verb-Subject?'. *Journal of Hebrew Scriptures* 11, article 14. doi.org/10.5508/jhs.2011.v11.a14.

Hornkohl, Aaron D. 2018. 'Biblical Hebrew Tense–Aspect–Mood, Word Order and Pragmatics: Some Observations on Recent Approaches'. In *Studies in Semitic Linguistics and Manuscripts: A Liber Discipulorum in Honour of Professor Geoffrey Khan,* edited by Nadia Vidro, Ronny Vollandt, Esther-Miriam Wagner, and Judith Olszowy-Schlanger, 27–56. Acta Universitatis Upsaliensis–Studia Semitica Upsaliensia 30. Uppsala: Uppsala Universitet.

Khan, Geoffrey, and Christo H. J. van der Merwe. 2020. 'Towards a Comprehensive Model for Interpreting Word Order in Classical Biblical Hebrew'. *Journal of Semitic Studies* 65 (20): 347–90.

Kuroda, Sige-Yuki. 1972. 'The Categorical and the Thetic Judgment'. *Foundations of Language* 9: 153 85

Lambrecht, Knud. 1994. *Information Structure and Sentence Form: Topics, Focus, and the Mental Representations of Discourse Referents.* Cambridge: Cambridge University Press.

Levinsohn, Stephen H. 2000. *Discourse Features of New Testament Greek: A Coursebook on the Information Structure of New Testament Greek.* 2nd ed. Dallas, TX: SIL International Publications.

Moshavi, Adina. 2010. *Word Order in the Biblical Hebrew Finite Clause.* Winona Lake, IN: Eisenbrauns.

Rashi. 1986. תורת חיים ספר בראשית, בראשית-חיי שרה. Jerusalem: Rav Kook.

Runge, Steven E. 2010. *Discourse Grammar of the Greek New Testament: A Practical Introduction for Teaching and Exegesis.* Bellingham, WA: Lexham Press.

Sasse, Hans-Jürgen. 1987. 'The Thetic/Categorical Distinction Revisited'. *Linguistics* 25: 511–80.

Van Valin Jr., Robert D., and Randy J. LaPolla. 1997. *Syntax: Structure, Meaning and Function*. Cambridge: Cambridge University Press.

COGNITIVE LINGUISTIC THEORY AND THE BIBLICAL LANGUAGES[1]

William A. Ross

Study of the Bible has always involved study of its languages. But the study of language has not always involved linguistic theory as such. It has only been over the past sixty years or so that western biblical scholarship has begun to appropriate and apply insights from general linguistics to better understand the ancient texts. Over that time, the bulk of linguistically-informed biblical language research has adopted formalist linguistic theories, such as structuralism or generativism.[2] This trend is due in part to the

---

[1] I am grateful to Elizabeth Robar, Travis Wright, and my two peer reviewers for their useful input on earlier versions of this chapter. My thanks go to Joey Hyatt for his capable research assistance preparing the bibliography.

[2] Taylor (2002, 4–5) concisely explains formalist approaches as those that "regard a language as a self-contained system, whose properties are encapsulated in a Grammar, i.e. a device which generates, or defines, the set of well-formed sentences which constitute the language. A general feature of formalist approaches is to regard a language as a disembodied object, which is independent, as it were, of the speakers who use it and the purposes for which they use it." More specifically with reference to mainstream generativism, 'formal' tends to mean

fact that formalist theories are older and better known in comparison with the alternatives. But it is also due to the tendency of interdisciplinary research never to be truly up-to-date on all fronts. That being the case, it is only in the last twenty years that biblical scholarship has come into direct contact with Cognitive Linguistics, a topic that is the focus of this chapter.

1.0. The History of Cognitive Linguistics

It is important to understand at the outset that Cognitive Linguistics is not a unified field of research. It is, as Geeraerts (2006b, 2) puts it, "an archipelago rather than an island," one whose members are described below (cf. Geeraerts and Cuyckens 2007a, 5–6). Even so, Cognitive Linguistics is a research perspective that is characterised by several key theoretical commitments concerning language, and these commitments do grant coherence and unity to the discipline as a whole, if not total uniformity. As discussed further below, it was not until the 1970s and 1980s that major developments—and controversies—in general linguistics at large created the necessary conditions from which the foundational pillars of Cognitive Linguistic theory would begin to emerge. But to understand why and how that happened requires a broader historical perspective than one might expect.

Cognitive Linguistics is not unique among theories for its focus on language as a mental phenomenon. Generativism, for example, is also 'cognitive' in a basic sense, in that it attributes a

---

explicit, non-embodied, and rationalist, which makes semantics describable with abstract, rule-governed predicate logic.

mental status to language.³ But Cognitive Linguistics does represent the revival of interest among linguists in the meaning-bearing function of language for communication alongside its psychological character. In other words, Cognitive Linguistic theory is interested not only in knowledge of a language, but also in language as a *form* of knowledge, even an "integral part of cognition" itself (Janda 2015, 131). For most of the twentieth century, this kind of outlook had receded entirely from view in linguistic theorising, in favour of an almost exclusive focus on extrapolating abstract structures or rules taken to account for language as a self-contained system. But it was not always so.

1.1. Early Modern Foundations

Linguistics emerged as a scientific discipline—if one wishes to use such terminology—in the nineteenth century, as it became distinct from the older and broader practices of philology.⁴ This was the era of diachronic, comparative linguistics.⁵ In many

---

[3] Hence the capitalisation of 'Cognitive Linguistics' as a point of distinction from other theoretical approaches that also consider cognitive aspects of language (Siewierska 2013, 485 n. 1).

[4] Linguists themselves disagree over whether and how linguistics can be considered a 'science', properly speaking. Harris (1993, 11) satisfyingly dismisses such bickering, saying that linguistics "is some sort of systematic, truth-seeking, knowledge-making enterprise, and as long as it brings home the epistemic bacon by turning up results about language, the label ['science'] isn't terribly important."

[5] Diachronic study looks at the development of phenomena over time, as compared with synchronic study, which looks at phenomena within a specific point or period of time.

ways, this phase of language study and its particular methods arrived upon the broader tide of historical reconstruction and comparativism that was rising throughout the academy at large in this period (De Maurio and Formigari 1990; Bod 2013, 143–83). Scholars tirelessly sought parallels in sound-meaning pairs as a way to chart the history of what would come to be known as the Indo-European language family.

Although many of their conclusions have stood the test of time remarkably well, nineteenth-century comparative linguists were also prone to indulging in wild speculation (see Eco 1995). These scholars were heirs to the old notion that languages are linked to the thought patterns of the people who use them (Robins 1997, 152–206). Some took this idea down dark, more deterministic pathways in the intensifying atmosphere of Romantic nationalism in *fin de siècle* Europe (see Olender 1992; Turner 2014, 125–46; Joseph 2020, 145–63). But at a general level, most scholars viewed the study of language as concerned with communication and also as a corollary in some way to the study of the mind and therefore to all of human society. Language was understood as essentially psychological and thus imbricated with human experience (Campbell 2003, 93–94; Geeraerts 2010, 9–16).

1.2. Formalist Peregrinations

The study of language changed shape at the turn of the twentieth century. Perhaps the most important bellwether was the posthumous appearance of the *Cours de linguistique générale* by Ferdinand de Saussure (1857–1913) in 1916, which set out to define the task of linguistics. Saussure's work had lasting effects. One was to reorientate linguistic inquiry away from diachronic questions of historical reconstruction, which had predominated previous scholarship, towards synchronic questions. Another was to move away from viewing language as a social phenomenon. Instead, Saussure distinguished linguistic behaviour (*parole*) from the supposed abstract system underlying it (*langue*). Only the latter was the proper object of linguistic research, understood as a self-contained system of interrelated signs.

This basic outlook became the foundation of structuralism as it took root in America in the work of Franz Boas (1858–1942), Edward Sapir (1884–1939), and especially Leonard Bloomfield (1887–1949). It was the latter in particular who dispensed with the mind as entirely irrelevant to linguistic inquiry and description. Bloomfieldian structuralism as it was articulated in his 1933 *Language* was highly systematic and method-orientated, positioning itself as having no overlap with other disciplines. Behaviourist theory helped justify the anti-psychological posture of structuralism, which instead focused on creating mechanisms to empirically verify linguistic descriptions of phonology and morphology. Ultimately, structuralism came to be entirely about the signifier but not at all about the signified; always the winter of grammar but never the Christmas of meaning. The latter was messy and much better left to the psychologists or sociologists (Bloomfield 1933, 140; cf. Harris 1993, 16–28; Robins 1997, 222–59; Campbell 2003, 95–100).

The face of linguistics changed again in the mid-twentieth century as the empiricist outlook of structuralism began to give way to the new theoretical paradigm developed by Noam Chomsky (1923–), the intellectual progenitor of transformational (later generative) grammar. The history and key commitments of generativism are recounted elsewhere in this volume (Naudé and Miller-Naudé) and need not be given in any detail here (see also Blevins 2013; Freidin 2013). But with Chomsky, linguistics became rationalist once again, turning attention back to the relationship between language and the mind. In broad strokes, Chomsky's approach focused on syntax and aimed to articulate the formal principles that describe how the mind of a speaker generates grammatical sentences given the parameters of a specific language. These principles were understood as being both universal across all languages and innate in the human mind. Generativism remained the predominant linguistic framework for most of the twentieth century, certainly in North America and in many cases elsewhere, until a theoretical parting of ways occurred in the 1980s (Robins 1997, 260–63; Campbell 2003, 100–03).[6]

1.3. Cognitive Realisations

The advent of Cognitive Linguistics is linked with a broader movement away from formalist theories that is known as functionalism (see Buth in this volume). Although generativism is interested in cognitive aspects of language as a system for expressing thought, it also gives little to no attention to the

---

[6] It is probably correct to say that generativism is still the dominant linguistic framework today, although only in certain areas, especially syntax.

communicative purpose of language, and intentionally so.[7] This orientation is not unique to generativism but can be traced back to Saussure's disinterest in *parole* in favour of *langue*. By contrast, functionalist theories focus on language as a means of communication and how grammar arises from use of the language. Functional and Cognitive Linguistics have distinct but very much overlapping histories, such that linguists disagree as to whether and how the latter is properly understood as part of the former (see Van Valin Jr. 2003; Nuyts 2010). Still, the two labels identify a set of theoretical frameworks that are rightly understood as fellow travellers on a road that has departed from the highway of generativism.

That departure was complete by the late 1980s, after over a decade of increasingly heated controversy within Chomskyan circles over theoretical developments known as Generative Semantics.[8] Certain participants in the debate were increasingly dissatisfied with the level of abstract restrictiveness that generativism had reached. In contrast to this formalism, the Cognitive

---

[7] In the words of Chomsky (2002, 76–77): "Language is not properly regarded as a system of communication. It is a system for expressing thought, something quite different." Another example is Chafe (1994, 8; quoted in Ariel 2010, 76), who states that "there are many important things about language that can never be understood by constructing sequences of words that begin with *John* and end with a period, and asking oneself whether or not they are sentences of English." Cited in Ariel (2010, 76). My thanks to Travis Wright for drawing my attention to these quotes.

[8] See the lively history by Harris (1993), now updated in an excellent second edition (2021).

Linguistic and functionalist approaches agreed that language is not an autonomous mental system but rather is integrated with human cognition as a whole.[9] One of the leading figures advancing this idea in the Cognitive Linguistics movement was George Lakoff (1941–), who in 1987 published one of the seminal texts in Cognitive Linguistics, entitled *Women, Fire, and Dangerous Things*. It was in that same year that Ronald W. Langacker (1942–) published *Foundations of Cognitive Grammar*, which would become another foundational text for Cognitive Linguistics, alongside *The Body in the Mind* by Mark Johnson (1987). As discussed in the next section, these texts and others soon to follow set out key theoretical commitments, largely in direct contrast to generativism, that make Cognitive Linguistics uniquely centred on the nature of linguistic meaning as part of human cognition as a whole. Today, Cognitive Linguistics is widely recognised as one of the major frameworks in theoretical linguistics as a discipline, and it continues to grow in popularity and application in numerous venues around the world (Taylor 2007, 566–71, 574–76; Nerlich and Clarke 2010, 590–92; see also Howe and Sweetser 2013, 123–24).[10]

---

[9] In generativism specifically, language is handled as a separate module within the human mind that is unconnected from other cognitive abilities, hence it is fundamentally disembodied.

[10] For a more in-depth discussion of the origins of Cognitive Linguistics, see Ross (forthcoming).

2.0. Key Theoretical Commitments and Major Concepts

Cognitive Linguistics as it has developed over the last forty years is focused on understanding the communicative function of language, specifically in terms of the experiential basis for structured relationships that exist between language and cognition. At a basic level, Cognitive Linguistics views language as a dynamic but shared repertoire of form-meaning pairings used to symbolically encode and transmit thought to others. Language in this sense involves a "repository of world knowledge, a structured collection of meaningful categories that help us deal with new experiences and store information about old ones" (Geeraerts and Cuyckens 2007a, 5).

2.1. Four Commitments

Four key theoretical commitments characterise Cognitive Linguistics as a whole and help bear out its view of language. The descriptions of these commitments below are brief and abstract, but are illustrated further below with the six concepts that flow out of them.

2.1.1. Language Arises from Embodied Cognition

Cognitive Linguistics hypothesises that the human mind has no autonomous or innate faculty of some kind where language processing occurs, separate from other cognitive processes, which is a basic assumption in Chomskyan generative grammar. Instead, Cognitive Linguistics maintains that linguistic knowledge is represented in the mind and processed in basically the same way as all other conceptual structures. Linguistic knowledge—the pairing of form and meaning—is therefore conceptual, an integral part of cognition in general, and organised and governed in the same ways as the cognitive abilities that are applied in other bodily tasks such as visual perception and sensorimotor activity. Language is distinguishable as a cognitive ability, but it is not unique in terms of the mental processes that are involved. An important corollary of this view of cognition is that linguistic meaning itself is embodied—not purely rational—since it reflects human experience in the world (Croft and Cruse 2004, 2–3; Geeraerts 2006b, 4–5; Janda 2015, 132–33).[11]

2.1.2. Language is Perspectivised

A fundamental commitment of Cognitive Linguistic theory is that conceptual structure—and thus also linguistic knowledge—is not reducible to mere truth-conditional correspondence to the external world. Rather, language bears meaning because it construes the world in a perspectivised, embodied way, imposing a structure upon it rather than just reflecting objective reality.[12] So in

---

[11] For example, in his discussion of the word *grasp* from a cognitive scientific perspective, Feldman (2008, 166) explains how "the embodied neural approach to language suggests that the complex neural circuitry that supports [the physical action of] grasping *is* the core meaning of the word."

[12] A basic example would be the word *sunset*, which only bears meaning (indeed only exists within language) because of the physical organisation of external objects relative to human perception. Note that this commitment does not entail an endorsement of philosophical relativism. From its earliest stages, theorists within the Cognitive Linguistic

Cognitive Linguistics, conceptual structure is likewise subject to construal in its organisation and how categories are formed. To articulate this commitment another way, grammar *is* conceptualisation, since linguistic structure reflects conceptual structure.[13] Cognitive Linguistics thus maintains that language provides various ways of portraying and profiling the information being communicated (Croft and Cruse 2004, 1, 3; Geeraerts 2006b, 4; Evans and Green 2006, 40–43).

2.1.3. Language is Symbolic

Cognitive Linguistic theory emphasises the primacy of meaning in linguistic analysis by assuming that the basic function of language is to express thought and therefore must involve meaning, including pragmatic meaning. The way language expresses thought is by using symbols, which consist of forms—whether spoken, written, or even signed—and meanings with which the forms are paired by convention. Linguistic symbols bear meaning that is associated not with a particular referent in the external world, but rather with a concept or mental representation, which itself is derived from categorisation of our experience in the

---

movement have argued against both foundationalism and relativism, as for example in Johnson (1987, 194–212). He argues (202) that "we *are* in touch with our world but always in a mediated fashion. There is thus no single, God's-Eye way of carving up the world. But it does not follow from this that we can carve it up any way we wish." See also Harder (2007, esp. 1253).

[13] Moreover, linguistic utterances are meant to elicit a shared conceptual structure between speakers.

external world. Notably, because Cognitive Linguistics hypothesises that linguistic cognition is indistinct from cognition in general (the first commitment), categorisation occurs not only with physical entities but also with language itself. As a result, linguistic phenomena are not strictly divided into the traditional 'levels' of phonology, morphology, syntax, and so on. Rather, language is viewed as a unified phenomenon for which these terms serve as convenient labels for what are in reality overlapping categories. (Evans and Green 2006, 6–7, 28–30; Geeraerts and Cuyckens 2007a, 5).

2.1.4. Language is the Conventions of Use

As noted above, Cognitive Linguistics shares with functionalism its focus on language as a means of communication and actual usage events among speakers. In Cognitive Linguistic theory, knowledge of language is understood to emerge from use, such that the abstraction of linguistic categories and structures by language learners and users occurs inductively. On this view, a language is nothing more than the set of form-meaning pairings used by convention in a speech community (Croft 2000, 26, 95–99).[14] Those form-meaning pairings, moreover, occur at every level of language, from morpheme all the way up to syntax and even discourse. A corollary of this commitment is the unpredictability of language owing to variability in usage events over time, which leads to language change. Language change occurs

---

[14] Cognitive Linguistics tends to use the term 'utterance' for communication usage events, which are understood as particular, actual instances of spoken or written forms by a language user (Evans 2007, 217–18).

not only because speakers themselves change, but because the external world does, too (Croft 1990, 257). At the same time, language change is not considered unpredictable. Although Cognitive Linguistics is not interested in uncovering linguistic universals in the same sense as in formalist theories, it does acknowledge universal tendencies in human language use that are constrained and motivated by shared cognitive abilities and processes, and therefore result in similar patterns of diachronic change across languages (Croft and Cruse 2004, 3–4, 71–73; Geeraerts 2006b, 4, 5–6).[15]

2.2. Six Concepts

In addition to these four key theoretical commitments in Cognitive Linguistic theory, there are numerous concepts that flow from them. While there are more than space allows for here, the six concepts discussed below are widely considered central to Cognitive Linguistics as a framework for the study of language. In anticipation of the next section, each concept discussed here is illustrated with reference to the biblical text and languages.

2.2.1. Image Schemas

Since Cognitive Linguistics understands conceptual structure to be grounded in embodiment, semantic structure is reckoned the same way. That is what it means for language to be embodied. In other words, part of what makes language meaningful is the

---

[15] On grammaticalisation theory, see especially Narrog and Heine (2011), Hopper and Traugott (2012), and Kouteva et al. (2019).

human embodied experience with which it is associated.¹⁶ One of the foundational ways of illustrating and accounting for this conceptual association between embodied experience and linguistic meaning is what Cognitive Linguistics calls the image schema, originally developed by Johnson (1987). According to Sullivan (2017, 398), image schemas are "simple cognitive structures that represent spatial configurations independently of a single sensory modality." They arise directly from repeated sensory interactions with the world, including the visual, auditory, haptic (touch), and vestibular (balance) systems of the body. Image schemas are not detailed ideas, but are rather abstract or 'schematic' in nature (hence the name), and thus provide a foundation for richer conceptual and semantic structures. In this sense, image schemas are pre-conceptual and subconscious.¹⁷

To label and describe image schemas, Cognitive Linguistics uses SMALL CAPITALS and simple diagrams, respectively. For example, because the human body has a unidirectional visual apparatus (i.e., eyes that look in one direction), axial orientation is inherently part of embodied experience. This simple reality of human embodiment gives rise to a number of image schemas,

---

[16] Or, as Evans and Green (2006, 158–60) put it, "Semantic structure is conceptual structure," and conceptual structure is embodied.

[17] In a series of studies, Mandler (1988; 1992; 1996; 2005; 2010) has shown how image schemas arise in conjunction with physical and psychological development during early childhood (even in the womb) through what she calls perceptual meaning analysis. See also Evans (2014, esp. 118–26; 2015, 122–53).

such as FRONT-BACK, LEFT-RIGHT, and—given the universal experience of gravity and three-dimensional space—UP-DOWN and NEAR-FAR as well. These image schemas are interconnected in human visual experience, as are many others. For example, Figure 1 shows the CONTAINER image schema at the far left. The diagrams in the centre and at right involve the CONTAINER image schema as well, but do so as part of the related image schemas for IN and OUT, respectively.[18]

Figure 1: Image schemas for CONTAINER, IN, and OUT

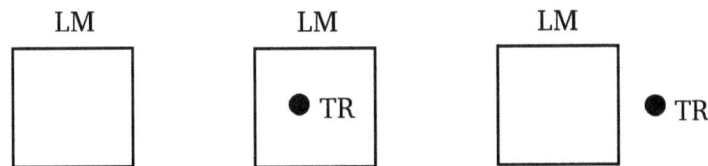

Note too the use of 'LM' and 'TR' in Figure 1, which stand for 'Landmark' and 'Trajector', respectively. These terms refer to elements that are related in any given construal, but are profiled in different ways as either focal (Trajector/TR) or non-focal (Landmark/LM). For example, in the centre diagram, the TR entity is IN the CONTAINER LM, while in the right diagram the TR is OUT (Evans and Green 2006, 176–91; Gibbs and Colston 2006; Evans 2007, 106–08; Oakley 2007).[19]

---

[18] Other image schemas that CONTAINER helps to structure could be elaborated, such as TOP-BOTTOM, OVER-UNDER, and FULL-EMPTY, etc.

[19] There are numerous image schemas that Cognitive Linguistics has collectively identified, although these are not exclusive of others that may be proposed. See Evans (2019, 235–36) for a synthesised list.

The notion of an image schema may seem simple, but because it helps analyse conceptual structures it also has significant explanatory power for linguistic structures, as illustrated in the clauses in example (1) below.

(1)   (a)   וַיֵּצֵא יוֹנָה מִן־הָעִיר

'Then Jonah went out of the city'

       (b)   וַיֵּשֶׁב מִקֶּדֶם לָעִיר

'and sat east of the city,'

       (c)   וַיַּעַשׂ לוֹ שָׁם סֻכָּה

'and he made a booth there for himself.'

       (d)   וַיֵּשֶׁב תַּחְתֶּיהָ בַּצֵּל

'And he sat under it in the shade' (Jon. 4.5a)

In (1a) Jonah is a TR that is portrayed as OUT of the boundaries of the city, which itself is construed as a CONTAINER LM. In addition, the verbal event in (1a) is structured by the SOURCE-PATH image schema that involves linear motion. Similarly, Jonah's resting place מקדם 'east' of the city in (1b) involves a CENTRE-PERIPHERY image schema in which the city is construed as central and Jonah's spatial position in (1b) as peripheral to the scene. (As discussed in more detail in §2.2.5 below, the geographical sense 'east' for מקדם arises from a FRONT-BACK image schema involved in the semantic structure of the word.) In (1d), Jonah is again a TR, but now profiled against two LMs, one being the booth as an elevated SURFACE under which Jonah sits and the other being the shade produced by the booth as a CONTAINER in which Jonah is located.[20]

---

[20] Note, too, that utterances involve perspective or situatedness in the spatial construal (Croft and Cruse 2004, 58–63). In (1) the construal is

2.2.2. Frame Semantics

An important aspect of the commitment to embodied cognition in Cognitive Linguistic theory is the related thesis that meaning is encyclopedic in nature. That is, semantic structure (form/meaning pairing) is inextricably linked—in fact it is understood to 'grant access'—to a complex inventory of structured knowledge about the world. That knowledge is encyclopaedic in that it derives from both physical and sociocultural dimensions of human experience.[21] The theories of Frame Semantics and Conceptual Domains are two approaches in Cognitive Linguistics to extrapolate this understanding of linguistic meaning. These theories are distinct, but in many ways complementary. This section focuses on Frame Semantics, leaving Conceptual Domains aside until the next section.[22]

A semantic frame is a schematisation of experience that is represented conceptually and held in long-term memory. In essence, a frame is a knowledge structure of interrelated concepts associated with an identifiable, culturally-embedded scene in human experience. Frames contribute to meaning construction by virtue of their gestalt quality. That is, without knowledge of the relationship structure of the frame as a whole, knowledge of

---

allocentric, taking a kind of bird's-eye view of the scene, rather than a 'Jonah's-eye view'. On the typological diversity of spatial models of construal, see for example Mawyer and Feinberg (2014).

[21] As van Wolde (2009, 51–103) puts it, words are "tips of encyclopedic icebergs."

[22] Frame Semantics originated with Fillmore (1982; 1985), while Conceptual Domains were developed by Langacker (1987).

any given concept within it is incomplete. Fillmore (2006, 373) makes this same point, explaining that a frame is "any system of concepts related in such a way that to understand any one of them you have to understand the whole structure in which it fits; when one of the things in such a structure is introduced into a text, or into a conversation, all of the others are automatically made available." For example, the concept associated with the word 'Monday' is linked to, prompts, and can only be fully understood within the frame WEEK, which is simpler and more basic than its parts.[23] Although frames are basic modes of knowledge representation in this sense, they are not static. Rather, a frame is updated, modified, and adapted on the basis of ongoing experience (see further Evans and Green 2006, 206–47; Ungerer and Schmid 2006, 207–18; Cienki 2007; Evans 2007, 85–86).

Understanding frame semantics comes more easily by illustration. In CL, a semantic frame is denoted using SMALL CAPITALS, much like an image schema. So, for example, the BAKING frame includes categories for at least one participant, the BAKER, who is in the BAKING role working with elements like INGREDIENTS and TOOLS that themselves have properties like WET, DRY, SHARP, and HOT. In an ancient Greek context, the BAKING frame provides the background and motivation for categories associated with words like σεμίδαλις ('fine flour'), ζύμη ('leaven'), ἀναμάσσω ('to knead'), φύραμα ('dough'), κλίβανος ('oven'), and ἄρτος ('bread loaf').

---

[23] I am grateful to one of my peer reviewers for his helpful illustration.

An interesting example of the BAKING semantic frame at work appears in Matthew 16. The following account appears as Jesus and his disciples are travelling by boat:

(2) (a) Καὶ ἐλθόντες οἱ μαθηταὶ εἰς τὸ πέραν ἐπελάθοντο ἄρτους λαβεῖν.
'And the disciples came to the other side and had forgotten to take bread.'

(b) ὁ δὲ Ἰησοῦς εἶπεν αὐτοῖς· ὁρᾶτε καὶ προσέχετε ἀπὸ τῆς ζύμης τῶν Φαρισαίων καὶ Σαδδουκαίων.
'And Jesus said to them, "Watch out and beware of the leaven of the Pharisees and Sadducees."'

(c) οἱ δὲ διελογίζοντο ἐν ἑαυτοῖς λέγοντες ὅτι ἄρτους οὐκ ἐλάβομεν.
'And they began to discuss among themselves, saying, "It is because we took no bread."'

(d) γνοὺς δὲ ὁ Ἰησοῦς εἶπεν· τί διαλογίζεσθε ἐν ἑαυτοῖς, ὀλιγόπιστοι, ὅτι ἄρτους οὐκ ἔχετε;
'But Jesus, aware of this, said, "You men of little faith, why do you discuss among yourselves that you have no bread?"' (Matt. 16.5–8)

With the note about their lack of bread in (2a), the scene is set for Jesus' comment in (2b). He cautions his disciples against ἡ ζύμη ('the leaven') of their religious opposition. In (2c) the disciples, having no bread with them but hearing Jesus mention ζύμη, become confused. Understanding how words grant access to semantic frames that structure encyclopaedic knowledge helps account for that confusion, as the word ζύμη naturally prompts the BAKING frame, although that is not the right frame for understanding Jesus' warning. The preceding events involving bread and the disciples' ongoing mental preoccupation with having forgotten to bring any on their journey further explain their initial (mis)interpretation in (2c) of Jesus' words in (2b). But as seen in (2d), Jesus' comment is in fact not straightforwardly about bread, but rather about teaching. The connections between those two ideas are extensive and rich, as are the implications, and they are explored in more detail in §2.2.4 below. Before doing that, however, another major concept within Cognitive Linguistics needs explanation.[24]

2.2.3. Domains and Conceptual Metaphor

One of the best-known parts of Cognitive Linguistics as a whole is conceptual metaphor theory, originally developed by Lakoff and Johnson (1980; see Tay 2014).[25] In essence, the theory holds that metaphor in language is no mere stylistic or rhetorical feature, but in fact helps to structure cognition and meaning itself via embodied experience. Conceptual metaphor involves two domains, a source and a target, the former being mapped or 'projected' unidirectionally onto the latter such that richer or more complex meaning arises through correspondence. A domain is

---

[24] Further illustration of frame semantics for Hebrew appears in Ziegert (2021, 29–31) and de Blois (2004). See also the application of frame semantics to English available online at https://framenet.icsi.berkeley.edu, accessed 29 June 2023, which also offers a very useful glossary of terms.

[25] Cognitive Linguistics has also proposed a theory of metonymy, which is not outlined here for reasons of space, though some have proposed metonymy as an even more basic cognitive process than metaphor. See Croft (2006); Evans and Green (2006, 310–27); Polzenhagen et al. (2014).

similar to a semantic frame, as discussed above, but is not necessarily associated with experience of a particular scene. Rather, domains are cognitive entities of varying levels of complexity and organisation that provide background information against which a concept is understood. Typically, concepts are structured with multiple domains in a kind of matrix.

Some domains are basic, deriving directly from embodied experience, and are thus pre-conceptual. As such, basic domains are similar to image schemas, but the latter are built upon the former, which are also not necessarily imagistic. Examples of basic domains, which again are denoted in Cognitive Linguistics using SMALL CAPITALS, would include SPACE, TEMPERATURE, TIME, VOLUME, and COLOUR, among others (see further in Evans and Green 2006, 234–35). These domains often provide the source in pervasive conceptual metaphors that structure linguistic meaning, but more complex domains may also appear. What makes these conceptual and not merely rhetorical metaphors is their motivation and usefulness at the level of thought itself. Several examples below will illustrate this theory (Evans and Green 2006, 230–47, 286–310; Ungerer and Schmid 2006, 114–27; Evans 2007, 33–35, 61–62; Grady 2007).

The first example demonstrates the pervasiveness of certain conceptual metaphors across languages and cultures owing to motivation by common human physical experience, as shown in example (3).

(3) (a) יִרְגְּזוּ כֹּל יֹשְׁבֵי הָאָרֶץ כִּי־בָא יוֹם־יְהוָה כִּי קָרוֹב

'Let all the inhabitants of the land tremble, for the day of the LORD is coming; it is near' (Joel 2.1)

(b)   כִּי אֶלֶף שָׁנִים בְּעֵינֶיךָ כְּיוֹם אֶתְמוֹל כִּי יַעֲבֹר

'For a thousand years in your sight are like yesterday when it is past' (Ps. 90.4)

One of the most pervasive conceptual metaphors is to understand TIME in terms of either SPACE or MOTION. In (3a) we see the FUTURE EVENTS ARE AHEAD metaphor, which arises from our experience of looking in the direction in which we are physically moving, so that as entities get closer to us they become visually larger. Physical movement through space also involves temporal progression, such that arrival at a distant destination corresponds to a future point in time. Along these same lines, a converse metaphorical entailment appears in (3b), where PAST EVENTS ARE BEHIND.

The second set of examples is more specific to the conceptual environment of ancient Israelite prophetic literature, in which the relationship between God and his people is portrayed as a marriage. This idea appears vividly in Ezekiel 16, where in verse 8 God says: "I also swore to you and entered into a covenant with you so that you became mine." In that chapter and others throughout the prophetical books there are statements like the following:

(4)   (a)   וַתִּבְטְחִי בְיָפְיֵךְ וַתִּזְנִי עַל־שְׁמֵךְ

'But you trusted in your beauty and became a whore because of your fame' (Ezek. 16.15)

(b)   כִּי עַל־כָּל־גִּבְעָה גְּבֹהָה וְתַחַת כָּל־עֵץ רַעֲנָן אַתְּ צֹעָה זֹנָה

'For on every high hill and under every green tree you have lain down as a whore' (Jer. 2.20b)

At the foundation of verses like these is the conceptual metaphor COVENANT IS MARRIAGE. However, a number of derivative metaphors also emerge as a result of the structure of MARRIAGE—at least as it was understood in the ancient Israel—as a conceptual domain. For example, in (4a) God's people are condemned in the broader contexts of the sentences in (4) on the basis of the metaphor IDOLATRY IS ADULTERY. The same metaphor appears in (4b), but with the additional implication that HIGH PLACES ARE SITES OF SEXUAL LIAISON. Of course, both examples in (4) are linked to the broader conceptual metaphor WORSHIP IS SEX.[26]

2.2.4. Mental Spaces and Conceptual Blending

Conceptual blending is a theory initially posited by Fauconnier (1994) and further developed by Fauconnier and Turner (2002), who argue that meaning is constructed in larger units of language (i.e., the sentence level and above) by integrating knowledge structures in novel and creative ways that give rise to a 'blend'. Conceptual blending is a basic, effortless cognitive process in human thought and imagination that is prompted directly in the dynamic context of communication. Again, Cognitive Linguistic theory hypothesises that language grants access to encyclopaedic knowledge of the external world as a kind of prompt for conceptualisation. This approach entails that meaning construction is grounded in language use, such that there is no principled division between semantics and pragmatics, as in formal approaches (Turner 1991, 206; Birdsell 2014).[27]

---

[26] Further illustration of conceptual metaphor theory for Hebrew appears in Ziegert (2021, 31–33).

[27] That is, they are not absolutely distinct. Cognitive Linguistic theory places semantics and pragmatics on a continuum of form-meaning pairings that may move from the pragmatic pole to the semantic pole

Meaning construction through conceptual blending involves the integration of mental spaces. Fauconnier (2007, 351) defines mental spaces as "very partial assemblies constructed as we think and talk for purposes of local understanding and action. They contain elements and are structured by frames and cognitive models... [and] are connected to each other by various kinds of mappings, in particular identity and analogy mappings." As Evans and Green (2006, 369) put it, "you can think of a mental space as a 'thought bubble'." Mental space theory is distinct from conceptual blending theory, but the two are closely related and function in a similar way to conceptual metaphor, though with important differences. Whereas conceptual metaphor involves unidirectional mapping of domains, conceptual blending involves selective integration of mental spaces into a novel elaboration. Whereas conceptual metaphors are stable and widely shared knowledge structures held in long-term memory, conceptual blends may be temporary and unique conceptualisations of information for creative purposes specific to ongoing discourse (although even blends may become conventionalised in long-term habitual cognitive structures).

Consider the example of conceptual blending in (5) below. This text is part of the same passage as example (2) above, and describes the resolution to the disciples' misconstrual of Jesus' warning.

---

as they become conventionalised in the language over time through entrenchment. On pragmatics within Cognitive Linguistics, see Panther (2022).

(5) (a) πῶς οὐ νοεῖτε ὅτι οὐ περὶ ἄρτων εἶπον ὑμῖν; προσέχετε δὲ ἀπὸ τῆς ζύμης τῶν Φαρισαίων καὶ Σαδδουκαίων.

"'How do you not understand that I did not speak to you about [actual] bread? But beware of the leaven of the Pharisees and Sadducees.'"

(b) τότε συνῆκαν ὅτι οὐκ εἶπεν προσέχειν ἀπὸ τῆς ζύμης τῶν ἄρτων ἀλλ' ἀπὸ τῆς διδαχῆς τῶν Φαρισαίων καὶ Σαδδουκαίων.

'Then they understood that He did not say to beware of the leaven of [actual] bread, but of the teaching of the Pharisees and Sadducees.' (Matt. 16.12–13)

Figure 2 presents a representation of the conceptual integration network involved in this passage, which could no doubt be further elaborated.

Figure 2: Conceptual integration network in Matt. 16.5–13

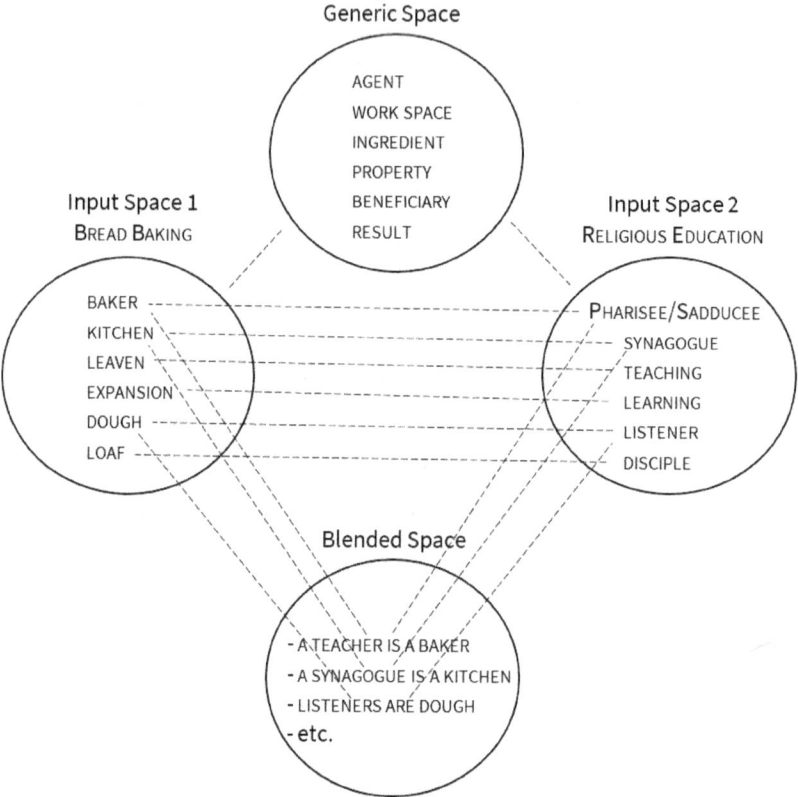

At the left and right are two mental spaces (called 'input spaces') represented by circles, each containing properties, roles, and relations and each structured by a semantic frame. The input spaces share features that are explicated in the generic space at the top of the figure. Through conceptually projecting and integrating input features, a novel conceptualisation emerges, represented at the bottom in the 'blended space'. Note that this mapping is selective; not all properties and elements in the input spaces are necessarily involved in the blend (Fauconnier 1994;

1997; Fauconnier and Turner 1998; Evans and Green 2006, 363–444; Evans 2007, 12–13, 114–15; Fauconnier 2007).

As noted above in §2.2.2, at first the disciples misunderstand because they are conceptualising Jesus' comments within the BAKING semantic frame alone. But after Jesus reminds them that obtaining actual bread for food is not the real problem (Matt. 16.9-10), they reconceptualise his words in terms of the blend portrayed in Figure 2. Jesus' clarification in (5a) prompts dynamic and temporary meaning construction in the context of their communication. As the features of each input space are integrated in the conceptual blend, novel meaning construction occurs. That meaning is represented in a limited way in the blended space, where the implications can be conceptually elaborated. For example, in the blend, the PHARISEES AND SADDUCEES (or perhaps just TEACHERS) ARE BAKERS, the SYNAGOGUE IS A KITCHEN, and anyone there as A LISTENER IS DOUGH. As Jesus explains, TEACHING IS LEAVEN, which has a disproportionate and determinative effect upon the outcome of DOUGH, for better or worse, when it is baked. In this sense, then, a DISCIPLE IS A LOAF OF BREAD. In a context where bread was a major part of daily diet and local bakers and bread quality would have been well known, this conceptual blend would have had readily accessible explanatory power.

2.2.5. Prototypes and Semantic Extension

The cognitive approach to lexical semantics understands words as lexical items whose meanings are associated with a complex but structured conceptual category (or categories). This view of categorisation was originally posited by Rosch (1978) and developed by Lakoff (1987), Taylor (2003), and others. Cognitive Linguistic theory hypothesises that conceptual categories form because humans gather as much information about our environment as possible with the least possible cognitive effort. The categorisation process also occurs because humans perceive consistent correlation between features of the external world. The principle of economy gives rise to differing levels of inclusiveness for categories and their members, while the principle of correlation informs the organisation of category members around a central exemplar, which is called a prototype. As such, the categories are radial, organised around the prototype to include other, gradually more peripheral members that are distinct but related. Prototype theory applies to lexical semantics insofar as any given word also forms a category—held in the 'mental lexicon'—with a prototypical meaning (or sense) at its centre and with other meanings extending from the prototype in a semantic network.[28] This model of lexical semantics integrates other aspects of Cognitive Linguistic theory, especially image schemas, semantic frames, and conceptual metaphor theory. It is primarily

---

[28] Note that prototype theory is applicable to both onomasiology and semasiology. The former deals with how words are used to categorise (or name) objects in the external world, whereas the latter deals with the network of concepts (or meanings) of a word understood as a category itself. Cognitive lexical semantics deals with both, but the discussion below is semasiological. The term mental lexicon refers to the inventory of words known by a language speaker, which is organised and detailed but nevertheless latent knowledge. See further Aitchison (2012); Taylor (2012).

by these cognitive mechanisms that Cognitive Linguistics has accounted for word meaning as a semantic network in which less prototypical senses derive from more prototypical senses through motivated (though not always predictable) meaning extension (Taylor 2003, 41–83; Evans and Green 2006, 328–63, 445–67; Geeraerts 2006c; Evans 2007, 175, 176–77; Lewandowska-Tomaszczyk 2007; Geeraerts 2010, 182–272; 2015).

To illustrate prototype theory, cognitive semantics, and embodied cognition, we will revisit מקדם from example (1b), above. This lexical item is a compound of the preposition מן ('from') and קדם, the latter of which will come into focus here first. The prototypical sense of this nominal appears to be *front* as an embodied, spatial concept. This sense appears in some texts, as in the adverbial uses in (6) below:

(6) (a) אָחוֹר וָקֶדֶם צַרְתָּנִי
'You encircle me in back and in front' (Ps. 139.5)

(b) הֵן קֶדֶם אֶהֱלֹךְ וְאֵינֶנּוּ וְאָחוֹר וְלֹא־אָבִין לוֹ
'Look, I go forwards and he is nowhere;
backwards, but I do not sense him' (Job 23.8)

In the HB, the spatial concept *front* is more often expressed using prepositional constructions involving the word פנה (the human 'face'), such as לפנים ('before', 'facing') or (על־)פני ('[at the] front of'). Even so, the *front* meaning associated with both פנה and קדם arose from the embodied construal of the human face as the axial front of a person given the orientation of visual perception.[29]

---

[29] The same construal underlies the verb קדם 'to meet, confront', which likely derived from the nominal.

Two other senses of קדם extend from the spatial prototype, each of which is motivated by different metaphorical construals of SPACE and TIME as semantic domains. Owing to embodied experience and encyclopaedic knowledge, the period of time categorised as a DAY is associated with the light of the SUN, which—as depicted with the arrow labelled A in Figure 3—follows a consistent directional trajectory from the temporal BEGINNING of the period in the east to its END in the west.[30]

Figure 3: Semantic extension of קדם

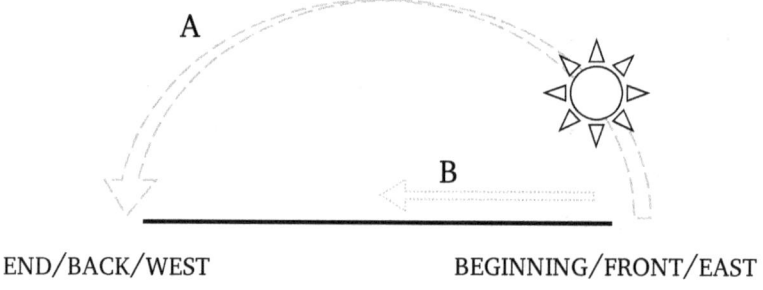

END/BACK/WEST   BEGINNING/FRONT/EAST

---

[30] Although space constraints prohibit fuller substantiation of this lexical semantic proposal, it is noteworthy that the polysemy of the Hebrew word ימין supports it, as the word can mean both *right* (*side*) or *south*. The former is the spatial prototype; the latter is a metonymic extension that can only be motivated within an eastward-facing construal, as I am proposing for קדם. It seems that eastwardness was construed as the unmarked/default directionality (e.g., Zebulun's boundary runs קדמה מזרחה, 'forwards, towards sunrise' to Gath-hepher in Josh. 19.13). In addition, eastward orientation was significant in other aspects of Israelite culture, as in the geographical orientation of the entrance to the Tabernacle and later Solomon's Temple (like many other ancient Near Eastern religious structures) towards the east (see Exod. 26.18–22; 1 Kgs 7; cf. Gen. 3.24 below).

Those earliest and latest temporal periods of the DAY period may be metaphorically construed as its spatial FRONT and BACK through the cognitively routine conceptual metaphor TIME IS SPACE, or, more specifically in this instance, THE BEGINNING IS THE FRONT. The texts in (7) illustrate this sense.

(7) (a) יְהוָה קָנָנִי רֵאשִׁית דַּרְכּוֹ קֶדֶם מִפְעָלָיו מֵאָז
'The LORD possessed me at the beginning of his way, before his deeds of old' (Prov. 8.22)

(b) וְהָיוּ בָנָיו כְּקֶדֶם וַעֲדָתוֹ לְפָנַי תִּכּוֹן
'Their children will be like before, and their congregation will be established in my presence' (Jer. 30.20a)

Given the movement of the SUN across the sky during the DAY period, this metaphor entails gradedness, such that EARLIER IS MORE FRONTWARD and vice-versa. It is in this way that the prototypical spatial meaning of קדם 'front' can extend metaphorically to the temporal sense 'before'.

A second semantic extension occurs, however, when the concept of directionality is added (with the affixed preposition מן) to the spatial construal of a DAY, as depicted with the arrow labelled B in Figure 3. The examples in (8) demonstrate this meaning, as does (1b) above.

(8) (a) וַיְגָרֶשׁ אֶת־הָאָדָם וַיַּשְׁכֵּן מִקֶּדֶם לְגַן־עֵדֶן אֶת־הַכְּרֻבִים
'So he drove out the man and positioned cherubim east of the garden of Eden' (Gen. 3.24)

(b) וַיַּעַל כְּבוֹד יְהוָה מֵעַל תּוֹךְ הָעִיר וַיַּעֲמֹד עַל־הָהָר אֲשֶׁר מִקֶּדֶם לָעִיר
'And the glory of the LORD went up from the middle of the city and stood over the mountain that is east of the city' (Ezek. 11.23)

This conceptualisation of קדם is also graded but involves geographical positionality of an entity relative to the SUN at the metaphorical FRONT of the DAY (מקדם). In this way, the third sense 'east' is motivated by the conceptual metaphor EASTWARDNESS IS PROXIMITY TO SUNRISE.[31]

2.2.6. Cognitive Approaches to Grammar

The study of grammar was at the centre of the emergence of Cognitive Linguistics out of generativism in the 1970s and 1980s. Since that time, two broad approaches to grammar have appeared as trunks of a single Cognitive Linguistic tree; distinct but grounded in the same spot. On the one hand there is Cognitive Grammar, a broad theoretical framework developed by Langacker (1987; 1991) that is to date the most influential (see the overviews in Langacker 2007 and Bennett 2014). It is also very detailed and expansive, to the extent that the introduction by Taylor (2002) covers topics ranging from phonology and morphology to verbal tense and idioms. On the other hand, there is

---

[31] The use of מן ('from') with קדם in this sense indicates a different construal of focal and non-focal entities as compared with English directional expressions. When correlating entities with cardinal directions, native English speakers construe eastward positionality as completed movement from the focal entity[1] to the non-focal entity[2] (e.g., Jonah[2] was [positioned *to* the] east of the city[1]). Hebrew speakers, however, appear to have had EAST as a directionally-stable third concept in the construal, such that eastward positionality of the non-focal entity[2] was construed as completed movement from the EAST[3] towards the focal entity[1] (e.g., Jonah[2] was [positioned *from* the] east[3] of the city[1]).

Construction Grammar, the roots of which appear in Kay and Fillmore (1999) and Goldberg (1995), and which was later developed by Croft (2001) and others.[32]

It is important to note that the six key concepts of Cognitive Linguistics discussed so far have been focused on semantics, specifically how meaning emerges in linguistic structures from conceptual structures. Cognitive approaches to grammar use these same key concepts to focus more directly on the linguistic system itself. In doing so, there are certainly differences between Cognitive and Construction Grammars, but they nevertheless share two guiding principles and are therefore compatible (see further Broccias 2006). The first is the symbolic thesis, which holds that the basic unit of grammar is a form-meaning pairing as a linguistic unit. In contrast to formalist approaches, this thesis entails that grammatical structure is not treated separately from meaning. Cognitive approaches to grammar take all form-meaning pairings into consideration as a unified and structured inventory of conventional linguistic units, from the level of bound morphemes, to lexical items, to syntactic configurations, understanding these units as existing along a continuum. The second guiding principle is the usage-based thesis, discussed above in §2.1.4. Within the realm of grammar, this thesis entails that each language user develops a kind of mental grammar through experience, with no sharp division between knowledge of a language

---

[32] See the overviews in Croft (2007) and Ramonda (2014). See also Hoffmann and Trousdale (2013) and the recent work by Hoffmann (2022). The earliest Construction Grammar proposal was Fillmore, Kay, and O'Connor (1988).

and use of a language (Croft and Cruse 2004, 225–90; Evans and Green 2006, 475–511; Ungerer and Schmid 2006, 244–56).

This section will focus only briefly on two examples to illustrate Construction Grammar in particular, building on §2.2.2 above. Construction Grammar helps to account for both 'irregular' idiomatic expressions as well as 'regular' syntactic expressions as linguistic units called constructions. While the former are not discussed here for reasons of space, the example in (9) below helps illustrate the latter in terms of the argument structure of constructions at the sentence level.

(9) Σπλαγχνισθεὶς δὲ ὁ κύριος τοῦ δούλου ἐκείνου ἀπέλυσεν αὐτὸν καὶ τὸ δάνειον ἀφῆκεν αὐτῷ.
'Then out of pity that servant's master released him and forgave him the debt.' (Matt. 18.27)

This use of ἀφίημι as a ditransitive verb meaning *forgive* is common in the New Testament (cf. Matt. 6.12; 12.31), involving a syntactic construction that we will call *Forgive Y Z* and that can be represented as X RESOLVES Y FOR Z (or, even more simply, CAUSE-RECEIVE with the Y resolution in view). In this construction, X is the AGENT, Y the PATIENT, and Z the BENEFICIARY (SVO^{dir}O^{ind}), with each argument expressed in the nominative, accusative, and dative cases, respectively.[33]

Goldberg's Construction Grammar approach to verb argument structure can also help account for sense distinctions by virtue of semantic frames. For example, the *Forgive Y Z* Construction in (9) involves the FINANCIAL TRANSACTION frame in which

---

[33] For further discussion of this construction and how it can be represented at semantic and syntactic levels, see Goldberg (2006, 20–22).

the conceptual metaphor SIN IS DEBT TO GOD appears. But the verb ἀφίημι also has a *permit* sense, which still has three arguments but involves a different construction and semantic frame, as shown in (10).

(10) καὶ οὐκ ἤφιεν λαλεῖν τὰ δαιμόνια, ὅτι ᾔδεισαν αὐτόν.
'And he would not permit the demons to speak, since they knew him.' (Mark 1.34b; cf. Matt. 8.22; Luke 8.51; Rev. 11.9)

The construction here might be called *Allow Y to Z* and can be represented as X ALLOWS Y TO PERFORM Z ACTION. This is a variation of the CAUSE-RECEIVE construction, where X is still the AGENT and Y the PATIENT, but Z is now another verb in the infinitive (SVOI), which will involve its own construction. The semantic frame varies depending upon what fills the Y and Z roles, but in many cases it is an AUTHORITY or CONTROL frame.

3.0. Cognitive Linguistics in Biblical Studies

Because Cognitive Linguistic theory itself is not a single set of clearly defined procedures and approaches, as noted above, it is no surprise that the use of Cognitive Linguistics within biblical scholarship is similarly variegated (Howe and Sweetser 2013, 122). The earliest application of Cognitive Linguistics to the study of the Bible and its languages was the use of conceptual metaphor theory by Brettler (1989), a substantial revision of his doctoral dissertation. 'Use' may be too strong a word, however, as the interaction is limited to five total citations of the work of Lakoff and Johnson (1980), all of which appear in the introductory chapter on method. The word 'cognitive' does not appear anywhere in Brettler's work and even 'conceptual metaphor' occurs only once (23).

Still, Brettler's study brought Cognitive Linguistics in its early phase to the attention of biblical scholarship, particularly in the study of Hebrew. Green and Howe (2014, 1) call this a "first wave," which was followed in the 1990s and early 2000s by a number of journal articles and conference papers that mostly applied Cognitive Linguistic theory to the Hebrew Bible. The "second wave" of influence they identify as the formation of 'The Use of Cognitive Linguistics in Biblical Interpretation' consultation at the 2006 annual meeting of the Society of Biblical Literature, under the leadership of Mary Therese DesCamp, Joel B. Green, Bonnie Howe, and Eve Sweetser. Howe and Sweetser (2013, 124–25) give a useful overview of the first six years of activity in this group, which ultimately culminated in the publication of a volume of collected essays that nicely balances Hebrew and Greek studies (Howe and Green 2014).[34]

Biblical scholars have of course continued to employ Cognitive Linguistic theory in their work to great effect, both independently and in connection with the SBL annual meeting. The following discussion highlights contributions in each of the respective biblical languages. Because Howe and Sweetser (2013, 125–

---

[34] It is my honour to serve presently as a member of the steering committee of the current iteration of this same group, now known as the Cognitive Linguistics in Biblical Interpretation programme unit. At present, members of the committee are working towards an edited volume introducing Cognitive Linguistics for biblical scholars that is to be published with SBL Press.

27) provide a useful survey of Cognitive Linguistics in biblical studies up through 2012, this section focuses on work that has appeared in the ten years since then, but is by no means exhaustive.[35]

As may be evident already in this section, it is true that most of the application of Cognitive Linguistics in biblical scholarship has so far gone to Hebrew. By far the best introduction to and overview of this Hebrew scholarship to date is van der Merwe (2021). In a bibliography of just over one hundred publications dealing with Cognitive Linguistics in biblical studies in the last ten years (which is nevertheless surely not exhaustive), almost sixty percent of the bibliography relates to Hebrew, with just under twenty percent to Greek. Overall, the great majority of publications are essay length, appearing in either journals or edited volumes. Despite their narrower scope, these contributions do not merely address finer linguistic matters. For example, Ross (2019) considers how attention to the conceptual blends constructed in Ps. 51 offers a different and perhaps better understanding of the final verses than has otherwise been considered. Many interpreters regard vv. 18–19 (Hebrew vv. 20–21) as a later interpolation, assuming that the plea that the LORD would "build up the walls of Jerusalem" is an abrupt change of topic that must have arisen in a postexilic context. But these verses in fact interact and cohere with the entire psalm to prompt a conceptual blend in which David himself is Zion/Jerusalem whose damaged spiritual walls require restoration by God the builder. This

---

[35] Key works from these earlier years would include, for example, Danove (2001) and van Wolde (2009), among others.

application of Cognitive Linguistics thus goes beyond language itself to help address interpretive debates and even compositional history.

In the scope of publications, far fewer in number are monographs that apply Cognitive Linguistics to the biblical languages. When these do appear, such studies tend to be the published form of doctoral dissertations (a notable exception here is van Wolde 2009). As such, these works can be extremely helpful on a broader topic, but of course still remain limited by default in what they address. A good example here is Robar (2015), who employs Cognitive Linguistics to address the function of the Hebrew *wayyiqtol* form at a discourse level to indicate schematic continuity (see also Robar 2021). Biblical scholarship has also begun to see Cognitive Linguistics applied in part or whole in collaborative edited volumes. For example, Ross and Runge (2022) present a collection of essays focused on understanding the semantics of postclassical Greek prepositions in Cognitive Linguistic perspective, particularly using prototype theory, pointing to new possibilities in lexicography and drawing out interpretative implications. Similarly, the volume edited by García Ureña et al. (2022) applies cognitive semantic theory to the lexicography of colour terms related to green within the Hebrew, Greek, and Latin Scriptures, analysing meaning at both the lexical and symbolic or cultural levels.

Rarest of all at this point are large-scale works that employ Cognitive Linguistics in the more standard or traditional categories of biblical studies publications. While there are some grammars, for example, that do reflect a much more up-to-date linguistic framework, such as van der Merwe, Naudé, and Kroeze (2017), to date none attempt to apply Cognitive Linguistics systematically. It is also fair to say that syntax has received virtually no attention within biblical scholarship from a Cognitive Linguistic perspective, despite the remarkable explanatory power of Construction Grammar for phenomena that so far have been examined only within a generative framework. Lexical semantics has fared better than syntax in biblical studies, but still lexicography proper has seen comparatively few results in print. However, following calls by van der Merwe (2006, 88–89) for attention to encyclopedic information in lexical entries, Reinier de Blois has been at work editing the *Semantic Dictionary of Biblical Hebrew*. Although the project is ongoing, its approach is based firmly in Cognitive Linguistic theory and the initial results are highly promising.[36]

4.0. Prospects for Research and Application

This essay has only begun to outline the theory and potential of Cognitive Linguistics, which is now widely recognised as one of the major linguistic frameworks, one that continues to grow in popularity and application in numerous venues around the world. One of those venues has certainly been biblical studies. Yet despite the fact that Cognitive Linguistics has been present within biblical scholarship for thirty years, its effects and influence are far from pervasive, for several reasons. One simple reason is that, while much of the activity in biblical studies involves

---

[36] The dictionary is freely available online at https://semanticdictionary.org/, accessed 4 May 2023.

the biblical languages, only a small proportion of scholarship focuses directly on refining contemporary understanding of the biblical languages themselves.[37] Another reason, alluded to at the outset, is that even scholars who engage regularly with the languages tend not to be acquainted with linguistic theory per se.[38] Knowledge of the differences between structuralism and generativism, for example, is nowhere within the expertise of many, perhaps most, biblical scholars. Given the scope and complexity of linguistics itself, that is rather unsurprising. But the practical effect is to leave biblical scholars in the dark as to what sort of theoretical framework underpins their favourite biblical language tool and what that might entail, if they even understand that there are indeed entailments. It is precisely this situation in the discipline that this volume seeks to remedy, at least in part (to mix several metaphors) by offering some teaser trailers, landmarks for orientation, and goods to test out.

In the end, however, biblical scholars must learn a hard lesson: If we truly wish to understand Cognitive Linguistics as a theoretical framework and apply it to better understand the ancient languages, it is directly to the primary literature itself

---

[37] One might add that there is a sizeable portion of biblical scholarship that gives little to no attention to the biblical languages at all. Proficiency in the biblical languages seems ever more to be a specialisation unto itself.

[38] There are exceptions that prove this general rule, notably the volume by Hornkohl and Khan (2021), which brings together specialists in Biblical and Rabbinic Hebrew and theoretical linguists.

that we must go. Although some may worry they have no business or no hope in so doing, it is worth noting that the abundant proliferation of introductions, handbooks, and companions over the last decade or so has not been limited to areas of biblical scholarship. Happily, the same phenomena characterise other disciplines as well, including linguistics. On a very simple level, then, one of the most promising prospects for Cognitive Linguistics in biblical studies is for biblical scholars to take up and read such resources as are listed in the section below. Understanding and applying Cognitive Linguistic theory is much more easily within reach than might be expected. For those already acquainted with Cognitive Linguistics—or at least those on their way—the prospects for research in the biblical languages and application in interpretation of Scripture are virtually limitless.

5.0. Further Reading

See the annotated bibliography in Howe and Sweetser (2013, 129–31). Note also the following resources:

5.1. Handbooks, Companions, Glossaries

1. Dancygier (2017)
2. Dąbrowska and Divjak (2015)
3. Taylor and Littlemore (2014)
4. Evans (2007)
5. Geeraerts and Cuyckens (2007b)

5.2. General Introductions

1. Croft and Cruse (2004)

2. Dirven and Verspoor (2004)
3. Evans and Green (2006), now updated by Evans (2019)
4. Geeraerts (2006a)
5. Ungerer and Schmid (2006)

5.3. Foundational Texts

1. Fauconnier (1994)
2. Fauconnier and Turner (2002)
3. Johnson (1987)
4. Langacker (1987; 1991)
5. Lakoff (1987)
6. Lakoff and Johnson (1980)
7. Talmy (1988)

References

Aitchison, Jean. 2012. *Words in the Mind: An Introduction to the Mental Lexicon*. 4th ed. Malden, MA: Wiley-Blackwell.

Ariel, Mira. 2010. *Defining Pragmatics*. Research Surveys in Linguistics. Cambridge: Cambridge University Press.

Bennett, Phil. 2014. 'Langacker's Cognitive Grammar'. In *The Bloomsbury Companion to Cognitive Linguistics*, edited by John R. Taylor and Jeanette Littlemore, 29–48. London: Bloomsbury Academic.

Birdsell, Brian J. 2014. 'Fauconnier's Theory of Mental Spaces and Conceptual Blending'. In *The Bloomsbury Companion to Cognitive Linguistics*, edited by John R. Taylor and Jeanette Littlemore, 72–90. London: Bloomsbury Academic.

Blevins, James P. 2013. 'American Descriptivism ("Structuralism")'. In *The Oxford Handbook of the History of Linguistics*, edited by Keith Allan, 419–37. Oxford: Oxford University Press.

de Blois, Reinier. 2004. 'Lexicography and Cognitive Linguistics: Hebrew Metaphors from a Cognitive Perspective'. *Davar-Logos* 3: 97–116.

Bloomfield, Leonard. 1933. *Language*. New York: Holt, Reinhart, and Winston.

Bod, Rens. 2013. *A New History of the Humanities: The Search for Principles and Patterns from Antiquity to the Present*. Oxford: Oxford University Press.

Brettler, Marc Z. 1989. *God Is King: Understanding an Israelite Metaphor*. Journal for the Study of the Old Testament Supplement Series 76. Sheffield: Sheffield Academic.

Broccias, Cristiano. 2006. 'Cognitive Approaches to Grammar'. In *Cognitive Linguistics: Current Applications and Future Perspectives*, edited by Gitte Kristiansen, Michel MAchard, René Dirven, and Francisco J. Ruiz de Mendoza Ibáñez, 81–115. Berlin: De Gruyter.

Campbell, Lyle. 2003. 'The History of Linguistics'. In *The Handbook of Linguistics*, edited by Mark Aronoff and Janie Rees-Miller, 81–104. London: Blackwell.

Chafe, Wallace L. 1994. *Discourse, Consciousness, and Time: The Flow and Displacement of Consciousness Experience in Speaking and Writing*. Chicago: University of Chicago Press.

Chomsky, Noam. 2002. *On Nature and Language*. Cambridge: Cambridge University Press.

Cienki, Alan. 2007. 'Frames, Idealized Cognitive Models, and Domains'. In *The Oxford Handbook of Cognitive Linguistics*, edited by Dirk Geeraerts and Herbert Cuyckens, 170–87. Oxford: Oxford University Press.

Croft, William. 1990. *Typology and Universals*. Cambridge: Cambridge University Press.

———. 2000. *Explaining Language Change: An Evolutionary Approach*. Longman Linguistics Library. Harlow: Pearson Education ESL.

———. 2001. *Radical Construction Grammar: Syntactic Theory in Typological Perspective*. Oxford: Oxford University Press.

———. 2006. 'Metonymy'. In *Cognitive Linguistics: Basic Readings*, edited by Dirk Geeraerts, 269–302. Cognitive Linguistics Research. Berlin: De Gruyter.

———. 2007. 'Construction Grammar'. In *The Oxford Handbook of Cognitive Linguistics*, edited by Dirk Geeraerts and Herbert Cuyckens, 463–508. Oxford: Oxford University Press.

Croft, William, and D. Alan Cruse. 2004. *Cognitive Linguistics*. Cambridge Textbooks in Linguistics. Cambridge: Cambridge University Press.

Dąbrowska, Ewa, and Dagmar Divjak (eds). 2015. *Handbook of Cognitive Linguistics*. Handbücher zur Sprach- und Kommunikationswissenschaft 39. Berlin: De Gruyter.

Dancygier, Barbara (ed.). 2017. *The Cambridge Handbook of Cognitive Linguistics*. Cambridge Handbooks in Language and Linguistics. Cambridge: Cambridge University Press.

Danove, Paul L. 2001. *Linguistics and Exegesis in the Gospel of Mark: Applications of a Case Frame Analysis and Lexicon*. Journal for the Study of the New Testament Supplement Series 218. Sheffield: Sheffield Academic.

De Maurio, Tullio, and Lia Formigari (eds). 1990. *Leibniz, Humboldt, and the Origins of Comparativism*. Amsterdam Studies in the Theory and History of Linguistic Science 49. Amsterdam: John Benjamins.

Dirven, René, and Marjolijn Verspoor. 2004. *Cognitive Exploration of Language and Linguistics*. 2nd rev. ed. Cognitive Linguistics in Practice 1. Philadelphia: John Benjamins.

Eco, Umberto. 1995. *The Search for the Perfect Language*. Oxford: Blackwell.

Evans, Vyvyan. 2007. *A Glossary of Cognitive Linguistics*. Edinburgh: Edinburgh University Press.

———. 2014. *The Language Myth: Why Language Is Not an Instinct*. Cambridge: Cambridge University Press.

———. 2015. *The Crucible of Language*. Cambridge: Cambridge University Press.

———. 2019. *Cognitive Linguistics: A Complete Guide*. Edinburgh: Edinburgh University Press.

Evans, Vyvyan, and Melanie Green. 2006. *Cognitive Linguistics: An Introduction*. Edinburgh: Edinburgh University Press.

Fauconnier, Gilles. 1994. *Mental Spaces: Aspects of Meaning Construction in Natural Language*. Cambridge: Cambridge University Press.

———. 1997. *Mappings in Thought and Language*. Cambridge: Cambridge University Press.

Fauconnier, Gilles, and Mark Turner. 1998. 'Conceptual Integration Networks'. *Cognitive Science* 22: 133–87.

———. 2002. *The Way We Think: Conceptual Blending and the Mind's Hidden Complexities*. New York: Basic Books.

———. 2007. 'Mental Spaces'. In *The Oxford Handbook of Cognitive Linguistics*, edited by Dirk Geeraerts and Herbert Cuyckens, 351–76. Oxford: Oxford University Press.

Feldman, Jerome. 2008. *From Molecule to Metaphor: A Neural Theory of Language*. Cambridge, MA: The MIT Press.

Fillmore, Charles. 1982. 'Frame Semantics'. In *Linguistics in the Morning Calm: Selected Papers from SICOL-1981*, edited by The Linguistics Society of Korea, 111–37. Seoul: Hanshin Publishing.

———. 1985. 'Frames and the Semantics of Understanding'. *Quaderni di Semantica* 6: 222–54.

———. 2006. 'Frame Semantics'. In *Cognitive Linguistics: Basic Readings*, edited by Dirk Geeraerts, 373–400. Cognitive Linguistics Research. Berlin: De Gruyter.

Fillmore, Charles, Paul Kay, and Mary Katherine O'Connor. 1988. 'Regularity and Idiomaticity: The Case of Let Alone'. *Language* 64: 501–38.

Freidin, Robert. 2013. 'Noam Chomsky's Contribution to Linguistics: A Sketch'. In *The Oxford Handbook of the History of Linguistics*, edited by Keith Allan, 439–67. Oxford: Oxford University Press.

García Ureña, Lourdes, Emanuela Valeriani, Anna Angelini, Carlos Santos Carretero, and Marina Salvador Gimeno (eds). 2022. *The Language of Colour in the Bible: Embodied*

Colour Terms Related to Greek. Fontes et Subsidia ad Bibliam pertinentes. Berlin: De Gruyter.

Geeraerts, Dirk (ed.). 2006a. *Cognitive Linguistics: Basic Readings*. Cognitive Linguistics Research. Berlin: De Gruyter.

———. 2006b. 'Introduction: A Rough Guide to Cognitive Linguistics'. In *Cognitive Linguistics: Basic Readings*, edited by Dirk Geeraerts, 1–28. Cognitive Linguistics Research. Berlin: De Gruyter.

———. 2006c. 'Prospects and Problems of Prototype Theory'. In *Words and Other Wonders: Papers on Lexical Semantic Topics*, 3–26. Berlin: De Gruyter.

———. 2010. *Theories of Lexical Semantics*. Oxford: Oxford University Press.

———. 2015. 'Lexical Semantics'. In *Handbook of Cognitive Linguistics*, edited by Ewa Dąbrowska and Dagmar Divjak, 273–95. Handbücher zur Sprach- und Kommunikationswissenschaft 39. Berlin: De Gruyter.

Geeraerts, Dirk, and Hubert Cuyckens. 2007a. 'Introducing Cognitive Linguistics'. In *The Oxford Handbook of Cognitive Linguistics*, edited by Dirk Geeraerts and Hubert Cuyckens, 3–21. Oxford: Oxford University Press.

——— (eds). 2007b. *The Oxford Handbook of Cognitive Linguistics*. Oxford: Oxford University Press.

Gibbs, Jr., Raymond, and Herbert L. Colston. 2006. 'Image Schema'. In *Cognitive Linguistics: Basic Readings*, edited by Dirk Geeraerts, 239–68. Cognitive Linguistics Research. Berlin: De Gruyter.

Goldberg, Adele. 1995. *Constructions: A Construction Grammar Approach to Argument Structure*. Cognitive Theory of Language and Culture. Chicago: University of Chicago Press.

———. 2006. *Constructions at Work: The Nature of Generalization in Language*. Oxford: Oxford University Press.

Grady, Joseph E. 2007. 'Metaphor'. In *The Oxford Handbook of Cognitive Linguistics*, edited by Dirk Geeraerts and Herbert Cuyckens, 188–213. Oxford: Oxford University Press.

Green, Joel B., and Bonnie Howe. 2014. 'Introduction'. In *Cognitive Linguistic Explorations in Biblical Studies*, edited by Bonnie Howe and Joel B. Green, 1–6. Berlin: De Gruyter.

Harder, Peter. 2007. 'Cognitive Linguistics and Philosophy'. In *The Oxford Handbook of Cognitive Linguistics*, edited by Dirk Geeraerts and Herbert Cuyckens, 1241–65. Oxford: Oxford University Press.

Harris, Randy Allen. 1993. *The Linguistics Wars*. Oxford: Oxford University Press.

———. 2021. *The Linguistics Wars: Chomsky, Lakoff, and the Battle over Deep Structure*. 2nd ed. Oxford: Oxford University Press.

Hoffmann, Thomas. 2022. *Construction Grammar: The Structure of English*. Cambridge Textbooks in Linguistics. Cambridge: Cambridge University Press.

Hoffmann, Thomas, and Graeme Trousdale (eds). 2013. *The Oxford Handbook of Construction Grammar*. Oxford: Oxford University Press.

Hopper, Paul J., and Elizabeth Closs Traugott. 2012. *Grammaticalization*. 2nd ed. Cambridge Textbooks in Linguistics. Cambridge: Cambridge University Press.

Hornkohl, Aaron D., and Geoffrey Khan (eds). 2021. *New Perspectives in Biblical and Rabbinic Hebrew*. Cambridge Semitic Languages and Cultures 7. Cambridge: Open Book Publishers.

Howe, Bonnie, and Joel B. Green (eds). 2014. *Cognitive Linguistic Explorations in Biblical Studies*. Berlin: De Gruyter.

Howe, Bonnie, and Eve E. Sweetser. 2013. 'Cognitive Linguistics and Biblical Interpretation'. In *The Oxford Encyclopedia of Biblical Interpretation*, edited by Steven L. McKenzie, 121–31. Oxford: Oxford University Press.

Janda, Laura A. 2015. 'Cognitive Linguistics in the Year 2015'. *Cognitive Semantics* 1: 131–54.

Johnson, Mark. 1987. *The Body in the Mind: The Bodily Basis of Meaning, Imagination, and Reason*. Chicago: University of Chicago Press.

Joseph, John E. 2020. *Language, Mind and Body: A Conceptual History*. Cambridge: Cambridge University Press.

Kay, Paul, and Charles Fillmore. 1999. 'Grammatical Constructions and Linguistic Generalizations: The *What's X Doing Y* Construction'. *Language* 75: 1–34.

Kouteva, Tania, Bernd Heine, Bo Hong, Haiping Long, Heiko Narrog, and Seongha Rhee (eds). 2019. *Word Lexicon of Grammaticalization*. 2nd ed. Cambridge: Cambridge University Press.

Lakoff, George. 1987. *Women, Fire, and Dangerous Things: What Categories Reveal about the Mind*. Chicago: University of Chicago Press.

Lakoff, George, and Mark Johnson. 1980. *Metaphors We Live By*. Chicago: University of Chicago Press.

Langacker, Ronald W. 1987. *Foundations of Cognitive Grammar*. Vol. 1, *Theoretical Prerequisites*. Stanford: Stanford University Press.

———. 1991. *Foundations of Cognitive Grammar*. Vol. 2, *Descriptive Application*. Stanford: Stanford University Press.

———. 2007. 'Cognitive Grammar'. In *The Oxford Handbook of Cognitive Linguistics*, edited by Dirk Geeraerts and Herbert Cuyckens, 421–62. Oxford: Oxford University Press.

Lewandowska-Tomaszczyk, Barbara. 2007. 'Polysemy, Prototypes, and Radial Categories'. In *The Oxford Handbook of Cognitive Linguistics*, edited by Dirk Geeraerts and Herbert Cuyckens, 139–69. Oxford: Oxford University Press.

Mandler, Jean. 1988. 'How to Build a Baby: On the Develompent of an Accessible Representational System'. *Cognitive Development* 3: 113–36.

———. 1992. 'How to Build a Baby II: Conceptual Primitives'. *Psychological Review* 99: 567–604.

———. 1996. 'Preverbal Representation and Language'. In *Language and Space*, edited by P. Bloom, M. A.. Peterson, L. Nadel, and M. F. Garrett, 365–84. Cambridge, MA: The MIT Press.

———. 2005. 'How to Build a Baby III: Image Schemas and the Transition to Verbal Thought'. In *From Perception to Meaning: Image Schemas in Cognitive Linguistics*, edited by Beate Hampe and Joseph E. Grady, 137–63. Berlin: De Gruyter.

———. 2010. 'The Spatial Foundations of the Conceptual System'. *Language and Cognition* 2: 21–44.

Mawyer, Alexander, and Richard Feinberg. 2014. 'Senses of Space: Multiplying Models of Spatial Cognition in Oceania'. *Ethos* 42 (3): 243–52.

Narrog, Heiko, and Bernd Heine (eds). 2011. *The Oxford Handbook of Grammaticalization*. Oxford Handbooks in Linguistics. Oxford: Oxford University Press.

Nerlich, Brigitte, and David D. Clarke. 2010. 'Cognitive Linguistics and the History of Linguistics'. In *The Oxford Handbook of Cognitive Linguistics*, edited by Dirk Geeraerts and Herbert Cuyckens, 589–607. Oxford: Oxford University Press.

Nuyts, Jan. 2010. 'Cognitive Linguistics and Functional Linguistics'. In *The Oxford Handbook of Cognitive Linguistics*, edited by Dirk Geeraerts and Herbert Cuyckens, 543–65. Oxford: Oxford University Press.

Oakley, Todd. 2007. 'Image Schemas'. In *The Oxford Handbook of Cognitive Linguistics*, edited by Dirk Geeraerts and Herbert Cuyckens, 214–35. Oxford: Oxford University Press.

Olender, Maurice. 1992. *The Languages of Paradise: Race, Religion, and Philology in the Ninteenth Century*. Translated by Arthur Goldhammer. Cambridge, MA: Harvard University Press.

Panther, Klause-Uwe. 2022. *Introduction to Cognitive Pragmatics*. Cognitive Linguistics in Practice. Amsterdam: John Benjamins.

Polzenhagen, Frank, Zoltán Kövecses, Stefanie Vogelbacher, and Sonja Kleinke (eds). 2014. *Cognitive Explorations into Metaphor and Metonymy*. Frankfurt am Main: Peter Lang.

Ramonda, Kris. 2014. 'Goldberg's Construction Grammar'. In *The Bloomsbury Companion to Cognitive Linguistics*, edited by John R. Taylor and Jeanette Littlemore, 60–71. London: Bloomsbury Academic.

Robar, Elizabeth. 2015. *The Verb and the Paragraph in Biblical Hebrew: A Cognitive-Linguistic Approach*. Studies in Semitic Languages and Linguistics 78. Leiden: Brill.

——. 2021. 'The Rise of *Wayyiqṭol*'. In *New Perspectives in Biblical and Rabbinic Hebrew*, edited by Aaron D. Hornkohl and Geoffrey Khan. Cambridge Semitic Languages and Cultures 7. Cambridge: Open Book Publishers.

Robins, R. H. 1997. *A Short History of Linguistics*. 4th ed. Longman Linguistics Library. London: Longman.

Rosch, Eleanor. 1978. 'Principles of Categorization'. In *Cognition and Categorization*, edited by Eleanor Rosch and Barbara B. Lloyd, 27–48. Hillsdale, NJ: Lawrence Erlbaum.

Ross, William A. 2019. 'David's Spiritual Walls and Conceptual Blending in Psalm 51'. *Journal for the Study of the Old Testament* 43: 607–26.

——. forthcoming. 'The History of Cognitive Linguistics'. In *Cognitive Linguistics for Biblical Studies: An Introduction*, edited by William A. Ross and Elizabeth Currier. Atlanta: SBL Press.

Ross, William A., and Steven E. Runge (eds). 2022. *Postclassical Greek Prepositions and Conceptual Metaphor: Cognitive Semantic Analysis and Biblical Interpretation*. Fontes et Subsidia ad Bibliam pertinentes 12. Berlin: De Gruyter.

Siewierska, Anna. 2013. 'Functional and Cognitive Grammars'. In *The Oxford Handbook of the History of Linguistics*, edited by Keith Allan, 487–501. Oxford: Oxford University Press.

Sullivan, Karen. 2017. 'Conceptual Metaphor'. In *The Cambridge Handbook of Cognitive Linguistics*, edited by Barbara Dancygier, 387–406. Cambridge Handbooks in Language and Linguistics. Cambridge: Cambridge University Press.

Talmy, Leonard. 1988. 'The Relation of Grammar to Cognition'. In *Topics in Cognitive Linguistics*, edited by Brygida Rudzka-Ostyn, 165–205. Amsterdam: John Benjamins.

Tay, Dennis. 2014. 'Lakoff and the Theory of Conceptual Metaphor'. In *The Bloomsbury Companion to Cognitive Linguistics*, edited by John R. Taylor and Jeanette Littlemore, 49–59. London: Bloomsbury Academic.

Taylor, John R. 2002. *Cognitive Grammar*. Oxford Textbooks in Linguistics. Oxford: Oxford University Press.

———. 2003. *Linguistic Categorization*. 3rd ed. Oxford Textbooks in Linguistics. Oxford: Oxford University Press.

———. 2007. 'Cognitive Linguistics and Autonomous Linguistics'. In *The Oxford Handbook of Cognitive Linguistics*, edited by Dirk Geeraerts and Herbert Cuyckens, 566–88. Oxford: Oxford University Press.

———. 2012. *The Mental Corpus: How Language is Represented in the Mind*. Oxford Linguistics. Oxford: Oxford University Press.

Taylor, John R., and Jeanette Littlemore (eds). 2014. *The Bloomsbury Companion to Cognitive Linguistics*. London: Bloomsbury.

Turner, James. 2014. *Philology: The Forgotten Origins of the Modern Humanities*. Princeton: Princeton University Press.

Turner, Mark. 1991. *Reading Minds: The Study of English in the Age of Cognitive Science*. Princeton: Princeton University Press.

Ungerer, Friedrich, and Hans-Jörg Schmid. 2006. *An Introduction to Cognitive Linguistics*. 2nd ed. Learning About Language. London: Routledge.

van der Merwe, Christo H. J. 2006. 'Biblical Hebrew Lexicology: A Cognitive Linguistic Perspective'. *KUSATU: Kleine Untersuchungen zur Sprache des Alten Testaments und seiner Umwelt* 6: 87–112.

———. 2021. 'Biblical Hebrew and Cognitive Linguistics: A General Orientation'. In *New Perspectives in Biblical and Rabbinic Hebrew*, edited by Aaron D. Hornkohl and Geoffrey Khan, 641–96. Cambridge Semitic Languages and Cultures 7. Cambridge: Open Book Publishers.

van der Merwe, Christo H. J., Jackie A. Naudé, and Jan H. Kroeze. 2017. *A Biblical Hebrew Reference Grammar*. 2nd ed. London: T&T Clark.

Van Valin Jr., Robert D. 2003. 'Functional Linguistics'. In *The Handbook of Linguistics*, edited by Mark Aronoff and Janie Rees-Miller, 319–36. Oxford: Blackwell.

van Wolde, Ellen. 2009. *Reframing Biblical Studies: When Language and Text Meet Culture, Cognition, and Context*. Winona Lake, IN: Eisenbrauns.

Ziegert, Carsten. 2021. 'Beyond Barr: Biblical Hebrew Semantics at its Crossroads'. *European Journal of Theology* 30: 19–36.

HISTORICAL LINGUISTICS AND THE BIBLICAL LANGUAGES

Kaspars Ozoliņš

The student of Biblical Hebrew can observe with relative ease that the language of the Old Testament not only differs from genre to genre and author to author, but also that it exhibits variation across its diachronically diverse writings.[1] Likewise, the classicist engaging with the Greek of the New Testament will note that it differs in important ways from the Greek of earlier time periods. Language change is a fact of life, and the biblical text is certainly no exception to this. Yet the rigorous application of the findings and methodology of historical linguistics to biblical studies has been less prevalent and less thorough than might be expected. This chapter provides a broad introduction to historical linguistics—the study of language change—especially as applied to biblical studies.

---

[1] This point, like almost anything in biblical scholarship, is disputed. Yet even those who would argue that the Old Testament is entirely the product of a single era still claim that certain authors employed an *archaising* style that reflects a diachronically earlier state of the language. See, e.g., Young, Rezetko, and Ehrensvärd (2008).

1.0. The History of Historical Linguistics

Although it has important historical precursors, modern linguistics developed in the wake of the Scientific Revolution of the sixteenth and seventeenth centuries in Europe. Historical linguistics in particular plays a special role in the *historical* development of linguistic inquiry, since the first systematic investigations into the nature of language were undertaken by scholars specifically interested in language change and the relationships among languages.[2]

Initial linguistic investigation, especially in the nineteenth century, was focused on the classification and comparison of the older languages of Europe and southwest Asia (the language family that came to be known as Indo-European). The growing impetus for these investigations occurred towards the end of the eighteenth century, as Europeans gradually became familiar with the languages and cultures of ancient India. In this connection, a famous statement from a speech delivered by Sir William Jones to the Asiatic Society in 1786 has been frequently quoted (Fortson 2010, 9):

> The *Sanscrit* language, whatever be its antiquity, is of a wonderful structure; more perfect than the *Greek*, more copious than the *Latin*, and more exquisitely refined than

---

[2] There are also other important terms that are used to describe the field. One is *comparative* linguistics, which emphasises the comparative method as a means for reconstructing linguistic history (see §2.2.3). Another is *diachronic* linguistics, a term that is perhaps less ambiguous than *historical linguistics*, since the latter could possibly be interpreted as the study of the history of the field of linguistics *in toto*.

either, yet bearing to both of them a stronger affinity, both in the roots of verbs and the forms of grammar, than could possibly have been produced by accident; so strong indeed, that no philologer could examine them all three, without believing them to have sprung from some common source, which, perhaps, no longer exists; there is a similar reason, though not quite so forcible, for supposing that both the *Gothick* and the *Celtick*, though blended with a very different idiom, had the same origin with the *Sanscrit*; and the old *Persian* might be added to the same family.

Jones' somewhat hyperbolic and subjective descriptions of these languages might strike the modern reader as being rather quaint. Nevertheless, a fundamental axiom of historical linguistics posits that descendent languages are related to one another via a now-lost parent language. Even geographically and chronologically diverse languages can be unexpectedly related. Table 1 compares cognates in English, ancient Greek, Latvian (a Baltic language spoken in Northern Europe), classical Latin, and Hittite (an extinct language originally spoken in present-day Turkey).

Table 1: Cognates in select Indo-European languages

English	Greek	Latvian	Latin	Hittite
water	ὕδωρ	ūdens	Umbr. *utur*	wāt-ar, -en-
brother	φράτηρ	brālis	frāter	negnaš
three	τρεῖς	trīs	trēs	tereš
cow	βοῦς	govs	bōs	GUD
(I) am	εἰμί	esmu	sum	ēšmi
night	νύξ	nakts	nox	nekuz

These languages exhibit similar basic vocabulary even though they range from the second millennium BC to the present day and from Turkey (Hittite) to Northern Europe (Latvian). The close resemblances demonstrate a genetic link between these geographically diverse languages (two modern, three ancient) and rule out accidental resemblance or borrowing. Following Jones, nineteenth-century scholars were preoccupied with the relationships of these similar languages and they endeavoured to reconstruct their parent language, which came to be called Proto-Indo-European.

However, after the appearance of Ferdinand de Saussure's classic *Cours de linguistique générale* in 1916, the diachronic dimension of language study became more of a minor player in linguistics and was replaced by a primary focus in the twentieth century on the *synchronic* study of language.[3] Such a neat bifurcation is of course an oversimplification, for diachrony and synchrony are always in relation with one another in language. In fact, a renewed appreciation for the centrality of diachrony in linguistics has grown in recent decades (see, for example, Bybee 2010; Hartmann 2021).

An overview of the history of the discipline will ideally focus on the study of the biblical languages, which are naturally of primary interest to biblical scholars. The languages of the Old and New Testaments (Hebrew, Aramaic, and Greek) belong to two linguistic families: Semitic and Indo-European. As such, it is appropriate to approach the field of historical linguistics from the perspective of these two language families. As it happens, most work in historical linguistics has thus far been done within these same two language families.

---

[3] Ironically, some of Saussure's greatest early work was in the area of historical linguistics (see §1.1. below).

1.1. Indo-European Studies

Koine Greek, the language of the New Testament era, belongs to the Greek (or Hellenic) branch of the Indo-European family of languages. The designation *Koine* (κοινή meaning 'common') refers to the *lingua franca* status of the Attic-Ionic dialect that spread throughout the Greek empire, launched by the conquests of Alexander the Great. Two earlier major periods in the written history of Greek may be identified: Classical/Archaic Greek and Mycenaean Greek (late second millennium BCE). The latter is of interest to Indo-Europeanists and other scholars because of its early attestation and its peculiar writing system, deciphered in the 1950s by Michael Ventris (see Ventris and Chadwick 1973).

The Indo-European family of languages contains several hundred languages (depending on classification) and is the largest such linguistic grouping in the world, by number of speakers. The designation *Indo-European* is intended to (roughly) encompass most of the languages spoken in the lands of Europe and Southwest Asia.[4] The major subfamilies are (in order of earliest written attestation): Anatolian, Indic, Iranian, Greek (or

---

[4] The German term *indogermanisch* is somewhat more precise, since the westernmost territory (namely, Scandinavia and Iceland) is inhabited by speakers of Germanic languages. (The equivalent term *Indo-Germanic* is now outdated in English.) The extinct Tocharian languages are a geographical outlier, having been spoken in the modern Chinese province of Xinjiang (in central Asia). A few languages in Europe are non-Indo-European, notably the Finno-Ugric languages Estonian, Finnish, and Hungarian. Basque (Spain and France) is a famous language isolate, while Maltese is a Semitic language.

Hellenic), Italic, Celtic, Germanic, Armenian, Tocharian, Slavic, Baltic, Albanian.[5] Several Indo-European languages enjoy a lengthy period of written attestation (rivalled only by some Semitic languages). The earliest attested written records are from the extinct Anatolian family (spoken in present-day Turkey), in particular, Hittite, dating back roughly to the Late Bronze Age.[6]

Early scholarly efforts at reconstructing Proto-Indo-European were influenced by the prestige of Sanskrit, the classical language of India (equivalent in status to that of Latin in Europe). This led scholars to reconstruct Proto-Indo-European with broadly similar features, especially in its vowel system. Subsequent study revealed that Greek, with its inherited five-vowel distinction, was in fact more archaic than the three-vowel distinction of Sanskrit.[7]

---

[5] Several larger subgroupings are typically made by scholars. The most clear is Indo-Iranian (Indic together with Iranian). Most scholars would also group together Baltic and Slavic (Balto-Slavic). Much more controversial is Italo-Celtic. Additionally, certain shared isoglosses lead many scholars to group together Balto-Slavic and Germanic in a northern dialect group, as well as Greek, Indo-Iranian, Armenian, and the poorly attested Phrygian into a southern dialect group.

[6] The earliest attested record of any Indo-European material is found in the form of Hittite loanwords in Old Assyrian texts from Kaniš, dating to the Middle Bronze Age (18th century BCE). See Kloekhorst (2019).

[7] Indo-Iranian (the sub-branch in which Sanskrit is located) distinguishes three vowel qualities ($\breve{\imath}$, $\breve{a}$, $\breve{u}$), with *$\breve{e}$ and *$\breve{o}$ having merged to $\breve{a}$. Note that the asterisk symbol is universally used in historical linguistics to denote a linguistic reconstruction that is prehistoric (i.e., prior to written records).

A major milestone in Indo-European studies was the reconstruction of a class of consonants called *laryngeals*, first hypothesised by Ferdinand de Saussure (1879). His rather brilliant reasoning is akin to the method now known as internal reconstruction.[8] The empirical existence of these consonants was confirmed by the discovery of Hittite (of the Anatolian branch) in the early twentieth century. The laryngeals were partly preserved intact in Anatolian, while in other branches they were lost, although they left various important traces (such as adjacent vowel colouring, compensatory lengthening, and other effects). Most scholars today reconstruct three laryngeals, conventionally designated $*h_1$, $*h_2$, $*h_3$. Their actual phonetic values are still unknown, though many scholars hypothesise that they were fricatives of some type, perhaps glottal and pharyngeal.[9]

---

[8] In retrospect, one can see a kinship between Saussure's later influential ideas on structuralism and the reasoning he employed here.

[9] An illustration of the crucial role that laryngeals play in Indo-European linguistics is seen, for example, in the interplay of morphological vowel alternations (called *ablaut*) and root structure in the singular and plural perfect stems of verbs like λείπω 'leave' (e.g., λέ-λοιπ-α and λε-λίπ-ομεν). Notice that the singular features an *o*-grade vowel in the root, whereas the plural lacks this. In another pair of forms, such as δέ-δω-κα (1 sg.) and δέ-δο-μεν (1 pl.), the difference observed is a vowel length distinction. However, with the postulation of a laryngeal for this second verbal root, the morphological symmetry is restored: $*de\text{-}doh_3\text{-}$ (sg.) ~ $*de\text{-}dh_3\text{-}$ (pl.). The loss of the laryngeal was not without effects: compensatory lengthening in the singular stem ($*de\text{-}doh_3\text{-}$ > δεδω-) and vowel epenthesis in the plural stem ($*de\text{-}dh_3\text{-}$ > δεδο-). Compare the reconstructed stems for λέλοιπα ~ λελίπομεν: $*le\text{-}loik^w\text{-}$ (sg.) ~ $*le\text{-}lik^w\text{-}$ (pl.).

A landmark multi-volume work appearing towards the end of the nineteenth century (1886–1900) is Brugmann and Delbrück's *Grundriß der vergleichenden Grammatik der indogermanischen Sprachen.* This represented the state of current knowledge at the time, prior to the discovery of Anatolian and Tocharian early in the following century. As it turns out, a considerable amount of time would pass before the insights of Tocharian, and especially Anatolian, were to alter the picture of Indo-European.

In recent decades it has become clear that Anatolian was the first to break off as a separate speech community (followed next by Tocharian). Some of the morphologically rich categories common to (Vedic) Sanskrit and Greek are now thought to have been later innovations shared by the core inner-IE branches after the breaking off of Anatolian (which appears to have lacked them).

A major ongoing area of study is the history and status of the so-called *-ḫi* and *-mi* conjugations in Anatolian and Indo-European. In core Indo-European, only the familiar *-mi* conjugation (cf. Gk δίδωμι 'give') is attested, though, interestingly, the long 1 sg. ending -ω of thematic verbs is standardly viewed as going back to *-o-h_2 (with the laryngeal ending ultimately related to the *-ḫi* conjugation).[10] Scholarship has demonstrated that the perfect tense-stem and the middle voice are clearly historically linked to the Anatolian *-ḫi* conjugation. The exact relationship is

---

[10] The so-called thematic verbs (much more common in Greek) belong to the same class as *-mi* verbs; compare the endings of Gk δίδωμι with the thematic verb *bhar-a-* 'bear; carry' in Sanskrit: 1 sg. *bhár-ā-mi* (from earlier **bʰarā*, cognate with Gk φέρω), 2 sg. *bhár-a-si*, 3 sg. *bhár-a-ti*.

controversial and has been much debated. A comprehensive theory of the Indo-European verb, developed by Jay Jasanoff since the 1970s, has been steadily gaining adherents (see Jasanoff 2003).

1.2. Semitic Studies

Hebrew and Aramaic, the languages of the Old Testament, belong to the Semitic family of languages, itself part of a larger grouping called Afro-Asiatic (which links Semitic with a number of languages spoken in northern and central Africa).[11] The immediate sub-branch to which both Hebrew and Aramaic belong is designated Northwest Semitic. Also classified as Northwest Semitic is Ugaritic, an extinct language spoken at Ugarit, a city state on the northern Levantine coast.[12]

Semitic linguistics has been shaped by particular constraints and methodological challenges. Semitic languages are characterised by a distinctive concatenative morphology, which features (mostly) triconsonantal verbal roots (C_1-C_2-C_3) combined with particular vowel patterns. For example, *k-t-b* 'write'

---

[11] Afro-Asiatic linguistics is still in its infancy, and many of the non-Semitic languages are poorly known and poorly attested. Additionally, the specific linguistic affiliation of the sub-branches is controversial.

[12] Discovered by accident in 1928, the archaeological site of Ugarit (Tell Ras Shamra) has yielded thousands of cuneiform tablets and other significant artefacts. Ugaritic studies over the past century has offered important linguistic, cultural, and theological insights into the Old Testament. For a broad introduction to Ugaritic studies, see Watson and Wyatt (1999).

combined with a particular vowel pattern to form a verbal adjective in Proto-Semitic: *kātib-* (Hebrew *qal* כְּתָב, Aramaic *peʿal* כְּתַב, Ugaritic G-stem *kātibu*, Arabic form I *kātibun*). A different vowel pattern with the same root yields a different grammatical form, e.g., the G-stem infinitive *katāb-*. Unfortunately, the reconstruction of the various vocalic patterns for both Proto-Semitic and intermediate branches is complicated by the fact that many ancient Semitic writing systems tended to leave out vowels. The writings of the Old Testament, for example, were originally written with a (largely) consonantal writing system, which was only later supplemented by the medieval Masoretic notation system of vowels (*niqqud*).

For example, the exact vocalisation of the Ugaritic word *šd* 'field' must be ascertained from other evidence (since the native Ugaritic orthography is largely consonantal). Its reconstructed form in Proto-Semitic featured an intervocalic glide (between the second root vowel and the case vowel): *ṣadayum*. The outcome of these so-called *triphthong* sequences varied from language to language.[13] In Biblical Hebrew, for example, III-ה nouns (originally derived from III-*y/w* roots) feature word-final *segol* in the absolute (e.g., שָׂדֶה 'field'), with regular loss of final **m*

---

[13] The term *triphthong* (derived from *diphthong*) is somewhat of a misnomer, as these sequences are better described from the standpoint of Semitic phonology as two vowels separated by an intervocalic glide: $V_1 w V_2$ and $V_1 y V_2$.

(originally used in Proto-Semitic to indicate unbound nominals).[14] Fortunately, among the archaeological finds at Ugarit are numerous cuneiform tablets which contain lists of Ugaritic words spelled with the logosyllabic orthography peculiar to Akkadian. One such example is *ša-du-u* 'field' (RS 20.123+), indicating to us that the outcome of this triphthong sequence in Ugaritic was /-ū/.

Another challenge historical linguists face in dealing with Semitic languages has been determining linguistic subgroupings. The most important criterion for establishing a subgroup is shared innovations between languages. Unfortunately, the significant linguistic contact between Semitic languages in the relatively small Middle East region has meant that genuine shared innovations are often hard to distinguish from borrowings. For more detail about the criteria of shared innovations, as well as the two major models of linguistic affiliation (the tree and wave models), see §2.1.4.

Important work by Robert Hetzron in the 1970s led to mainstream adoption of a Central Semitic node which, in the current standard view, includes three main sub-branches: Northwest Semitic, Arabic, and Old South Arabian (Ṣayhadic). The primary shared innovation justifying this node was the replacement of the imperfective *yaqaṭṭal* verbal form with the *yaqtulu* form (the ancestor of the familiar *yiqtol* form in Hebrew).

Some scholars have rejected Hetzron's model, pointing out that there appears to be a set of shared features justifying a

---

[14] The less common biform שָׂדַי 'field' indicates the original III-y root shape.

'south' Semitic branch.[15] For example, Arabic, Old South Arabian, and Modern South Arabian, as well as Ethiopian, all exhibit a distinctive *p > f sound change. Furthermore, the phenomenon of so-called 'broken' (or internal) plurals is widespread among these languages, whereas it is less prevalent (and never occurs without an overt plural suffix) in Northwest Semitic. Huehnergard and Rubin (2011) argue persuasively that these (and other) features are in some cases trivial, while in other cases they provide evidence for intensive contact between the 'southern' languages *after* the split of Central Semitic from the rest of West Semitic.[16]

The status of some other sub-groupings in Semitic also continues to be debated. Potentially of interest to biblical scholars is the ongoing discussion about the status of Aramaic, Ugaritic, and the Canaanite dialects (including Hebrew) within Northwest Semitic (see Pat-El and Wilson-Wright 2018).

2.0. Key Theoretical Commitments and Major Concepts

In historical linguistics, several crucial theoretical commitments are a necessary foundation for the investigation of language change in all its dimensions. These are described below, followed by an exploration of some of the field's major concepts.

---

[15] The 'south Semitic' view was standard among earlier generations of Semitists.

[16] Kogan's recent detailed lexical study (2015) of Semitic isoglosses, including between Arabic and Northwest Semitic, finds additional support for a Central Semitic node.

2.1. Theoretical Commitments

Any scientific discipline contains within it various assumptions (sometimes unstated or otherwise unknown to non-specialists) without which its specific concepts and methods could not be coherent or justified. Four such primary commitments are sketched here.

2.1.1. Pervasiveness of Language Change across All Levels

Human language is the object of all linguistic investigation. A *sine qua non* within the subfield of historical linguistics is the assumption that *all* natural human languages are everywhere and always subject to continuous and perpetual language change at all levels. Consider the somewhat idealised Figure 1 below. All subsystems within a given language (whether phonetics, phonology, etc.) are subject to change over time.[17] This process is generally gradual (although it is not always uniform in intensity), such that speakers do not generally perceive the change to be very great within their own lifetimes. Over a larger timespan, however, such as centuries or millennia, the accumulated changes can result in drastic differences.

---

[17] This neat segmentation is of course conceptual, and in reality all schools of linguistic thought acknowledge that the boundaries between language domains are highly permeable and interconnected (hence terms such as *morphosyntax*, *pragmatico-semantic*, etc.).

Figure 1: Multi-level language change

Time →			
Language states			
Phonetics$_1$	Phonetics$_2$	...	Phonetics$_x$
Phonology$_1$	Phonology$_2$	...	Phonology$_x$
Morphology$_1$	Morphology$_2$	...	Morphology$_x$
Syntax$_1$	Syntax$_2$	...	Syntax$_x$
Semantics$_1$	Semantics$_2$	...	Semantics$_x$
Pragmatics$_1$	Pragmatics$_2$	...	Pragmatics$_x$

Historical linguists assume that any natural language—even if poorly understood or as yet unknown—will be subject to this phenomenon.[18]

2.1.2. The Regularity of Sound Change

The study of sound change lies at the heart of the discipline of historical linguistics. One key reason for this is the *regularity* of sound change in all human languages—a far-reaching theoretical commitment. Early nineteenth-century observers of language change (e.g., Rasmus Rask, August Schleicher, Franz Bopp, etc.)

---

[18] In fact, one of the distinguishing factors in classifying languages as 'living' (as opposed to 'extinct' or 'dead') is whether they are (or were) in the process of undergoing change. Nevertheless, the classification of a language as 'dead' is somewhat controversial, given phenomena such as the widespread use of Latin in medieval Europe, for example.

noted systematic sound correspondences between sets of cognate vocabulary, leading them to postulate consistent sound laws to account for these differences (see §2.2.3. on the comparative method). The consistency of the sound correspondences was seen to apply across the board in a given language (for example, the same sound change affected verbs, nouns, adjectives, etc., without exception). The regularity of sound change is largely what makes linguistic reconstruction of prehistoric language states possible. In its strongest form, this claim is linked to the nineteenth-century German Neogrammarians (Ger. *Junggrammatiker*), especially expounded in Osthoff and Brugmann (1878).

The actual degree of regularity of sound changes is a topic of some controversy in historical linguistics. Some types of processes (for example, dissimilation and metathesis) appear to be less than fully regular. Closely tied to this issue is the question of the actual locus of sound change. Does it take place mainly during the language acquisition process of children? Or is it rather to be located in fluent adult speakers? Or both? What is the relationship and interplay between 'regular' sound change and other types of change in language (especially analogy)? For our purposes, it is enough to note that most scholars accept a *general* regularity in language sound change (what could be perhaps termed 'qualified exceptionlessness').

2.1.3. Linguistic Reconstruction from Sound Change

Linguistic reconstruction is the systematic recovery of chronologically earlier language states (often thousands of years earlier). This process includes proto-languages, intermediate daughter branches, and all other intermediate language states. The end goal of linguistic reconstruction is to provide as comprehensive a history as possible for a given language within its language family. This activity is a constant work-in-progress for scholars engaging with each language family, and in some cases, scholarship has been working towards this goal for centuries.

Although all levels of language are subject to change over time as seen above, the investigation of sound change (phonetics and phonology) in language is agreed to be the major *starting* point and the foundation for the entire enterprise of linguistic reconstruction. This is partly due to the regularity of sound change, discussed above, but there are additional reasons. Language subsystems exist in a roughly hierarchical arrangement, hence sound change naturally becomes the foundation for other, higher-level linguistic reconstruction. This is because higher language domains (such as morphosyntax) ultimately terminate at the phonological/phonetic domains.

All syntactic constructions, for example, consist of a discrete sequence of morphemes. Each morpheme in turn consists of a discrete sequence of phonemes (contrastive speech sounds within a given language).[19] Finally, each phoneme is an abstract representation of a set of phones (the final, phonetic domain), whose distribution in the language is governed by complex language-specific rules.

---

[19] Naturally, some morphemes in languages can consist of only a single phoneme; but a conceptual distinction between the two is still necessary.

As an example, Figure 2 below illustrates the hierarchical relationships in the Classical Greek present participle γιγνόμενα 'the things taking place'.[20] Notice that the complete word (level III) consists of five discrete morphemes in the morphological level (II), of which the first, a present-stem reduplicant gi-, is especiallly noteworthy.[21] Finally, the five morphemes comprise nine distinctive phonemes in the phonological level (I).

Figure 2: Morphological hierarchy of γιγνόμενα

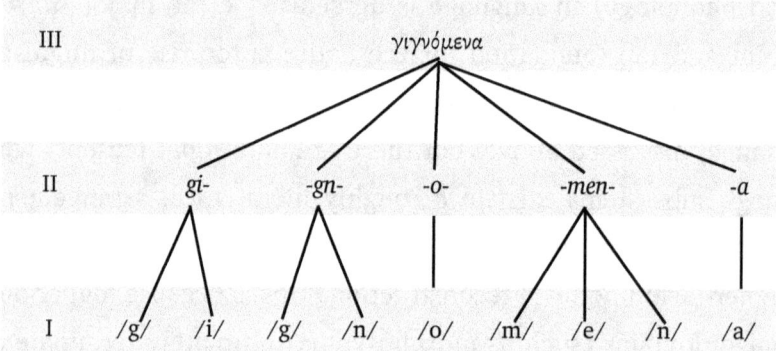

However, a consequence of this bottom-up schema is that any sound changes will have cascading consequences for higher-level domains. For example, the historic loss of the preconsonantal phoneme /g/ in post-classical Greek (/gignomena/ > /gīnomena/) occasioned compensatory lengthening of /i/ > [iː]. This is evidenced by the consistent spelling of {ει} in this and related

---

[20] This schema is necessarily simplified, and therefore does not capture the internal hierarchical structures at each of the three levels.

[21] Not to be confused with the perfect-stem reduplicant C_1e- (cf. γέγονα).

present-tense forms in the biblical manuscript tradition, e.g., Luke 9.7: P⁷⁵ ℵ D {γεινομενα}.[22]

This change in the language, although originating at the phonetic/phonological level, has consequences for higher levels of the language. In place of a clear phonological boundary between the present-stem reduplicant *gi-* and the root *-gn-*, one observes a new opaque present-stem *gīn-*. Speakers would now internalise a quasi-suppletive set of verbal stems (e.g., present *gīn-* [γείνεται], aorist *-gen-* [ἐγένετο], perfect *-gon-* [γέγονε]). This new structure is depicted in Figure 3 below.

Figure 3: Revised morphological hierarchy of γιγνόμενα

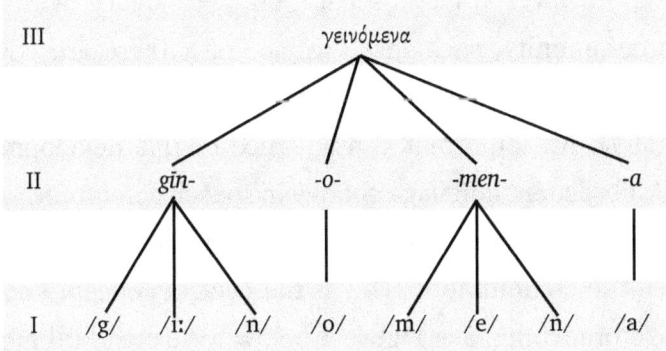

From this illustration one sees the foundational role that sound change plays in linguistic structures, as well as how it enjoys a certain priority in historical linguistics. Although language change can occur in any language domain, the most secure and

---

[22] See Williams (2018) for a defence of the view that {ι} ~ {ει} spelling interchanges are not uniformly haphazard, as is usually assumed (part of a larger phenomenon known as 'itacism').

logical foundation for *linguistic reconstruction* is the phonetics/phonology domain (i.e., sound change).[23]

2.1.4. Language Branching and Speech Communities

A language or dialect is a more or less unified speech community with a set of shared (though unconsciously accepted) conventions that constitute a particular *grammar*. A grammar may be conceived of as a collection of form-and-meaning pairings.

The language of such a speech community (say, speech community x) undergoes innovations over time, such that all of its members (= speakers) essentially hold together linguistically. Suppose, however, that a separation takes place within this speech community, such that in place of x there are now two separate speech communities, y and z (typically separated by geography). An important consequence of this development is that all subsequent language change in speech communities y and z will be distinctive, unless language contact is reestablished between the communities. This is the central concept known as language branching. See Figure 4 below for a standard model of Northwest Semitic.

---

[23] In practice, this usually means that the most developed linguistic reconstructions tend to be phonological in nature, followed by morphosyntax and semantics (though these other, less well-developed areas of study in Indo-European historical linguistics have experienced significant advances in recent decades).

Figure 4: Standard model of Northwest Semitic

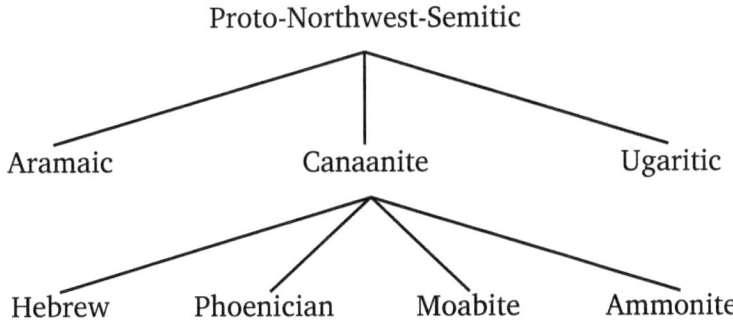

Over time, the iterative branching process yields a family 'tree', where each 'twig' (or dialect) is linked to a larger series of 'branches' (or distinctive languages), while all branches ultimately converge into a single 'trunk' (the proto-language).[24] While all speech communities are ultimately related to one another within a given family, a hierarchical structure relates each language in a more precise way that captures the individual relationships between any two members.

Once separated, the different changes that two speech communities undergo are generally not predictable beforehand. Within a given language family, when speech communities are no longer in contact with one another, the changes they subsequently undergo will not always be identical.[25] The more time

---

[24] This specialised field, known as *cladistics* (from Gk κλάδος 'branch'), is also important for several other non-linguistic scientific disciplines, for example, textual criticism.

[25] An active topic of discussion among historical linguists is the degree to which linguistic trajectories can be mapped out, given the common starting point of separated speech communities. In part, this depends on whether language change is best characterised as *prophylactic* or

that passes, the more distinctive each speech community becomes. Here, the imprecise, yet useful, terms *dialect* and *language* apply. Given enough time, separated speech communities sharing a language will develop distinctive dialects. These dialects will grow progressively less mutually intelligible, until, at some point, they are conventionally considered distinctive languages.[26]

In reality, this neat model is complicated by the phenomenon of language contact between distinctive speech communities. Prolonged language contact (whether minor or intensive) can lead to new shared linguistic innovations over time. These innovations (or *isoglosses*) can create challenges in the establishment of linguistic affiliations between the languages of a language family (as even in the example of Northwest Semitic; see §1.2).

To capture this reality, an alternative (but complementary) *wave model* has been used by historical linguists to account for features and changes that spread throughout any speech communities in contact with one another (whether they are linguistically homogeneous or not). The metaphor of a spreading wave (or better: ripples in a pond) nicely illustrates how language change

---

reparative. In other words, does language change primarily occur in order to avoid certain phenomena that are unconsciously disfavoured by speakers, or, rather, does language change occur as a subsequent tool for repairing already existing changes which themselves are disfavoured?

[26] Something of the imprecision in these categories may be observed when considering that the Scandinavian *languages* (Swedish, Norwegian, and Danish) are largely mutually intelligible, yet the numerous *dialects* of Modern Arabic or the varieties of Chinese are not.

is often much more complex than imagined. The wave model is popular with dialectologists, especially in the context of the study of a dialect continuum (or language continuum). Many linguists today do not view the tree and wave models as mutually exclusive, but in fact as complementary, the former accounting for *genetic* relationships, the latter accounting for subsequent external linguistic influences.

2.2. Major Concepts

Building on the previous section, the following is a necessarily brief exploration of some of the methods and tools used by historical linguists in their exploration of language change.

2.2.1. The Role of Philology

As we have seen, linguistics was birthed in the context of the study of ancient languages, which is described in part as philology. Nevertheless, historical linguistics eventually grew to be a separate scientific discipline in its own right, distinct from philology. Consequently, the term *philology* nowadays more properly describes the various tools employed by scholars (not just linguists) in order to study ancient texts. Philology, which has been neatly encapsulated as the art of reading slowly, includes diverse disciplines such as archaeology, paleography, textual criticism, and other historical fields of inquiry.

These tools are still highly relevant for historical linguists, since scholars prize the early written records of a language as a means of conducting linguistic reconstruction. Unfortunately, the quality and accuracy of such data are uneven for the documentation of a historically prior stage of a spoken language (irrespective of whether that language is currently extinct or living). Knowledge about writing systems (paleography, etc.) is vital for understanding the conventions that native (and non-native) speakers chose in representing a given language. Furthermore, if an ancient text can only be accessed by scholars as the product of a chain of textual transmission (i.e., scribal copying), the discipline of textual criticism must be employed in order to sort out genuine linguistic data from non-linguistic scribal errors or supposed corrections that have arisen in the manuscript tradition.

In fact, any written representation of language, whether ancient or modern, is always incomplete and imprecise due to various factors. To begin with, speakers do not require or depend on a precise phonetic (or even phonological) transcription of language in order to achieve comprehension. An illustration of various levels of transcriptional detail in the Masoretic system and the International Phonetic Alphabet (IPA) is given in the example below.

(1) (a) אפדנו ('his palace'; Dan. 11.45)
Consonantal representation
(b) אַפַּדְנוֹ
Approximate phonemic representation
(c) /ʔapːadno/
Broad (phonemic) IPA transcription
(d) אַפַּדְנוֹ
Approximate suprasegmental representation
(e) [ʔap.pað.'noː]
Narrow (phonetic) IPA transcription

Varying levels of detail and accuracy are presented for the hapax אַפַּדְנוֹ 'his palace' (Dan. 11.45) in the example, on a spectrum from (a)–(e). Notice, however, that each non-IPA representation is not fully consistent (hence the designation 'approximate'). This is an artefact of complex historical factors. For example, the consonantal representation is not fully consonantal, since it includes a final vowel letter (וֹ–).[27] Additionally, while the Masoretic system itself accounts for vowel quality and generally indicates suprasegmental stress, it does not record vowel length, even though this is generally thought to have been at least partly phonemic in Tiberian Hebrew.[28]

What is particularly interesting about this example, however, is that it is plausibly one of a select few examples of a non-aspirated /p/ in the entire Masoretic reading tradition of the Old Testament. We know from Latin and Greek transcriptions that the normal pronunciation of פ appears to have been not [p], but an aspirated stop [pʰ], e.g., וְאַרְפַּכְשַׁד (Gen 10:22) // Αρφαξαδ. Geoffrey Khan adduces testimony from the medieval grammarian Saadya Gaon for the hapax legomenon אַפַּדְנוֹ 'his palace' at Dan. 11.45,

---

[27] The use of vowel letters can be documented from the early first millennium BCE, and it is generally thought that the initial point of contact was the monophthongisation of particular diphthongs in Northwest Semitic. Thus, for example, *mawt {mwt} > mōt {mwt} 'death' (cons.), where w came to represent ō.

[28] There has been something of a revolution in our understanding of the phonology of Tiberian Hebrew in recent decades, largely thanks to the detailed work of Geoffrey Khan. For an excellent brief overview of the history of scholarly interpretation of the Masoretic vocalic system, see Suchard (2018).

which he describes as "between *bet* and *pe* with *dagesh*" (Khan 2020, 215). This appears to be an attempt to capture the hearer's perception of a non-aspirated stop (since *bet* was not aspirated). Khan argues that the reading tradition for this loanword essentially inherited its non-aspiration from its Old Persian source (which lacked aspiration), probably with pharyngealisation, as a phonetic approximation of the loanword in Hebrew. Incredibly, there is even some corroborating evidence for this pronunciation from Latin and Greek transcriptions: e.g., απαδανω (Theodoretus, fifth century AD).[29]

As can be seen from just one example, historical linguists rely heavily on the methods and findings of philology in order to do good linguistic work on language states that are inaccessible with traditional field work methodology. The soundness of their reconstructions and theoretical models in large part depends on sound philological work.

2.2.2. Borrowing[30]

Linguistic borrowing is in fact a pervasive feature of many distinctive speech communities in human societies, since they are frequently in contact (sometimes extensive contact) with other language communities. This contact can take many different

---

[29] For the full argument, as well as more complete evidence, see Khan (2020, 214–20).

[30] This discussion on borrowing is deliberately placed prior to the sections that follow because discerning and eliminating borrowed linguistic material is an important criterion for establishing legitimate correspondence sets when using the comparative method.

forms. Sometimes it is limited and sporadic; at other times and contexts it can be significant, such that a high level of bilingualism exists between two speech communities.[31] The term *borrowing* generally refers to lexemes and semantic notions which are transferred from one speech community to another. (Note that this excludes other types of linguistic influence, such as syntax, which are no less genuine.)

The actual process of borrowing, like with other diachronic aspects of language, is not instantaneous. A borrowed lexeme begins life as a recognisably foreign element that over time may become progressively integrated into a speech community, such that eventually its users will no longer perceive it as foreign, but perfectly native. When examining lexical material in a speech community, or even in an ancient text (say, that of the Bible), it is important to ascertain where on the scale of adoption a given lexical item is diachronically situated (at the time of its usage). Depending on the analysis, foreign words in a text might be described either as *loanwords* or alternatively as an example of *code-switching*.

A helpful illustration for understanding borrowing is the so-called 'Latinisms' in the Gospel of Mark. As shown in Table 2, these include the following (adapted from Zeichmann 2017):

---

[31] Various complex factors (linguistic and non-linguistic) can play a role in determining the degree of contact, such as the linguistic relatedness of the two speech communities, their relative social ranking, and the degree of societal integration between them.

Table 2: Latin-Greek Borrowing

Latin	Greek	References (GMark)
grabātus 'cot'	κράβατος	2.4, 9, 11, 12; 6.55
modius 'a measure'	μόδιον	4.21
legiō 'legion'	λεγιών	5.9, 15
speculātor 'scout'	σπεκουλάτωρ	6.27
dēnārius 'a day's wage'	δηνάριον	6.37; 12.15; 14.5
pugnus 'fist'	πυγμή	7.3
sextārius 'a measure'	ξέστης	7.4
cēnsus 'census'	κῆνσος	12.14
Caesar 'Caesar'	καῖσαρ	12.14, 16, 17 [2×]
quadrāns 'a coin'	κοδράντης	12.42
vae 'woe'	οὐαί	13.17; 14.21
flagellō 'to whip'	φραγελλόω	15.15
praetōrium 'palace'	πραιτώριον	15.16
centuriō 'centurion'	κεντύριων	15.39, 44, 45

The presence of so many Latin words in Mark's Gospel has been taken by many commentators as fairly strong evidence for a Roman (i.e., Western) provenance for the writing. Other scholars, however, argue for a Syrian or Palestinian setting. Zeichmann examines the character of these Latinisms and concludes that they are poorly internalised borrowings. Some of the senses Mark uses for the Latin words are quite atypical (for example πυγμή as 'hand'). The very presence of Latinisms most likely indicates a post-70 CE writing date if in Palestine (when the Roman occupation, the use of Latin, and the prevalence of Roman items, such as coins, increased dramatically). On the other hand, Mark's rather rough and irregular use of Latin words may indicate only a rudimentary acquaintance with the language, which is consistent with a Roman provenance.³²

Another application of studies in loanwords and linguistic borrowing for biblical studies is the use of loanwords to obtain relative dates for the composition of a text. If the historical time period during which cultural and linguistic contact took place between two speech communities is known, in theory approximate dates of composition could be assigned to texts containing particular loanwords. For example, the presence of Greek loanwords in the book of Daniel has frequently been used as an argument in favour of a Hellenistic-era composition. A recent re-examination of the evidence by Benjamin Noonan (2018), however, argues that the phonological makeup of these Greek loanwords (mainly musical terms) indicates that they were borrowed from a non-Attic source (i.e., not the dialect which spread as a consequence of Alexander's Hellenisation). This debate illustrates that linguistic evidence can play a role in assessing the date of a text's composition, but that one should be cautious in relying on such evidence for a conclusive decision (see §3.0 below).³³

---

³² Zeichmann himself favours a post-war Syrian or Palestinian provenance, though this is on the assumption that "the author of Mark was [not] a Judaean denizen writing from Rome or a refugee of the Jewish War" (Zeichmann 2017, 47).

³³ A vivid illustration of such overconfidence is the famous assessment of S. R. Driver (1900, lxiii, emphasis original) with regard to the date of Daniel: "The verdict of the language of Daniel is thus clear... the Greek words *demand*, the Hebrew *supports*, and the Aramaic *permits*, a date *after the conquest of Palestine by Alexander the Great*."

2.2.3. The Comparative Method

The comparative method has already been mentioned, but in this section it is explained in more detail, especially as a process. This is one of the most important tools historical linguists make use of when conducting research into a family of languages. As its name suggests, the method involves a *comparison* of assembled lexical items between two or more genetically related languages. It is important to state at the outset that the method is necessarily iterative by nature, as several assumptions required by the method are themselves clarified in the course of implementing the selfsame method. In the initial phase, of course, it may not necessarily have been established that the languages in question are in fact related, as superficial resemblances are not enough to establish such a link (since they could be chance similarities). Hence, there is a necessary element of circularity in the method; an initial provisional hypothesis is usually sufficient to begin. The pervasive presence of a core set of vocabulary that appears to be shared between two languages is a valid starting point for the application of the comparative method.[34]

The first step involves the assembling of a list of lexical items which are plausibly cognate with one another. At this stage, it is critical to exclude any borrowed lexemes in any language, since they would inevitably skew the analysis (see the previous section). This, too, is not always easy to accomplish, as there is a

---

[34] Sometimes the similarities between two languages have been much obscured by many layers of sound change. For example, it was not immediately obvious to scholars that Old Irish was Indo-European until the meticulous work of Franz Bopp.

degree of circularity in ascertaining which lexemes are borrowed and which ones are inherited.[35] Table 3 below shows a sample correspondence set between Hebrew, Aramaic, and Ugaritic.[36] Although of course these three languages are now known to be genetically related to one another, it is helpful to see exactly how this claim can be established. As one examines the list of correspondences, certain observations emerge. (In the following, only the voiced coronal consonants /d/, /z/, and /ð/ will be examined, though the correspondence sets above also reveal other patterns.) Not only do most of the words look fairly similar to one another, but particular patterns are evident.

For example, sometimes all three witnesses agree in sharing the same consonant /d/: דָּם ‎| דמא ‎| *dm* 'blood'. This is also found in קָדוֹשׁ ‎| קַדִּישׁ ‎| *qdš* 'holy' and צֶמֶד ‎| צמדא ‎| *ṣmd* 'holy', as well as דֶּלֶת ‎| דלתא ‎| *dlt* 'door'.[37] In another set, there is also agreement among the three languages with regard to /z/: זַיִת ‎| זיתא ‎| *zt* 'olive'. However, sometimes the languages disagree: זבח ‎| דבח ‎| *dbḥ* 'sacrifice' and זָהָב ‎| דְּהַב ‎| *ḥrṣ* 'gold'. (Further examination reveals

---

[35] In some cases, heavy lexical borrowing can eliminate much core vocabulary, which presents a unique set of challenges to scholars. One such example is Armenian, whose vocabulary is much more strongly shaped by Middle Iranian languages than English is by Norman French. It took quite a bit of careful work in the late nineteenth century, for example, to establish that Armenian constitutes a unique branch of Indo-European and that it is not an Iranian language.

[36] This example concerns the reconstruction of Proto-Northwest-Semitic; see Figure 4 in §2.1.4 above.

[37] Note that vowels are included in Table 3 only where there is evidence, but are omitted for verbs.

that in the last set, Ugaritic ḫrṣ must be removed from consideration as it is clearly cognate with a poetic equivalent חָרוּץ in Hebrew; the cognate of זָהָב has apparently been lost in Ugaritic.)

Table 3: Example cognate words in Hebrew, Aramaic, and Ugaritic

	BHebrew	BAramaic	Ugaritic
a.	זָהָב 'gold'	דְּהַב 'gold'	ḫrṣ 'gold'
b.	זַיִת 'olive'	JArm. זיתא 'olive'	zt 'olive'
c.	זֶה dem. pron.	דִּי rel. pron.	d/ḏ rel. pron.
d.	דֶּלֶת 'door'	JArm. דלתא 'door'	dlt 'door'
e.	שַׁעַר 'gate'	תְּרַע 'door'	ṯġr 'gate'
f.	דָּם 'blood'	JArm. דמא 'blood'	dm 'blood'
g.	זבח 'sacrifice'	דבח 'sacrifice'	dbḥ 'sacrifice'
h.	קָדֵשׁ 'holy'	קַדִּישׁ 'holy'	qdš 'holy'
i.	שָׁלֹשׁ 'three'	תְּלָת 'three'	ṯlṯ 'three'
j.	תַּחַת 'below'	תְּחוֹת 'under'	tḥt 'under'
k.	צוּר 'rock'	טוּר 'mountain'	ġr 'mountain'
l.	צֶלֶם 'image'	צְלֵם 'image'	ṣlm 'image'
m.	אֶרֶץ 'earth'	אֲרַע/אֲרַק 'earth'	arṣ 'earth'
n.	צַלְמָוֶת (?)	חֲשׁוֹךְ 'darkness'	ġlmt/ẓlmt 'darkness'
o.	צֶמֶד 'yoke'	JArm. צמדא 'yoke'	ṣmd 'team'
p.	מחץ 'strike'	מחא 'strike'	mḫṣ 'fight'

Once this is done, however, there remains a discrepancy between the /d/ of Aramaic and Ugaritic, on the one hand, and the /z/ of Hebrew, on the other. A final correspondence set, the relative/demonstrative pronoun זֶה | דִּי | d/ḏ reveals that Ugaritic apparently features two (dialectal) outcomes of the same segment. All these correspondences are then conveniently tabulated on a separate chart (Table 4 below). The next step is the analysis of the sets of segments in order to propose a single reconstructed phoneme per set. The full agreement between the three languages with regard to sets 1 (/z/) and 3 (/d/) allows us to hypothesise that the immediate ancestor of the languages (Proto-Northwest-Semitic) featured a phonemic inventory with the same two segments: *z and *d.

Table 4: Segment correspondence in Hebrew, Aramaic, and Ugaritic

	Hebrew	Aramaic	Ugaritic
Set 1	/z/ז	/z/ז	z /z/
Set 2	/z/ז	/d/ד	ḏ /ð/ ~ d /d/
Set 3	/d/ד	/d/ד	d /d/

This is the most economical explanation, as it would be highly unlikely that each language independently innovated in the same direction, resulting in such correspondences.

Set 2, however, presents some challenges. Which segment ought we to reconstruct? In the majority of cases, Ugaritic agrees with Aramaic in sharing a /d/ segment (over against the /z/ of Hebrew). The interesting case of the relative pronoun ḏ /ð/, however, reveals that in at least some cases, the reflex of this correspondence set in Ugaritic was a voiced interdental fricative. A feature analysis (Table 5) shows that /ð/, although a fricative, is not a sibilant like /z/, and is therefore situated midway between /d/ and /z/. Cross-linguistic patterns further show that it is quite common for interdental fricatives to become sibilants (e.g., *ð > /z/; viz. Hebrew), or else to be 'strengthened' to a stop (e.g., *ð > /d/; viz. Aramaic).

Table 5: Feature analysis of /z/, /ð/, and /d/

	Coronal	Voiced	Sibilant	Stop
/z/	+	+	+	−
/ð/	+	+	−	−
/d/	+	+	−	+

As there is nothing apparent in the environment of these words (from the correspondence sets) to motivate a change in Aramaic or Ugaritic, we must instead hypothesise that an *unconditioned* merger took place in Hebrew between *ð and *z (> /z/) that is absent in Aramaic. Correspondingly, a separate unconditioned merger must have taken place in Aramaic between *ð and *d (> /d/). The reconstructed segments in each of the correspondence sets are given below in Table 6 in the left column.

Table 6: Reconstructed segments of *z, *ð, and *d

	Hebrew	Aramaic	Ugaritic
*z	ז /z/	ז /z/	z /z/
*ð	ז /z/	ד /d/	ḏ /ð/ ~ d /d/
*d	ד /d/	ד /d/	d /d/

The results of this analysis indicate that Proto-Northwest-Semitic featured a series of three voiced coronal phonemes, which were reduced to two in Hebrew and Aramaic (though in different ways).

2.2.4. A Typology of Sound Change

The previous discussion illustrated the importance of understanding the phonology of the segments in correspondence sets assembled between cognate languages. Additionally, knowledge of common patterns of sound change in other languages provides valuable information for the comparative method. This section provides a brief overview of various types of phonological processes.

A pervasive phenomenon in sound change is *lenition*, or consonantal weakening. In general, consonantal segments frequently tend to change along certain common pathways, potentially leading to segment loss. In table 7 below, three different places of articulation (bilabial, alveolar, and velar) are arranged in parallel to show common pathways towards ∅ (though other pathways are also possible). For example, a common process in languages is for geminated segments to be degeminated. Voiceless (non-geminated) stops will often become voiced in the environment of surrounding vowels (which are usually voiced in most languages).

Table 7: Pathways towards consonantal weakening

	Bilabial	**Alveolar**	**Velar**
Geminate	/p:/	/t:/	/k:/
Degemination	/p/	/t/	/k/
Voicing	/b/	/d/	/g/
Spirantisation	/β/	/ð/	/ɣ/
Debuccalisation	/h/	/h/	/h/
Segment loss	∅	∅	∅

The final stage prior to segment loss is called *debuccalisation*, in which the oral segment loses its original place of articulation, moving to the glottis (/h/).[38]

Consider an example of lenition from Biblical and Byzantine Greek. The spelling of Σιλουανοῦ (m. gen. sg.) 'Silvanus' at 2 Cor. 1.19, a loanword from Latin *Silvānus* /silwaːnus/, varies somewhat in the manuscript tradition (in which we also find lunate sigma):

(2) (a) ϲιλουανου

P46ᶜ ℵ A B C K L P Ψ 1739 *rell*

(b) ϲιλβανου

P46* D F G

---

[38] A far less common cross-linguistic process than lenition is its reverse, called *fortition*. The change of *ð > /d/ in Aramaic is one such example.

The spelling ciλβανου in (2b) indicates that for some later Byzantine scribes, the phoneme represented by {β} had already shifted from a voiced stop /b/ to a fricative /β/, which was perceived as the closest rendering of the Latin proper name (with /w/).[39]

Another common category of sound change is the loss of vocalic segments. Syllables which have lost articulatory prominence in words tend to lead to vowel reduction, and finally loss, which is called *apocope*. The loss of word-internal vowels is called *syncope*. A pervasive example of apocope in Hebrew is the loss of old Semitic case vowels (e.g., nominative *malk-u*, genitive *malk-i*, accusative *malk-a*, all losing their final vowel in מֶלֶךְ 'king').[40]

The juxtaposition of a consonantal segment next to a following sound articulated close to the palate of the mouth (whether a vowel or consonant) leads to a common sound process in many languages called *palatalisation*. For example, in Pre-Greek, the co-occurrence of certain consonants before the palatal glide /j/ (usually spelled as a *y* in English) led to a series of widespread sound changes, including changes in place of articulation (/l/ > /lʲ/, with a palatal co-articulation), changes in manner of articulation (stop > affricate), among others. The examples in (3)

---

[39] The IPA symbol for a voiced bilabial fricative is a Greek *beta*. Manuscript data taken from Royse (2007, 852). Note that the use of {ου} is itself an attempt to render Latin /w/ in Greek.

[40] An intermediate step was the form *malk*, which subsequently developed an anaptyctic vowel to break up the final consonant cluster *-lk*. This widespread phenomenon in Hebrew is termed *segolisation* (after the name of the final vowel seen in the so-called segolates).

below in Greek are illustrations from various present formations with the Indo-European *-jo- suffix (contrasted with aorist):

(3) (a) *bal-jo- > *balʲo- > *baʎ:o- > βάλλω 'throw' (present); *(e-)bal- > ἔβαλον (aorist)

(b) *klep-jo- > *klepʲo- > *kleptʃo- > κλέπτω 'steal' (present); *(e-)klep-sa- > ἔκλεψα (aorist)

(c) *pʰulak-jo- > *pʰulakʲo- > *pʰulatʃ:o- > φυλάσσω 'guard' (present); *(e-)pʰulak-sa- > ἐφύλαξα (aorist)

A very common process in sound change is the assimilation of a segment (or segments) in part or in whole to the features of an adjacent segment. For example, in Biblical Hebrew *hitpaʿʿel* stems, certain features of the root-initial segment spread backwards to the alveolar *t* of the stem prefix. This is referred to as *regressive* assimilation (the reverse is called *progressive* assimilation). For instance, the verbal root דבר formed a *hitpaʿʿel* with regressive voicing assimilation: e.g., *mit-dabir- > *mid-dabir- > מְדַבֵּר (Num. 7.89).

Sometimes this assimilation in *hitpaʿʿel* stems was combined with yet another (often seemingly sporadic) process called metathesis, which involves the exchange of two or more segments, sometimes even when they are non-adjacent. This is a well-known phenomenon in *hitpaʿʿel* stems with roots which begin with a sibilant. For example, the verbal root צדק 'to be just' formed a *hitpaʿʿel* in which the emphatic feature of the root-initial sibilant spread to the adjacent dental of the prefix (assimilation). Additionally, the emphatic sibilant was swapped with the dental prefix: *nit-ṣadiq- > *niṣṭadiq- > נִצְטַדָּק (Gen. 44.16; pausal form).

2.2.5. Analogy

In some ways, the two great 'engines' of language change are sound change and analogy (often competing with one another in terms of their effect on a given language). Analogy may be described as the process whereby speakers, in perceiving similarities (potentially of various kinds) between two linguistic structures, proceed to further advance the similarities in other aspects of the same linguistic structures.

For example, some scholars hold that the *weqaṭal* form in Biblical Hebrew is perhaps an analogical development drawing from the *wayyiqṭol*. When final short vowels were lost, the Semitic jussive-preterite form *yaqṭul* merged in most contexts with the imperfective *yaqṭulu*. In Biblical Hebrew, the old (short) *yiqṭol* lives on mainly in the *wayyiqṭol* form. The imperfective (long) *yiqṭol*, by contrast, is used to indicate various modal nuances, as well as imperfective aspect. Later speakers, unaware of this earlier development, could have perceived in the prefixed *waw* of the *wayyiqṭol* as having a 'converting' effect, transforming an imperfective *yiqṭol* into a perfective preterite (hence the *waw*-conversive terminology in some Biblical Hebrew pedagogy). The analogy comes into play when speakers took the suffix conjugation form, prefixed it with *waw*, and 'converted' its meaning from perfective to imperfective (i.e., the inverse of *wayyiqṭol*). Thus the *wayyiqṭol*, on this analysis, represents a direct historical development of the original jussive-preterite *yaqṭul*, while the *weqaṭal* represents an analogical development that was constructed on the model of *wayyiqṭol*.

When engaging in the task of linguistic reconstruction, it is critical to distinguish between genuine historical sound changes and various analogical effects (which sometimes even serve to undo particular sound changes in languages). One common form of analogy is *paradigm levelling*. Speakers over time tend to reduce inflectional distinctions in verbal or nominal paradigms, usually triggered by various kinds of analogy. For example, the 3mp prefix conjugation in Ugaritic features a *t-* element (thus in contrast to the *y-* of Biblical Hebrew). An example may be cited from a letter, KTU 2.63: *ilm tġrk tšlmk* 'may the gods (mp) guard you [and] keep you'. Notice that both verbs have a masculine subject (*ilm* 'gods'), yet feature a *t*-prefix. Likewise, an Amarna Canaanite letter (*EA* 252) contains an unambiguous example of a 3mp prefix conjugation form with a *t-* element: *ti-ma-ḫa-ṣú-ka* 'they strike you'.

This feature (from second millennium BCE Amarna Canaanite and Ugaritic) is used by Robyn Vern in part to argue against the view that there is such a thing as 'archaic' Biblical Hebrew Poetry. For her, one would need to demonstrate the presence of traces of this feature (among others) in Biblical Hebrew passages that are presumed to be archaic in order to sustain such a claim: "If there is sustainable evidence that there are second millennium remnants of the 3mp *t*-preformative, these poetic texts may be considered of second millennium typology with regard to this particular linguistic feature" (Vern 2011, 203).

Yet a consideration of two alternative models for the reconstructed paradigm of the prefix conjugation in Northwest Semitic indicates that the change of *ya- → ta-* is analogically justified with Reconstruction B, while the reverse is manifestly not under either A or B.[41] It seems that paradigm levelling in Amarna Canaanite and Ugaritic was brought about by the pressure to unify all plural prefixes (apart from 1c) under *ta-*, a scenario favouring Reconstruction B. See Figure 5 below for an illustration of this mechanism.

Figure 5: Reconstructed paradigm of the prefix conjugation in Northwest Semitic

	Reconstruction A	**Reconstruction B**
3m	**ya-qtul-ū*	**ya-qtul-ū*
3f	**ya-qtul-na*	**ta-qtul-na*
2m	**ta-qtul-ū*	**ta-qtul-ū*
2f	**ta-qtul-na*	**ta-qtul-na*
1c	**na-qtul*	**na-qtul*

In considering two alternative reconstructions, historical linguists generally favour paradigmatic *heterogeneity* (all things being equal).

A final type of analogy to be discussed is *folk etymology*. A classic example in Biblical Hebrew is the traditional rendering of צַלְמָוֶת 'shadow of death', which occurs eighteen times in the Old Testament (most famously in Psalm 23.4). This understanding is based on a morphological segmentation צל 'shadow' + מות 'death'. Such an interpretation is already seen in the ancient translations, e.g., the Septuagint (σκιὰ τοῦ θανάτου 'shadow of death') and the Targums (טולא דמותא 'the shadow of death'). Its

---

[41] Some scholars make use of an arrow (→) or a double greater-than sign (≫) in order to distinguish analogical change from sound change (>). Note that Reconstruction A is based on the homogeneity (with **ya-*) exhibited by all major, early languages.

parallels in poetry, however, imply that the word is somehow associated with darkness, which is not a necessary interpretation of the phrase 'shadow of death'. An apparent cognate in Ugaritic, ġlmt 'darkness' (variant spelling ẓlmt), suggests that צלמות should probably be segmented as a derivative in -ūt from an unattested stative root צלם* 'to be dark' (cf. Akkadian ṣalāmu 'to be dark'). One can grasp by this example how folk etymology works. It occurs when speakers accidentally reinterpret a word or a phrase by morphological resegmentation. The original word צַלְמוּת* 'darkness' would have been reanalysed as צל 'shadow' + מות 'death', leading to sound change (מוּת- > מָוֶת-) that appears to be irregular.

2.2.6. Other theoretical concepts

Space precludes discussion of the many other kinds of language change (including syntactic change and semantic change), as well as additional methods historical linguists use to recover such changes (for example, internal reconstruction). As with many other fields of linguistics, historical linguistics is a broad field, with many sub-disciplines. Scholars continue to make progress in a number of increasingly specialised fields, while at the same time interdisciplinary approaches are growing in popularity, even drawing on fields outside of linguistics (for example, the recent application of Bayesian phylogenetics to language classification).

3.0. Historical Linguistics in Biblical Studies

The methods and tools of historical linguistics have been applied to biblical studies with ever growing intensity over the past few decades. The main area of application by far has been the Old Testament, which by its nature is arguably more amenable to such research. Despite this, improvement in work done in both the Old and New Testaments is a *desideratum*, as some of it can be uninformed at times about a number of generally accepted assumptions of historical linguistics.

Within Old Testament studies, historical linguistics has been applied most significantly (and increasingly controversially) to the question of the dating of its various texts. Fassberg (2016) offers an excellent overview of the history of scholarship in this area. He outlines three major time periods, the first beginning in the nineteenth century with the publication of Gesenius' *Geschichte der hebräischen Sprache und Schrift* (1815) and concluding with the publishing of the first fragments of Ben Sira in 1896 by Solomon Schechter. The second period continues with the incorporation of the insights about the language of Ben Sira, as well as that of the Damascus Document (published in 1910), until the discovery of the Dead Sea Scrolls (DSS) in 1947. The third period continues unto the present day, as the data about the DSS and especially the language contained in its non-biblical texts continues to be analysed. Especially noteworthy are the rigorous methodological principles for dating texts developed by Avi Hurvitz and continued by his students. A significant monograph that represents the cumulation of this research is Hurvitz's lexicon of Late Biblical Hebrew (2014).

Rezetko and Young (2019) argue persuasively that a fourth period may be discerned, which began in the 2000s. Within this current period, the heretofore accepted practice of dating biblical texts by means of linguistic features began to be seriously challenged by a number of scholars, most particularly in a series of works by Ian Young, Robert Rezetko, and Martin Ehrensvärd (Young, Rezetko, and Ehrensvärd 2008; Rezetko and Young 2014). Their work has generated intense debate and fresh research in this area. In the last decade, several major monographs on the question of diachrony in biblical Hebrew have emerged (e.g., Miller-Naudé and Zevit 2012; Moshavi and Notarius 2017). Although a definitive consensus has not yet emerged from all the debate, the discussions have fostered much more methodological caution in deriving actual dates (or even rough time periods) from the results of investigations into the language of particular texts of the Old Testament. To take but a single example, consider the presence of the apparent Aramaism יְתַנּוּ 'they recount' (Judg. 5.11) in the linguistically archaic Song of Deborah and Barak.[42] The presence of Aramaisms in Biblical Hebrew texts is typically taken to be evidence of a late date of composition. Yet this is probably an oversimplification, since there would have been early language contact between Aramaic-speaking peoples and those of Canaanite stock (such as Biblical Hebrew speakers). Such forms indicate that care must be taken in assigning dates to the language of biblical texts.

---

[42] The Old Greek rendering δώσουσιν 'they give' appears to be an alternative vocalisation reflecting an expected יִתְּנוּ.

An overall assessment of the debate can be briefly offered here. It seems that the confidence exhibited by an earlier generation of scholars has been tempered somewhat. (One thinks of Driver's [1900, lxiii] famously confident assertion about the dating of Daniel over a century ago, also mentioned in §2.2.2 above: "The verdict of the language of Daniel is thus clear… the Greek words *demand*, the Hebrew *supports*, and the Aramaic *permits*, a date *after the conquest of Palestine by Alexander the Great*" [emphasis original].) Even if absolute dates for language states could be established, there is no exact correspondence between language states and ancient biblical texts, which are composite documents received via centuries of textual transmission.

Furthermore, the contributions of scholars such as Gary Rendsburg have helpfully introduced the dialectal dimension to the diachronic debate: the language variation we see in the Old Testament text should not only be attributed to diachronic factors. To this might also be added other sociolinguistic phenomena such as register and even an author's idiolect.

At the same time, the extreme scepticism of Rezetko, Young, and Ehrensvärd seems unwarranted. As Aaron Hornkohl (2017, 75) notes: "We may… reasonably accept that BH has a history and that the general lines of this history may be traced in the Masoretic editions of biblical literature." The textual tradition for the Old Testament is reasonably secure (certainly for the purposes of detecting diachronic change). The Masoretic tradition has been demonstrated to have faithfully preserved minute linguistic nuances (even comparing favourably to many earlier texts from the Dead Sea, which exhibit a degree of linguistic updating and harmonisation).

The scholarship of Avi Hurvitz and his students has produced fairly rigorous criteria for evaluating potential diachronic changes. For example, the criterion of linguistic opposition establishes evidence for real linguistic change in the complementary distribution of lexemes such as שֵׁשׁ 'linen' (Classical Biblical Hebrew) and בוּץ 'linen' (Late Biblical Hebrew). Furthermore, although the extra-biblical evidence is meagre, it corroborates the picture we see within the biblical texts.

In short, while the vigorous debate in recent decades has produced positive improvements in methodology and it has helpfully tempered some of the more confident claims of an earlier generation of scholarship, it does not seem to have overturned the basic consensus: the Old Testament is a collection of texts produced over a period of several centuries, and these texts give evidence of diachronic linguistic development.

4.0. Prospects for Further Study and Application

No such equivalent application of the methods and tools of historical linguistics currently exists in New Testament studies. New Testament Greek, however, is a potential growth area and historical linguistics may well provide some tools for better understanding the Greek verb (especially from its Indo-European vantage point). A promising development in this regard is the recent publication of *The Greek Verb Revisited* by editors Steven Runge and Christopher Fresch (2016). Within this collection of essays, one sees a new focus on the diachronic dimension as a necessary dialogue partner in the serious current scholarly disputes of the nature of the Koine Greek verb (see in particular the essays by Rutger Allen, Peter Gentry, and Amalia Moser).

Historical linguistics as a discipline stands as a welcome tool to scholars of all backgrounds engaged in the study of the biblical languages (as well as other ancient languages). Even the study of a single time period of a language is the study of a language in a state of perpetual (though gradual) diachronic flux and transition. This chapter has hopefully demonstrated that the tools and methods that historical linguists employ can be profitably used by biblical scholars as a means of advancing the state of our exegetical and historical knowledge of the biblical texts.

5.0. Further Reading

5.1. Handbooks, Companions, Etymological Dictionaries

1. Greek morphonology: Rix (1992)
2. Greek etymology: Chantraine (2009)
3. Greek verb: Runge and Fresch (2016)
4. Hebrew morphonology: Blau (2010)
5. Hebrew and Aramaic: Noonan (2020)
6. Non-Semitic Loanwords: Noonan (2019)
7. Hebrew vowels: Suchard (2019)
8. Semitic etymology: Kogan (2015)

5.2. General Introductions

1. Historical linguistics: Campbell (2021)
2. Indo-European: Fortson (2010)
3. Greek: Horrocks (2014)
4. Semitic: Rubin (2010)
5. Hebrew: Sáenz-Badillos (1993)
6. Aramaic: Gzella (2021)

5.3. Foundational Texts

1. Indo-European: Klein, Joseph, and Fritz (2017)
2. Wackernagel's 1918–19 lectures: Langslow (2009)
3. Historical linguistics: Hock (1991)
4. Indo-European: Kuryłowcz and Mayrhofer (1968)
5. Semitic: Huehnergard and Pat-El (2019)

References

Blau, Joshua. 2010. *Phonology and Morphology of Biblical Hebrew*. Linguistic Studies in Ancient West Semitic 2. Winona Lake, IN: Eisenbrauns.

Bybee, Joan. 2007. 'Diachronic Linguistics'. In *The Oxford Handbook of Cognitive Linguistics*, edited by Dirk Geeraerts and Hubert Cuyckens, 945–87. Oxford: Oxford University Press.

———. 2010. *Language, Usage, and Cognition*. Cambridge: Cambridge University Press.

Campbell, Lyle. 2021. *Historical Linguistics: An Introduction*. 4th ed. Cambridge, MA: The MIT Press.

Chantraine, Pierre. 2009. *Dictionaire étymologique de la langue grecque: Histoire des mots*. Librairie Klincksieck: Serie linguistique. Paris: Klincksieck.

de Saussure, Ferdinand. 1916. *Cours de linguistique générale*. Paris: Payot.

———. 1879. *Memoire sur le système primitif des voyelles dans les langues indo-européennes*. Leipzig: Vieweg.

Driver, S. R. 1900. *The Book of Daniel: With Introduction and Notes*. Cambridge: Cambridge University Press.

Fassberg, Steven E. 2016. 'What is Late Biblical Hebrew?'. *Zeitschrift für die alttestamentliche Wissenschaft* 128 (1): 1–15.

Fortson, Benjamin W. 2010. *Indo-European Language and Culture: An Introduction*. Malden, MA: Wiley-Blackwell.

Gesenius, Friedrich H. W. 1815. *Geschichte der hebräischen Sprache und Schrift*. Leipzig: Vogel.

Gzella, Holger. 2021. *Aramaic: A History of the First World Language*. Translated by Benjamin Suchard. Grand Rapids: Eerdmans.

Hartmann, Stefan. 2021. 'Diachronic Cognitive Linguistics: Past, Present, and Future'. *Yearbook of the German Cognitive Linguistics Association* 9 (1): 1–34.

Hock, Hans Henrich. 1991. *Principles of Historical Linguistics*. Trends in Linguistics 34. Berlin: Mouton de Gruyter.

Hornkohl, Aaron. 2017. 'All Is Not Lost: Linguistic Periodization in the Face of Textual and Literary Pluriformity'. In *Advances in Biblical Hebrew Linguistics: Data, Methods, and Analyses*, edited by Adina Moshavi and Tania Notarius, 53–80. Linguistic Studies in Ancient West Semitic 12. Winona Lake, IN: Eisenbrauns.

Horrocks, Geoffrey C. 2014. *Greek: A History of the Language and its Speakers*. Hoboken, NJ: Wiley-Blackwell.

Huehnergard, John, and Aaron Rubin. 2011. 'Phyla and Waves: Models of Classification'. In *The Semitic Languages: An International Handbook*, edited by Stefan Weniger, 259–78. Berlin: De Gruyter.

Huehnergard, John, and Na'ama Pat-El. 2019. *The Semitic Languages*. London: Routledge.

Hurvitz, Avi. 2014. *A Concise Lexicon of Late Biblical Hebrew*. Supplements to Vetus Testamentum 160. Leiden: Brill.

Jasanoff, Jay H. 2003. *Hittite and the Indo-European Verb*. Oxford: Oxford University Press.

Khan, Geoffrey. 2020. *The Tiberian Pronunciation Tradition of Biblical Hebrew*. Vol. 1. Cambridge Semitic Languages and Cultures 1. Cambridge: Open Book Publishers.

Klein, Jared, Brian Joseph, and Matthias Fritz (eds). 2017. *Handbook of Comparative and Historical Indo-European Linguistics*. Handbücher zur Sprach- und Kommunikationswissenschaft 41. Berlin: De Gruyter Mouton.

Kloekhorst, Alwin. 2019. *Kanišite Hittite*. Handbook of Oriental Studies, Section 1: The Near and Middle East 132. Leiden: Brill.

Kogan, Leonid. 2015. *Genealogical Classification of Semitic: The Lexical Isoglosses*. Berlin: De Gruyter.

Kuryłowcz, Jerzy, and Manfred Mayrhofer. 1968. *Indogermanische Grammatik*. Heidelberg: Carl Winter Universitätsverlag.

Langslow, David. 2009. *Jacob Wackernagel, Lectures on Syntax: With Special Reference to Greek, Latin, and Germanic*. Oxford: Oxford University Press.

Metcalf, George J. 1974. 'The Indo-European Hypothesis in the Sixteenth and Seventeenth Centuries'. In *Studies in the History of Linguistics: Traditions and Paradigms*, edited by Dell H. Hymes, 233–57. Bloomington, IN: Indiana University Press.

Miller-Naudé, Cynthia, and Ziony Zevit (eds). 2012. *Diachrony in Biblical Hebrew*. Linguistic Studies in Ancient West Semitic 8. Winona Lake, IN: Eisenbrauns.

Moshavi, Adina, and Tania Notarius (eds). 2017. *Advances in Biblical Hebrew Linguistics: Data, Methods, and Analyses*. Linguistic Studies in Ancient West Semitic 12. Winona Lake, IN: Eisenbrauns.

Noonan, Benjamin. 2018. 'Daniel's Greek Loanwords in Dialectal Perspective'. *Bulletin for Biblical Research* 28 (4): 575–603.

———. 2020. *Advances in the Study of Biblical Hebrew and Aramaic: New Insights for Reading the Old Testament*. Grand Rapids: Zondervan Academic.

Osthoff, Hermann, and Karl Brugmann. 1878. *Morphologische Untersuchungen auf dem Gebeiete der indogermanischen Sprachen*. Vol. 1. Leipzig: Verlag von S. Hirzel.

Pat-El, Na'ama, and Aren Wilson-Wright. 2018. 'Features of Aramaeo-Canaanite'. *Journal of the American Oriental Society* 138 (4): 781–806.

Rezetko, Robert, and Ian Young. 2014. *Historical Linguistics and Biblical Hebrew: Steps Toward an Integrated Approach*. Ancient Near East Monographs 9. Atlanta: SBL Press.

———. 2019. 'Currents in the Historical Linguistics and Dating of the Hebrew Bible: Report on the State of Research as Reflected in Recent Major Publications'. *HIPHIL Novum* 5 (1): 3–95.

Rix, Helmut. 1992. *Historische Grammatik des Griechischen: Laut- und Formenlehre*. Darmstadt: Wissenschaftliche Buchgesellschaft.

Royse, James R. 2007. *Scribal Habits in Early Greek New Testament Papyri*. New Testament Tools, Studies, and Documents 36. Atlanta: SBL Press.

Rubin, Aaron D. 2010. *A Brief Introduction to the Semitic Languages*. Gorgias Handbooks 19. Piscataway, NJ: Gorgias Press.

Runge, Steven E., and Christopher Fresch. 2016. *The Greek Verb Revisited: A Fresh Approach for Biblical Exegesis*. Bellingham, WA: Lexham Press.

Sáenz-Badillos, Angel. 1993. *A History of the Hebrew Language*. Translated by John Elwolde. Cambridge: Cambridge University Press.

Suchard, Benjamin. 2018. 'The Vocalic Phonemes of Tiberian Hebrew'. *Hebrew Studies* 59: 193–207.

Ventris, Michael, and John Chadwick. 1973. *Documents in Mycenaean Greek*. Cambridge: Cambridge University Press.

Vern, Robyn. 2011. *Dating Archaic Biblical Hebrew Poetry: A Critique of the Linguistic Arguments*. Perspectives on Hebrew

Scriptures and its Contexts 10. Piscataway, NJ: Georgias Press.

Watson, Wildred, and Nicolas Wyatt. 1999. *Handbook of Ugaritic Studies*. Handbook of Oriental Studies, Section 1: The Near and Middle East 39. Leiden: Brill.

Williams, Peter J. 2018. 'Semitic Long /i/ Vowels in the Greek of Codex Vaticanus of the New Testament'. In *Studies in Semitic Linguistics and Manuscripts: A Liber Discipulorum in Honour of Professor Geoffrey Khan*, edited by Nadia Vidro, Ronny Vollandt, Esther-Miriam Wagner, and Judith Olszowy-Schlanger, 15–26. Studia Semitica Upsaliensa 201. Uppsala: Acta Universitatis Upsaliensis.

Young, Ian, Robert Rezetko, and Martin Ehrensvärd. 2008. *Linguistic Dating of Biblical Texts*. 2 vols. London: Equinox.

Zeichmann, Christopher B. 2017. 'Loanwords or Code-Switching? Latin Transliteration and the Setting of Mark's Composition'. *Journal of the Jesus Movement in its Jewish Setting* 4: 42–64.

COMPUTATIONAL LINGUISTIC ANALYSIS OF THE BIBLICAL TEXT

Willem Th. van Peursen

1.0. History and Development of the Theory

1.1. Introduction

The application of computational linguistics to the Bible is part of the broader field of 'Bible and Computer' as it was coined in the 1970s and which encompasses, besides linguistic research, an ever-increasing field of computational textual analysis applied to the biblical text. It takes place at the intersection of biblical studies and the rapidly developing field of Digital Humanities.

This chapter deals with computational linguistics as a method, besides the other methods described in this volume. It should be recalled, however, that computational linguistics is interwoven with other approaches. When we compare the various available syntactic databases of the Hebrew Bible, we can observe, for example, that of the three most well-known databases the Andersen–Forbes database is explicitly eclectic in its linguistic theory (cf. Andersen and Forbes 2012).[1] On the other

---

[1] For project documentation and bibliographical references, see http://andersen-forbes.org, accessed 1 May 2023.

hand, the ETCBC database or BHSA (cf. Kingham and Van Peursen 2018) builds on the form-to-function approach developed by Jaap Hoftijzer and Wolfgang Richter (Van Peursen 2007, 140–41) and is influenced by the text-syntactic approach developed by Harald Weinrich and Wolfgang Schneider (Van Peursen 2020a, 140–55). Holmstedt's and Abbegg's Accordance Hebrew Syntax Database (Holmstedt and Cook 2018) is highly informed by generative linguistics (Accordance documentation 2014).[2]

Because of these observations, it would be an oversimplification to treat computational linguistics as a method distinct from, for example, generative linguistics or Cognitive Linguistics. Each computational linguistic analysis uses a digital corpus and each of these corpora is rooted in linguistic theories (see below, §2.3). Moreover, computational linguistics is a broad field that includes various approaches such as rule-based computer-science, statistics, Artificial Intelligence, and Deep Learning.[3] All these approaches have been applied to the biblical languages, and hence this chapter will present various approaches rather than one single method. Nevertheless, we shall see that these computational approaches have some common features that justify treating them together and that they have developed further in ways that are typical for computational corpus linguistics and go

---

[2] For other database projects on Biblical Hebrew that were active over the last decades see Kroeze (2013).

[3] In addition, computational linguistics as a discipline also covers approaches such as speech recognition or natural language generation that fall outside the scope of the current chapter. For an overview see, e.g., Clark, Fox, and Lappin (2010); Jurafsky and Martin (2021).

beyond the linguistic theories underlying the annotations in the respective databases. This reality justifies a separate chapter in the current volume devoted to computational linguistics as a method by itself.

1.2. The Beginnings

From our remarks in the introduction, it will be evident that it is impossible to give a historical survey of the application of computational linguistics to Biblical Hebrew without considering the wider context. This is the context of text and computing as an emerging field of studies in the twentieth century. Leaving aside for the moment predecessors such as the mechanical machines that were made, or at least designed, in the nineteenth century, such as the design for a mechanical general purpose computer by Charles Babbage, we will start this survey with the emergence of the forerunners of the modern computers in the 1940s and 1950s. In this period, we see the transformation of the calculation machine into the universal machine: that is, a machine that can do any task for which it is programmed. In these early years, Robert Busa started his famous project of the *Index Thomisticus*, which involved the complete lemmatisation of the works of Thomas Aquinas (which consists of 181 works, comprising 11 million words). This monumental project started in 1949 and lasted about thirty years.

The first universal computers created were not primarily meant for text processing. It should be recalled that the combination of text/language and computation/calculation is not as self-evident as it now seems. Even long before the emergence of computers, the fuzziness and ambiguity of natural language frustrated projects like those of Wilhelm Leibniz (1646–1716), who for "his whole life... continued to believe in the construction of a language consisting of logical symbols that could be manipulated by means of a calculator. Such a language, and a machine to 'calculate' it, would enable any philosophical debate to be settled with the click of a button" (Van der Weel 2011, 106). Likewise, "around a hundred years ago, polymaths like Bertrand Russell were furiously fighting to capture the nuances of language with a view to developing a universal formal language," which remained an ongoing academic pursuit that continued in the field of computer science, but appeared to be a highly challenging project (see action.ai 2021).

It was only in the 1960s and the 1970s that the marriage between computer and text took place. In the 1960s, computers became able to process text. A milestone was the first edition of the ASCII standard in 1963. This standard involved a 7-bit encoding in which, for example, 1000000 stands for @, 1000001 for A, and 1000010 for B, and 1000011 for C. In total, the ASCII standard contained 128 codes. Accordingly, the first attempts to create electronic versions of the Hebrew Bible had to accommodate this standard.

These attempts started in the 1970s. In 1970, Francis Andersen and Dean Forbes started a project that finally resulted in the Andersen–Forbes database. In the same year, Christof Felix Hardmeier (1970) from Greifswald reported on his own experiments in his article on the new potential of electronic data processing. Somewhat later, in 1977, the Werkgroep Informatica

Vrije Universiteit (WIVU) was established in Amsterdam under the guidance of Eep Talstra (after whom the WIVU was rebaptised as the Eep Talstra Centre for Bible and Computer [ETCBC] in 2013), which marked the start of the WIVU/ETCBC database. At Westminster Theological Seminary in Philadelphia, J. Alan Groves started pioneering work which initiated the research at what is now called the J. Alan Groves Center for Advanced Biblical Research. This work resulted in the Westminster Leningrad Codex (first released in 1987), to be followed by the Westminster Hebrew Morphology (also known as the Groves-Wheeler morphology) and the Westminster Hebrew Syntax.

Pioneers such as Andersen, Forbes, Hardmeier, and Talstra found each other in the *Association Internationale Bible et Informatique* (AIBI), which was established in 1982 and held its first conference in 1985 in Louvain-la-Neuve. Besides the pioneers already mentioned (and others such as Marc Vervenne or Emanuel Tov), a driving force behind this organisation was R. F. Poswick from the Benedictine monastery of Maredsous. The theme of the first AIBI conference was 'the text', and that was precisely the main challenge during those years: how to represent the Hebrew text and linguistic annotations. There was no Unicode, no markup language like HTML and XML, and not even a PC back then. The first challenge these pioneers faced was building electronic text corpora, displaying them on the screen, and handling the right-to-left writing direction for Hebrew.

1.3. Interface, Office and Network

Major changes took place in the 1980s and 1990s, which were related to such terms and abbreviations as GUI (Graphical User Interface), the DTP (Desktop Publishing) revolution, and WYSISWYG (What You See Is What You Get). These changes can be illustrated by the introduction of the Apple Lisa in 1983, the first version of the program PageMaker in 1984, and the first release of Microsoft Office in 1989. These developments marked a change in the application of the computer towards more office-related activities. With this development, the use of the computer became much more widespread, both in number of users and in types of applications. In the field of biblical studies this resulted in the appearance of software packages such as BibleWorks (first release in 1992) and Accordance (first release in 1994).

These new tools became extremely helpful for biblical scholars. One could now display the Hebrew Bible and the ancient versions side by side, search for words and word combinations in the electronic text instead of consulting a printed concordance, and store large commentaries on one's disk rather than on one's bookshelves.[4] A side-effect of this development, however, was a shift of focus. The early pioneers of 'Bible and Computer' were mainly concerned with the computer as an analytical tool, but in practice, it rather became a useful office tool. Being able to search for a word with a query instead of looking

---

[4] But often, again, the computer was used to generate concordances that were published in print. Thus, e.g., Postma, Talstra, and Vervenne (1983); cf. Oosting (2016, 195).

it up in a printed concordance may be a little bit faster, but it is not a methodological improvement. A burning question that occupied the early pioneers but seemed to be hardly a concern for the broader community of biblical scholars was: How can we go beyond the imitation of the traditional instruments?[5]

Another effect of the developments in the 1980s described here was that some of the databases that were initiated in the 1970s and 1980s became commercial products. To my best knowledge, it is only the ETCBC database that is publicly available,[6] while the Andersen–Forbes database is only available in the commercial Bible software packages of Logos and Accordance, and the more recent Holmstedt–Abbegg database only in Accordance.[7] This has hindered further development within the scholarly community, because one of the primary conditions of

---

[5] See the telling title of Talstra and Dyk (2006): 'The Computer and Biblical Research. Are there Perspectives beyond the Imitation of Classical Instruments?'

[6] https://github.com/ETCBC/bhsa, accessed 4 May 2023. Recently, also the MACULA Hebrew syntax trees have become available at https://github.com/Clear-Bible/macula-hebrew, accessed 4 May 2023. These syntax trees have been developed by Clear Bible, Inc. together with the Groves Cente and build on the Westminster Hebrew Syntax Without Morphology and the Open Scriptures Hebrew Bible morphology (serving in place of the Westminster Hebrew Morphology). The Groves Center has also released the Westminster Hebrew Syntax Without Morphology at https://github.com/Clear-Bible/macula-hebrew/tree/main/sources/GrovesCenter, accessed 4 May 2023.

[7] Cf. Accordance documentation (2014), for the advantages that Holmstedt and Abbegg considered for integrating their database into the Accordance software right from the start.

computational linguistics is that the analyses are retrievable and that the underlying algorithms are available on online platforms such as GitHub (cf. below, §4.3).

In the 1990s, a new element radically changed the digital landscape: networking. The World Wide Web was launched in 1991 and in the same year the first version of Unicode was released. These two milestones were closely related, because only with the unequivocal definition of characters in Unicode was it possible to exchange text that remained stable regardless of the environment in which it was read. For PC users, the internet became accessible through the browsers that came onto the market, such as Netscape Navigator in 1994 and Internet Explorer in 1995.

This new development was also soon picked up by biblical scholars. Electronic journals in the field of biblical studies were initiated, such as *TC: A Journal of Biblical Textual Criticism* and the *Journal of Hebrew Scriptures*, which both started in 1996.[8]

At the turn of the century, a new stage started with the introduction of more interactive forms of publication and communication, in which the users became both consumers and contributors and in which the dividing line between information consumption and information creation was blurred. This is often labelled 'Web 2.0'. Milestones include the launch of Wikipedia (2001) and the emergence of social media such as Facebook (2004) and Twitter (2006).

---

[8] Mention should also be made here of *Hugoye*, a journal in the field of Syriac studies, which started in 1998.

This ever-growing field of textual and social computer applications affected biblical studies. The use of electronic tools was no longer the privilege of biblical scholars. More and more, everyone had an increasing number of online Bibles and Bible study tools at their disposal. Likewise, the field of 'Bible and Computer', as defined by the AIBI, was expanding as well. At the sixth AIBI conference held in Stellenbosch in 2000, there were sections on grammar, statistics, and discourse, but also on education, multi-media, publishing, and community, all in relation to the Bible and the computer.

1.4. Reorientation: Methodological Innovation?

The development described above was not the programme that the pioneers of the 1970s and 1980s had in mind when they started their work. A re-orientation took place in the first decade of the twenty-first century. The seventh AIBI conference (convened by Marc Vervenne, Leuven, 2004) and the eighth conference (convened by Luis Vegas Montaner, Madrid, 2008) were both presented as expert meetings focusing on the question of how the computer can play an innovative role in biblical scholarship.[9] How could the computer be used as an analytical tool, rather than merely as a library, an office tool, and an imitation of traditional tools, which it apparently had become in the 1990s?

The question regarding the role of the computer in methodological innovation touched upon the more encompassing

---

[9] See the overview given in Poswick (2010), but note that the Leuven 2004 conference is absent from Poswick's overview.

question regarding textual scholarship as a humanities discipline in relation to computer science, which typically belongs to the sciences. Computation and the related scientific mode of inquiry gave the ability to sort, quantify, reproduce, and report text, but how could this be fruitfully combined with interpretation as the valued mode of assigning or discovering meaning as understood in traditional scholarship and the related reflexive concepts of individualism and subjectivity (Van Peursen 2010)?

The final decades of the twentieth century had witnessed a shift in the humanities from the hermeneutic and critical tradition of the nineteenth and twentieth centuries towards the identification and representation of patterns by digital means in the second half of the twentieth and the early years of the twenty-first century. Rens Bod (2013) coined the two phases 'Humanities 1.0' and 'Humanities 2.0'. (Note that '2.0' is used here differently to in 'Web 2.0' discussed above). Humanities 1.0 embodied the traditional understanding of the humanities as it was framed at the end of the nineteenth century. Wilhelm Dilthey (1833–1911) and others advocated a clear-cut distinction between the humanities and the sciences, the first mainly involved in *Verstehen* (understanding) the second in *Erklären* (explanation). This distinction had a significant impact on modes of scholarship, but also on the organisation of academia, where most institutions have separate departments for the humanities and the sciences. With the appearance of the computer as a tool for textual scholarship (Humanities 2.0), this distinction was blurred. How could this distinction be maintained now that computer scientists seemed to be analysing texts in the same way in which natural scientists analysed DNA structures? Rens Bod (2013, 177) has argued that this new mode of scholarship should not be the end point, but that a next step should be taken (which he labelled Humanities 3.0), in which Humanities 1.0 and Humanities 2.0 are combined and in which the hermeneutic and critical tradition of Humanities 1.0 should be applied to the tools and patterns obtained by Humanities 2.0.

1.5. From Rule-Based Analysis to Machine Learning

While biblical scholars and textual scholars in general were busy incorporating computer science into their disciplines, computer science itself developed further with astonishing speed. Let us illustrate this with the example of machine translation. From the early days of computational linguistics, it was evident that it would be tremendously useful if the computer could be used to translate a text from one language into another. As early as the 1970s, attempts were made to achieve this task by rule-based machine translation. In this approach, the input that the computer receives is the text to be translated and language rules. These rules include, for example, a bilingual lexicon, morphology, and syntax. The more refined those rules, the fewer errors the translation contains and the better it becomes. However, after decades of improvements, the results did not meet the high expectations. Natural language appeared more unruly than people thought (cf. above, §1.1). The rule-based techniques of the 1970s to the 1990s were replaced by statistical approaches in the 1990s until the 2010s. However, although there was significant progress, the real breakthrough came only with the application of machine learning. Here the input is no longer a text to be translated and a set of rules to carry out this task, but rather a large collection of training data, in this case of parallel texts in two languages, from which the computer itself can learn how to translate. Although the mechanisms that are at work are largely hidden, the performance is outstanding.

If we define machine learning more precisely, we can say that it is the ability to learn without being explicitly programmed. It is a subgroup of Artificial Intelligence, which refers to any technique that enables computers to mimic human behaviour or, more precisely, the effort to automate intellectual tasks normally performed by humans. Artificial Intelligence (AI) went through various stages by itself, from symbolic AI, which was prevalent until the 1980s and involved the application of explicit rules and the manipulation of logic, to machine learning, where the computer goes beyond the instruction and rules it is given and learns by itself how to perform a certain task. A subgroup of machine learning is deep learning, which refers to the extraction of patterns from data with the help of neural networks. In the case of machine learning, we can distinguish between supervised machine learning, in which the machine learns from human-labelled examples, and unsupervised learning, in which the machine has to detect patterns in the unlabelled data by itself. Supervised methods include attempts for text classification. In biblical studies, an example is Dicta (see n. 10), which provides an exciting collection of tools for author recognition and text classification, such as the Tiberias Stylistic Classifier (cf. below,

§§2.5 and 3.3).¹⁰ These tools can be used, for example, to classify a text of debated origin along the lines of early and late Biblical Hebrew.

Experts may challenge the rather simple definitions given here for machine learning, deep learning, and Artificial Intelligence, and there is much debate about the exact nature and definitions of the various designations given here. But the main point to be made is that a major shift has taken place, which affects our whole understanding of using the computer in linguistic analysis. Elsewhere I have suggested that the transformations that are taking place now with the transition from rule-based approaches to machine learning may even mark a more drastic discontinuity with existing methods of biblical interpretation than the appearance of the computer as an exegetical tool in the last decades of the twentieth century (Van Peursen 2020b, 310). Whereas many of the rule-based approaches could somehow mimic traditional approaches (e.g., queries replacing concordances or manually created lists), machine learning opens up completely new avenues of scholarship that may lead to new forms of human-computer interaction in the interpretation of texts.

1.6. Corpora and Fuzzy Data

The application of computational linguistics to the Bible implied that the Bible was considered a corpus, and thus it entered the field of corpus linguistics. However, in this field of studies, the

---

¹⁰ See https://tiberias.dicta.org.il/, accessed 4 May 2023.

Hebrew Bible did not match the corpora from other languages and periods. There are huge differences between, for example, the British National Corpus (BNC) and the Hebrew Bible. The BNC has more than 100 million words, as against 420,000 words in the Hebrew Bible. The BNC has extensive metadata about, for example, author and date of origin, whereas for almost every part of the Hebrew Bible authors and provenance are debated issues. The BNC has been carefully selected to create a representative linguistic corpus, whereas the Hebrew Bible, whatever the selection processes that made it the biblical canon that we now have, was never intended to be linguistically representative and was selected along completely different criteria. Accordingly, at least until the turn of the century, the computational analysis of the Hebrew Bible was a questionable undertaking according to the developing standards of computational linguists. When in the early 1990s Eep Talstra once presented his research on Deuteronomy to an audience of computational linguists, he met with much misunderstanding. How could he study a corpus of which he did not know the date of origin? Unaware of the complex questions regarding sources and editorial processes in the Hebrew Bible that have puzzled biblical scholars for centuries, one of the respondents suggested that Talstra should first clean up his data (that is: stripping it of any later additions so that what remains is a corpus of which the date and provenance are clear) before any linguistic or textual analysis could start (Talstra 2010, 54).

This situation has completely changed since the above-mentioned emergence of Web 2.0. Currently, much linguistic research is conducted on tweets, blogposts, and other digitally born texts that represent a kind of fuzzy data, with little context and little metadata, all of which resembles the Hebrew Bible much more than the BNC does. Thanks to these developments, computational research into the Bible has found a better connection with the wider field of Digital Humanities than in the last three to four decades of the twentieth century.

2.0. Key Theoretical Commitments and Major Concepts

2.1. Solid Criteria instead of Subjective Intuition

Biblical scholars were among the first who experimented using the computer as a tool for the study of texts and languages. In the 1970s, at the dawn of computer-aided textual analysis and more specifically in the newly emerging field of 'Bible and Computer', the mission of the pioneers (above, §1.2.) was clear: Make meaningful, substantiated statements about the Bible. Such an effort did not guarantee the correct interpretation, but at least it could identify interpretations that did not match the facts. Traceability and transparency played an important role in this development.[11]

---

[11] A typical example is Hardmeier's above-mentioned article. Addressing the question as to whether the computer can help in traditional source criticsm, Hardmeier (1970, 180) argues: "Die maschinelle Konkordanzarbeit ermöglicht dagegen ein Zweifaches: Einmal kann der Kriterienkatalog über die Wortschatzstatistik hinaus auf neue, rein formale Struktureigentümlichkeigen bestimmter Texte ausgedehnt werden (…) Zum anderen kan überprüft werden, wieweit lexikalische und formale Merkmale für bestimmte Textschichten überhaupt charakteristisch sind." It was, however, only after the emergence of machine

This mission fit in a positivist, modernist climate, and was especially opposed to an unbridled theologising based on individual words and etymologies, which has made, among others, Kittel's *Theologisches Wörterbuch zum Neuen Testament* (1942–1979) famous (or infamous). In the 1960s, James Barr assessed this approach critically on the basis of general linguistic and philological insights (see Barr 1961). Talstra, who earlier in the 1970s had studied with Barr in Manchester, would certainly agree with Barr's criticism, and started creating a database that was not focused on etymology and semantics, but on syntax.

This mission of those pioneers in Digital Humanities (at that time other labels were used such as Alpha-Informatics) still plays an important role and is reflected in open science practices. Statements about occurrences of words or patterns can be made traceable and reproducible, for example by publishing queries on the SHEBANQ website of the ETCBC.[12] At the same time, we have also seen developments in computational textual analysis that run counter to the ideals of the pioneers (above, §1.3).

2.2. Deep Blue and AlphaGo

The introduction of the computer in the workplace of the exegete in the last decades of the twentieth century enabled the biblical scholar to be more systematic, objective, and quantitative. The qualification 'objective' does not mean that computational data

---

learning that the computer was used fruitfully to address the traditional source-critical questions; cf. below, §3.3.

[12] See https://shebanq.ancient-data.org, accessed 4 May 2023. For the underlying ideas and the role of annotation, see Roorda (2018).

is theory-neutral or that the computer provides the final answer (as it is sometimes misunderstood), but it does indicate another mode of scholarship. The added value of this work lies in its systematic approach, which reduces the role of intuitive *ad hoc* interpretations, on the one hand, and in the increasing complexity of searches and analyses, on the other.

In the 1970s–2000s, the claim that the computer was more systematic and objective was frequently met with scepticism by traditional scholars, who often found those computer guys weird and imagined that using the computer as a tool in biblical studies was in fact building an echoing well: what you get out of the computer depends on what you put into it. Often the question was raised: What does the computer deliver that could not be delivered without it? To parry this criticism, I often used the analogy of the chess computer, which seemed especially apt since Deep Blue had beaten Gary Kasparov in 1997. The mind of the human chess player works efficiently because it recognises patterns and therefore has a useful selection mechanism, whereas the computer, so to speak, calculates everything (still an interesting study is De Groot 1946). However, the speed with which the computer does so (which has increased over the years) is so immense that it surpasses human capacities. Likewise, once you have an annotated database, questions that would take months or years when addressed manually—e.g., a statistical overview of *plene* or defective spellings, or a collection of all clause patterns in the Hebrew Bible where the object precedes the verb (for examples, see §3 below)—can now be answered in very short time periods.

Whereas the analogy of the chess computer worked well until the first years of the twenty-first century, it does not capture the developments that have taken place over the last two decades, described above (§1.5), such as the emergence of machine learning. For these developments, we can rather use the analogy of the Go computer (see Dorobantu 2022). Whereas the human world champion of chess was defeated by the computer in 1997, it took until 2016 before a computer program defeated the human world champion in Go. The difference between chess and Go is that with Go the complexity of the game and the number of possible continuations is exponentially higher than with chess. Moreover, in Go there is also a strong aesthetic aspect. Because of the infinite number of possibilities and the aesthetic aspects, computational calculation power is not enough to win the game. Rule-based approaches (enabled by calculation power) were insufficient, but learning capabilities (enabled by pattern recognition) succeeded. Likewise, in textual analysis the computer is no longer merely a powerful calculation or sorting machine. It has become a much more complex instrument, and to some extent less dependent on human input (above, §1.5).

2.3. The Role of Linguistic Theory in the Creation of Text Databases

The different endeavours to create linguistic databases of the Hebrew Bible reflected the different approaches that were and are current in biblical linguistics. Each approach has its advantages and disadvantages. And even in those cases where the builders of a database try to be as theory-neutral as possible, it will be evident that any database and any choice that is made is informed by one's position about Biblical Hebrew and about language in general. This is not only a challenge for computational approaches. It is the case in any linguistic or textual study of the Hebrew Bible or Greek New Testament.

Let us have a look how linguistic theory functions in the three most well-known databases (above, §1.1; see also Miller-Naudé and Naudé 2018, 7), which we will discuss in the order of their age. First, the Andersen–Forbes database is eclectic and hence somewhat ambiguous in its relation to generative grammar. Andersen and Forbes explicitly reject Chomskyan linguistics but also "find much of value in the work of the generativists, especially generalized phrase structure grammar" (Andersen and Forbes 2012, 14; see also Van Peursen 2015, 301). One of the main reasons for their rejection of Chomskyan linguistics is their claim that Biblical Hebrew belongs to the non-configurational languages, which are "a serious impediment to the transformationalists' quest for Universal Grammar" (Andersen and Forbes 2012, 87).[13] Andersen was also influenced by structuralism and by Kenneth Pike's tagmemics (Miller-Naudé and Naudé 2018, 7). Informed by syntax, function, and semantics, they developed a rich set of annotation labels, including, among others, seventy-six part-of-speech labels.

Second, the ETCBC tried to be more independent of linguistic theory by following the principles of distributional analysis,

---

[13] For a different view on the question as to whether Biblical Hebrew is a configurational language, partly in response to Andersen and Forbes, see Kaajan (2019).

form-to-function, and bottom-up. Unlike the Andersen–Forbes database, the ETCBC database has a rather minimal parts-of-speech set (Kingham 2018). And unlike the other databases, the ETCBC database does not immediately assign functions to forms, but starts with a distributional analysis of linguistic phenomena (at all levels, for example varying from morphemes to clause patterns) before functional labels are assigned. Moreover, the deduction of functions from formal criteria is transparently and traceably documented in auxiliary files that are part of the data creation workflow (Kingham 2018; Kingham and Van Peursen 2018).

The 'bottom-up' description is used for approaches that start from the identification of morphemes and word level analysis and move from there to the higher levels of phrases, clauses, sentences, and text-syntactic relations. It is often combined with the form-to-function principle, which holds that we should first make a distributional analysis of forms and patterns before any function can be deduced. It starts from the awareness that we know little about the biblical languages and that to avoid creating an echoing well out of our own analysis or database, we should start with observable textual phenomena before we proceed to function or even semantics.

'Bottom-up' is often contrasted with 'top-down'. In Biblical Hebrew linguistics, the latter is represented, for example, in the textlinguistic approach of Robert Longacre (1989), which is much more informed by cross-linguistic evidence and applies categories known from other languages (such as narrative, predictive, hortatory, or expository genres; techniques for, for example, distinguishing between mainline and offline information or for indicating the peak of a text or discourse). Likewise, the distributional analysis of forms and patterns, which to some extent is like Construction Grammar or exemplar-based syntax as it developed in the 1980s and 1990s, is often considered as a counter-reaction to the generative linguistic framework.

Third, the Holmstedt–Abbegg database, also called the Accordance Hebrew Syntactic Database, is based on a generative framework (cf. Accordance documentation 2014). Whereas the Andersen–Forbes and ETCBC databases started in the 1970s, the Holmstedt–Abbegg database started more recently, in 2008. Their intention was to create a database upon a model of Hebrew syntax that differed from the two existing databases, with "a tight focus on syntax, grounded in (but not bound by) Chomskyan generative linguistic theory" (Holmstedt and Cook 2018, 2).[14] More specifically, they adhered to Chomskyan minimalism, which was developed in the 1990s from the Government-and-Binding model that was prevalent in the 1980s, but they also realised that "to base the database and its underlying tagging scheme on a fully articulated minimalist framework would be inappropriate." For this reason, they combined their adherence to Chomskyan theory with the motto "data primary, theory wise" (Holmstedt and Cook 2018, 3).

That the Holmstedt–Abbegg database is grounded in Chomsky's generative approach is visible, among other things, in the inclusion of so-called null constituents. Because of the

---

[14] For other databases, which are not yet available publicly, such as Richter's database, see Kroeze (2013).

generative principle that every phrase has a 'head', a null marker has been inserted in every phrase that lacks an overt head. That Holmstedt et al. were not bound by the generative approach is visible, for example, in their non-binary hierarchical clause analysis, thus differing from Chomsky's minimalist syntax (as well as the Government-and-Binding model), which adopts a strictly binary approach to constituent structure (Holmstedt and Cook 2018, 10).

2.4. Back to the Black Box?

The emergence of author recognition techniques, neural networks, Artificial Intelligence, and machine learning in recent years provided new potential for biblical studies, but it also posed new challenges. The results are astonishing, but exactly what the algorithms do takes place in an impenetrable 'black box'. (The reality of machine learning is that the computer pieces together a set of patterns increasingly sophisticated until they fit the starter data, and then these patterns are used to interpret new texts. There is no known way to describe or articulate these patterns, however, which is why machine learning algorithms are spoken of as a 'black box'.) This seems to be a development that is the reverse of the openness and traceability that the 'Bible and Computer' pioneers stood for. The attempts to make Artificial Intelligence understandable to humans in the field of 'explainable

AI' (for example, in the DIANNA project [Deep Insight in Neural Network Analysis]) is still in its infancy.[15]

These transformations are perhaps even more drastic than those of the 1970s. That early period from the 1970s showed, to some extent, a continuation of pre-digital scholarly practices. For example, it became possible to look up words with a search query in a digital text file instead of a paper concordance, but that did not imply any methodological innovation.

In recent years, there have been various attempts to integrate these new developments into biblical studies by making use of advanced statistical analysis (Naaijer 2020; cf. below, §3.2), topic modelling (Vlaardingerbroek 2017), Markov Chains (Kingham et al. 2018), stylometrics (Van Hecke 2018; Van Hecke and De Joode 2021), and neural networks (Van der Schans et al. 2020; Naaijer 2020, 149–75). Here the main challenge is to determine how the results of the 'black box' relate to current scholarship.[16]

A case in point are the projects in which text clustering methods are applied to questions related to linguistic dating to see whether we can distinguish certain groups or collections of

---

[15] See 'Deep Insight And Neural Network Analysis—DIANNA', https://www.esciencecenter.nl/projects/deep-insight-and-neural-networks-analysis-dianna/, accessed 25 May 2023.

[16] Most examples in this section are taken from the ETCBC, because the present author is most acquainted with it, but the situation with other institutions and with individual researchers seems to be similar. Scholars recognise the great potential of recent developments in computer science but are still in an experimenting phase to find out how it can be made useful to biblical studies.

texts that agree with current scholarly notions such as Standard Biblical Hebrew versus Late Biblical Hebrew. The challenge is, if the outcomes agree with current scholarship, the computational analysis does not really add to our knowledge, except for confirming existing theories. But if the outcome seems to be at odds with current scholarship, should we search for explanations that still fit the traditional framework (e.g., labelling outliers in an alleged early corpus as later additions), or should we rather challenge and tweak the algorithms? And if we improve the algorithms so that they better yield the expected results, how do we avoid the risk of creating a circular argument?[17]

For all the layers of linguistic analysis that were explored with rule-based approaches and distributional analysis from the 1970s onwards, these new approaches have the potential to accelerate, refine, or automate analytical procedures. Although there are now various databases containing a morphological analysis of the Hebrew Bible, when extending the corpus to other Hebrew texts or corpora of other Northwest-Semitic languages, machine learning can be used to accelerate the process of the morphological analysis.[18] Likewise, with the search for phrase patterns, new methods searching for patterns using n-grams, flex

---

[17] Cf. below, §3.3, for the example of the distinction between P and non-P by author-clustering algorithms.

[18] Thus, the eScience Center project 'Morphological Parser for Inflectional Languages Using Deep Learning' aims to accelerate the analytical procedures by having the computer make more accurate predictions about the morphological analysis based on the ETCBC's existing Hebrew- and Syriac-encoded texts (Naaijer and Van Peursen 2022).

grams, etc. can replace the pattern-matching tools that functioned in the distributional analysis with which the ETCBC started (or the manual assignment of phrase patterns based on human intuition in other projects).[19] In the text-syntactic analysis, automatic anaphora resolution can complement existing methods of computer-assisted, text-hierarchical analysis based on clause relations (cf. Erwich 2021). The identification of participants is the first step to establishing their relationships as the basis for social network analysis, and other emerging approaches in which computational linguistics and literary analysis meet (cf. Canu Højgaard 2021).

2.5. From Talstra to Tiberias

The projects and experiments described in §2.4 show a difference from the various approaches in the early years of 'Bible and Computer'. In the projects of Andersen, Forbes, and Talstra, the lucidity of the rules that were applied served as an argument for the validity of the analysis. In those new approaches, the proof for the validity is not so much the structure of the algorithms or the analytical steps, but rather the results of test cases.[20] In, for example, the author-clustering tools that are used for Tiberias (above, §1.5), what counts as convincing argument for the analysis is the

---

[19] This happens in the CLARIAH Fellowship project 'PaTraCoSy: PAtterns in TRAnslation: Using COlibriCore for the Hebrew Bible corpus and its SYriac translation' (Coeckelbergs 2022).

[20] In the case of the Tiberias Stylistic Classifier (see the following discussion), at the moment of this writing the algorithms used are not publicly available.

results of a test set.[21] In their case they point to the successful deconstruction of an artificially mixed book, consisting of randomly merged segments from Jeremiah and Ezekiel, coined 'Jeriel'. The algorithms successfully distinguished between the two components of this artificial book with an accuracy of 89 to 95 percent (Dershowitz et al. 2015).

In conclusion, the potential of the machine learning algorithms is unprecedented, and the results are impressive. However, what exactly those algorithms do, and how they arrive at their results, is beyond human understanding. The insightful and traceable analyses that were the showpiece of emerging computational Bible research (above, §2.1) are now giving way to a black box that, while yielding great results, allows little insight into what goes on inside that box. Even if the output of the algorithms provides some insights (e.g., the Tiberias programs list the phenomena on which the results are based, such as typical linguistic elements of a selected corpus, which distinguish it from another corpus), the human researchers will have to find out by themselves the typical linguistic or stylistic features of a certain corpus or collection (cf. below, §3.3).

---

[21] The term 'author clustering' is in this context more precise than 'author recognition'; cf. Dershowitz et al. (2015, 255).

3.0. Use and Contributions in Biblical Studies to Date

3.1. Orthography

After the emergence of databases of the Hebrew Bible, it soon became clear that computational analysis enabled types of research that were hardly imaginable without digital tools. As early as the 1980s, Francis Andersen and Dean Forbes (1986) published their monumental work on spelling in the Hebrew Bible, filled with tables and mathematical formulas to investigate the distribution of *matres lectionis* over the entire biblical corpus. They could make observations about the extent to which these vowel letters were used in the biblical corpus, about the relation of the Masoretic Text to the more defective pre-exilic inscriptions and the more *plene* spellings of the last centuries BC, and about differences between the various parts of the Hebrew Bible, with the Pentateuch having the most conservative spelling. More recently, Johan de Joode and Dirk Speelman (2020) have applied quantitative linguistic methods to the orthographic heterogeneity within the Hebrew Bible and the Dead Sea Scrolls.

3.2. Syntax

When syntactic databases became available, all kinds of research questions could be addressed more effectively, ranging from major questions about diachronic developments (Siebesma-Mannens 2014), to the extent to which poetic structure affects clause patterns (Bosman 2019), to corresponding phrase and clause patterns in the Hebrew Bible and the Peshitta (Van

Peursen 2007; Dyk and Van Keulen 2013), and to the interpretation of specific grammatical phenomena or translation issues. It is now easy to find parallels for the construction in the phrase וַתָּשַׁר דְּבוֹרָה וּבָרָק בֶּן־אֲבִינֹעַם בַּיּוֹם הַהוּא 'On that day Deborah and Barak son of Abinoam sang (f. sg.)' (Judg. 5.1), where the verb preceding the compound subject agrees with the first element of this subject. Those parallels show that this is a common phenomenon and that an emendation of the verb or the deletion of the second part of the subject ('and Barak…') is not needed (Sandborg-Petersen 2011; Meeuse 2021, 10). Likewise, a careful analysis of the verb valence pattern used shows that the phrase וַיָּשֶׂם יְהוָה לְקַיִן אוֹת (Gen. 4.15) should be translated 'And the LORD set a sign in place on behalf of Cain' rather than with 'And the LORD put a mark on Cain', which is the rendering of the NRSV and many other translations (Dyk, Glanz, and Oosting 2013, 30–32; Meeuse 2021, 6–7).

The more advanced applications of statistical analysis and machine learning enable new possibilities for charting the distribution of clause patterns over the Hebrew Bible in relation to various parameters, such as assumed date of origin, genre, text type, and sentence pattern. An interesting case concerns the distribution of 'to be' constructions. In Biblical Hebrew, there are five ways in which 'to be' can be expressed: Bipartite and tripartite nominal clauses; constructions with the particles יֵשׁ ('there is') and אֵין ('there is not'); and clauses containing the verb הָיָה ('to be'). On the basis of quantitative analysis taking all these parameters into account, Martijn Naaijer (2020) has convincingly argued that in the alleged Early Biblical Hebrew corpus the so-called narrative text type and the direct speech sections differ considerably, and that the direct speech sections show similarities with the Late Biblical Hebrew texts (regardless of the distinction between narrative and direct speech in the latter). In other words: in late texts, there is less of a difference between narrative and direct speech.

3.3. Author Clustering

Perhaps the most cutting-edge application of machine learning and computational linguistics to biblical studies can be found at the research group at Bar Ilan University that is responsible for the Tiberias Stylistic Classifier for the Hebrew Bible (above, §§1.5., 2.4., and 2.5.). Their tools distinguished between Priestly (P) and non-Priestly (non-P) texts in the Pentatcuch, thus agreeing with a major conclusion of the Documentary Hypothesis (Dershowitz et al. 2015).[22] This is not only a milestone in the application of computational linguistics in biblical studies. It also shows where the interaction between computational linguistics and biblical scholarship can now take place, because the outcome of the computational analysis is not merely an 'objective proof' of a scholarly hypothesis, but rather the start of new scholarly reflection as articulated and tested with the iterative development and application of computer algorithms. Questions that arise are: How can we account for the few verses that have been classified as non-P in traditional scholarship, but were assigned

---

[22] Another interesting case study is the assignment of Isaiah 34–35, for which it has been argued that these chapters were written by Deutero-Isaiah (Berman 2021).

P in the computational analysis and vice versa? Do they reveal flaws in the algorithms, or should we rather reconsider their assignment to P or non-P? (For this dilemma see also above, §2.4.) What does the outcome tell about the other elements of the Documentary Hypothesis, such as the J, E, and D sources, that cannot be distinguished by the algorithms?[23] Would scholars ever have set out to answer such a question with computational linguistics if the hypothesis had not already existed? The algorithm's ability to distinguish between P and non-P means they consistently differ, but what confidence do we have that they differ in the way scholars have claimed they do (e.g. in terms of authorship and date)?

Another question relates to the notion of author recognition and computer programs that are built to detect unconscious individual elements of language use and an author's "subtle stylistic preferences" (Dershowitz et al. 2015, 253). How can such an approach be applied to compositions such as P that in Old Testament scholarship are usually considered the work of groups of scribes, or as consisting of successive editorial layers?[24] The algorithms will not reproduce S. R. Driver's (1913, 131–35) list of words and phrases typical of P, and the notion of an author as an individual that can be identified on the basis of unconscious

---

[23] Cf. Dershowitz et al. (2015, 270): "There appear to be two possible explanations for this: (1) the J and E source are not sufficiently distinct from one another in terms of word usage (…); (2) the traditional J/E division is flawed."

[24] See, e.g., Smend (1978, 57), on the supposed successive stages of the composition of P.

authorial fingerprints seems to be remote from the priestly circles like the alleged *Sitz im Leben* of P in traditional Old Testament scholarship. Yet, traditional source criticism and cutting-edge author-clustering algorithms largely arrive at a similar distinction between P and non-P. Here is both the requirement and opportunity to reconcile the claims of what has been called 'algorithmic criticism' (Verhaar 2016) with those of traditional scholarship. Or in other words, to proceed from Humanities 1.0 (traditional source criticism) through Humanities 2.0 (source detection with author-clustering algorithms) to Humanities 3.0 (cf. above, §1.4).

4.0. Prospects for Further Study, Application, and Collaboration

4.1. Syntax and Semantics

Most of the database projects that began in the 1970s and the 1980s started with syntax. The Andersen–Forbes database also includes semantic roles, but the way in which the labels have been assigned is not always clear and hence they are difficult to reproduce (and therefore assess). The other databases currently available also have a strong focus on syntax. This focus is understandable from the positivist climate in which these projects originated and the uneasiness that was felt with contemporaneous etymologising lexicographical approaches. But now, about half a century later, it is crucial to investigate how computational linguistics can be applied to the semantics of Biblical Hebrew. Otherwise, what happens is that advanced syntactic databases are enriched with digital representatives of the scholarly knowledge of the nineteenth and twentieth centuries as it is codified, for example, in Brown, Driver, and Briggs's 1910 lexicon. This is what we see happen in the commercial or semi-commercial Bible software packages in which both the advanced syntactic databases discussed in this chapter and the older lexicographical resources have become available.

There are two clear ways in which the current syntactic databases could be extended towards semantic analysis. The first relates to the intersection of syntax and semantics. The search for valence patterns provides new insights about the meaning and usage of a verb. Hence one way to proceed is to enrich the syntactic labels with verbal valence patterns and the associated semantic roles according to strict criteria of how valence patterns and meaning interrelate (cf. Dyk 2016). For the study of verbal valence and clause patterns, the application of existing approaches, especially those that have been applied successfully in computational linguistics such as Role and Reference Grammar, appears to be promising (cf. Canu Højgaard 2019).

Another way in which the current database could be extended to semantic analysis is the application of methods that have been developed in computational lexicography and semantics to the Hebrew Bible. Obviously, not everything that has been developed in this field is applicable to the Bible, which is, linguistically speaking, a limited corpus without native speakers. Thus, building a WordNet for Biblical Hebrew would meet with many complications. What could be promising, however, is to experiment with approaches such as co-occurrence analysis, topic modelling, and similar methods to establish the relations between words.[25]

4.2. Linked Data and Geospatial Analysis

An extension of semantic and lexicographic information may be the interlinking with other resources. In recent years, the ETCBC has explored the potential use of Linked Data in which textual data is linked to encyclopedic or geospatial data. Pilot projects include Linking Syriac Data (2017–2018);[26] Linking Syriac Liturgies (Van Peursen and Veldman 2018); and Linking Syriac Geographic Data (see Van Peursen 2018). Although it is wonderful that this brings the textual data (in these projects: Syriac data) into the Linked Data universe, there is the danger that encyclopedic information takes the place of sound syntactic analysis. If, for example, we want to map all the geographical entities mentioned in the Syriac Book of the Laws of the Countries, we have to decide how to identify the places mentioned or to locate the peoples mentioned in those texts. The same can be said of the famous catalogue of nations and peoples gathered at Jerusalem in Acts 2:9–11 (Van Altena 2022, 135–57). Such questions may

---

[25] Such new initiatives could be linked with or even incorporated in the most up-to-date digitally-available lexicographical and semantic resources, such as those of the Semantic Dictionary of Biblical Hebrew (https://semanticdictionary.org, accessed 4 May 2023) and the Semantics of Ancient Hebrew Database (https://www.sahd.div.ed.ac.uk, accessed 4 May 2023) projects.

[26] See https://github.com/hvlaardingerbroek/LinkSyr, accessed 4 May 2023.

be even more challenging in the case of biblical studies, because of the debate over the extent to which the biblical accounts can be related to the history and geography of ancient Israel and given the uncertainties about the identification of places and events in the Bible.

In addition to these interpretive difficulties, there is the challenge that we mentioned in §1.3 above. If linked geospatial data do not go beyond a mere digital representation of the well-known traditional atlases of the Bible, or of the maps of Jerusalem, ancient Israel, the ancient Near East, and the Roman Empire often included in printed Bibles, this only serves practical purposes, rather than representing a methodological innovation. However, given the 'spatial turn' in biblical studies (cf. Van Altena 2022, 41), it is to be expected that geospatial analysis, when applied properly, can lead to new insights and a better understanding of the Bible, even though its application to the Bible is still in its infancy.

4.3. Collaboration and Open Science

Another field where progress can be made is the comparison of the various linguistic databases of the Hebrew Bible. Each database has its specific approach, and the user is most helped by being able to compare the various databases, their underlying assumptions, and the way in which these assumptions resulted in the annotations in each verse of the Bible.[27] It is a pity, however, that anyone who wants to compare the three most elaborate

---

[27] A nice comparison is made in Miller-Naudé and Naudé (2018).

databases available to date (cf. §§1.1 and 2.3) needs to purchase them in commercial software packages. Only the ETCBC database and the Westminster Hebrew Syntax Without Morphology (cf. n. 6 above) are publicly available. Bringing the other databases into the open access domain is easier said than done, given copyright issues and business models, as well as practical challenges, but hopefully these challenges can be resolved in the near future. This will be necessary to enable scholarly pursuits engaging with all the databases.

Open Science, however, is more than making databases available. It relates also to the transparency of analytical procedures and the availability of queries and algorithms. A breakthrough in the application of computational linguistic analysis to the Hebrew Bible would be the availability of the workflows of the data creation processes and the programs that have been used in the creation of those databases and of the algorithms that are currently being developed for advanced cutting-edge approaches as those mentioned in §§2.4. and 3.3.

4.4. Computational Linguistics and the New Testament

This chapter focused on the use of computational linguistics in Old Testament studies. In New Testament studies we see parallel developments, although syntactic databases emerged somewhat later than in Old Testament studies.[28]

---

[28] For the pioneering work in the 1970s and 1980s see Mealand (1988). However, in the first decades of the emerging field of 'Bible and Computer' relatively more attention was paid to the Old Testament and

The morphological encoding started, as in the case of the Old Testament, in the 1970s, with, e.g., the GRAMCORD Greek New Testament (first published 1977); the work of Timothy and Barbara Friberg, who produced the Analytical Greek New Testament (first published 1981); and MorphGNT, which was initiated in the 1980s by Robert Kraft at the University of Pennsylvania's Center for Computer Analysis of Texts (CCAT) and received major updates and corrections by James Tauber from the 1990s onwards.[29]

The computational syntactic analysis of the New Testament received an impetus from two projects that started in the first years of the twenty-first century.[30] The first project is the Greek

---

Hebrew than to the New Testament and Greek. This is reflected, for example, in the contributions to the AIBI conferences (cf. above, §1.2). The contributions to the first AIBI conference (Leuven, 1985) included twelve contributions that dealt exclusively with Hebrew and the Old Testament and only four that dealt with Greek and the New Testament (besides eight other contributions). The second conference (Jerusalem, 1988) showed similar statistics. It contained seventeen contributions on Hebrew and the Old Testament, two on the Septuagint, two on Greek and the New Testament and one on the Greek works of Gregorius of Nyssa (besides thirteen other on general issues or discussing both the Old and the New Testament).

[29] Available on GitHub: https://github.com/morphgnt, accessed 4 May 2023.

[30] Because of copyright issues, these open-source projects are often based on the older editions by Nestle, Tischendorf and Westscott, and Hort, or on the SBL Greek New Testament, rather than on the most recent Nestle-Aland edition. For a morphologically annotated version of

New Testament of the OpenText.org initiative by Stanley E. Porter at McMaster Divinity College and partners. The goal of this project is, according to its website, "to construct a representative corpus of Hellenistic Greek (including the entire New Testament and selected Hellenistic writings of the same period) to facilitate linguistic and literary research of the New Testament documents." At clause level their annotations include four major categories: Subject, Predicator, Complement, and Adjunct.

Some more syntactic categories (e.g., object, second object) are distinguished in a project of the Asia Bible Society, namely the Greek syntax trees produced by Andi Wu and Randall K. Tan (who was also involved in the OpenText.org project) and made available through Clear Bible (formerly Global Bible Initiative).[31] These data interact well with other tools such as the Lowfat Syntax Tree Browser.[32]

---

the Byzantine Text see https://github.com/byztxt, accessed 4 May 2023.

[31] Greek syntax trees: https://github.com/biblicalhumanities/greek-new-testament/tree/master/syntax-trees, accessed 4 May 2023; Clear Bible: https://www.clear.bible, accessed 4 May 2023.

[32] See https://github.com/biblicalhumanities/greek-new-testament/tree/master/syntax-trees/reader/doc, accessed 4 May 2023. For a newer release see https://github.com/Clear-Bible/macula-greek, accessed 4 May 2023.

A project to bring the data from the OpenText project and those from the Asia Bible Society together in Text-Fabric is carried out by Oliver Glanz at the Center of Biblical Languages and Computing (CBLC) at Andrews University.[33]

Whereas computational Old Testament studies had a strong linguistic focus from the 1970s onwards, in New Testament studies there were other areas in which the potential of the computer was explored first, such text editing, stemmatology, and manuscript studies. The computer program Collate, developed by Peter Robinson in the late 1980s (succeeded in 2010 by Collatex[34]) was soon adopted by New Testament scholarship in Birmingham and Münster for text comparison and text editing. In the early 1990s, Gerd Mink, one of the editors of the *Editio Critica Maior* (ECM) of the Greek New Testament, developed the Coherence-Based Genealogical Method (CBGM; Wachtel 2019). This method was particularly apt to deal with the typical features of the transmission of the New Testament, such as the high degree of contamination, which hinders the traditional genealogical tree-model (Gurry 2016).

New Testament scholarship has also made great progress in manuscript imaging (see various contributions in Hamidović et al. 2019). Hundreds of manuscripts have been digitised and high-quality images can be studied and annotated in the Virtual Manuscript Room of the *Institut für Neutestamentliche Textforschung*

---

[33] See https://github.com/CenterBLC/NA, accessed 4 May 2023.

[34] See https://collatex.net/about, accessed 4 May 2023.

(INTF) in Münster.[35] And as in the case of Old Testament studies, new experiments with data meaning, text reuse detection, and the use of NLP for semantic information extraction have appeared on the scene (for examples see Hamidović et al. 2019).[36]

5.0. Further Reading

The various databases discussed in this chapter do not provide final answers, but are useful tools, each of them situated in the complex field of linguistic theories. It is therefore extremely important to use them in consultation with the documentation listed below.

Those who want to do more advanced analysis are advised to develop some basic programming skills and use the datasets that are available as a whole on GitHub or another platform, rather than only with a user-friendly search interface.

In the case of the ETCBC database, for example, Meeuse (2021) is a good starting point for exploring the database through the user interface of the SHEBANQ website, but much more advanced research (as in the examples mentioned in §3.2) is possible for those who have mastered Python and use the Python package Text-Fabric to analyse the Hebrew Bible.[37]

---

[35] See https://ntvmr.uni-muenster.de, accessed 4 May 2023.

[36] See also above, §4.2 on geospatial analysis in New Testament studies.

[37] SHEBANQ website: https://shebanq.ancient-data.org; ETCBC database on GitHub: https://github.com/ETCBC/bhsa; Text-Fabric: https://github.com/annotation/text-fabric; Python courses: https://www.codecademy.com or https://www.udemy.com/user/fredbaptiste. All accessed 4 May 2023.

5.1. Computational Linguistics

1. Clark, Fox, and Lappin (2010)
2. Jurafsky and Martin (2021)

5.2. Hermeneutical Implications of Computational Text Analysis

1. Bod (2013)
2. Clivaz (2019)
3. Van der Weel (2011)
4. Van Peursen (2010)

5.3. History of the Discipline

1. Oosting (2016)
2. Poswick (2010)

5.4. Database and Tools

5.4.1. General Overview and Methodological Issues

1. Kroeze (2013)
2. Miller-Naudé and Miller (2018)

5.4.2. Andersen-Forbes Database

1. Andersen and Forbes (2012)

5.4.3. Accordance Syntactic Database

1. Accordance documentation (2014)
2. Holmstedt and Cook (2018)

5.4.4. ETCBC Database

1. Kingham (2018)
2. Kingham and Van Peursen (2018)
3. Meeuse (2021)

5.4.5. Tiberias Stylistic Classifier

1. Berman (2021)
2. Dershowitz et al. (2015)

5.4.6. New Testament Databases

1. Porter et al. (2019)

References

Accordance documentation. 2014. 'Holmstedt–Abegg Hebrew Syntactic Database. Principle and Parameters, v. 5.0 (rev. October 2014)'. https://www.accordancefiles1.com/exchange/downloads/documents/holmstedt_syntax_14.pdf, accessed 23 May 2022.

action.ai. 2021. 'Natural Langauge is an Unruly Beast: How We Tame Her in Order to Create Groundbreaking Conversational AI'. https://action.ai/what-happens-when-we-speak-a-brief-foray-into-language-and-how-we-artificially-process-it/, accessed 29 June 2022.

Andersen, Francis I. and A. Dean Forbes. 1986. *Spelling in the Hebrew Bible*. Biblica et Orientalia 41. Rome: Biblical Institute Press.

———. 2012. *Biblical Hebrew Grammar Visualized*. Linguistic Studies in Ancient West Semitic 6. Winona Lake, IN: Eisenbrauns.

Barr, James. 1961. *The Semantics of Biblical Language*. Oxford: Oxford University Press.

Berman, Joshua. 2021. 'Measuring Style in Isaiah: Isaiah 34–35 and the Tiberias Stylistic Classifier for the Hebrew Bible'. *Vetus Testamentum* 71 (3): 303–16. doi.org/10.1163/15685330-12341070.

Bod, Rens. 2013. 'Who's Afraid of Patterns? The Particular versus the Universal Meaning of Humanities 3.0'. *BMGN Low Countries Historical Review* 128: 171–9.

Bosman, Hendrik-Jan. 2019. 'Prosodic Influence on the Text Syntax of Lamentations'. PhD dissertation, Vrije Universiteit Amsterdam.

Canu Højgaard, Christian. 2019. 'Semantic Mapping of Participants in Legal Discourse'. *HIPHIL Novum* 5 (2): 136–42.

———. 2021. 'Roles and Relations in Biblical Law: A Study of Participant Tracking, Semantic Roles, and Social Networks in Leviticus 17–26'. PhD dissertation, Vrije Universiteit Amsterdam.

Clark, Alexander, Chris Fox, and Shalom Lappin. 2010. *The Handbook of Computational Linguistics and Natural Language Processing*. Malden, MA: Wiley-Blackwell.

Clivaz, Claire. 2019. *Ecritures digitales: Digital Writing, Digital Scriptures*. Digital Biblica Studies 4. Leiden: Brill.

Coeckelbergs, Mathias. 2022. 'From Pattern to Interpretation. Using Colibri Core to Detect Translation Patterns in the

Peshitta'. In *LREC 2022 Conference Proceedings*, edited by Nicoletta Calzolari et al., 4270–74. Paris: ELRA, 2022.

de Groot, A. D. 1946. *Het denken van den schaker: Een experimenteel-psychologische studie*. Amsterdam: Noord-Hollandsche Uitgevers Maatschappij.

de Joode, Johan, and Dirk Speelman. 2020. 'A Hermeneutic of Variation? The Orthographic Variability of the Hebrew Bible and the Larger Dead Sea Scrolls'. *Journal for Semitics* 29 (2) [24 pages]. doi.org/10.25159/2663-6573/6633.

Dershowitz, Idan, Navot Akiva, Moshe Koppel, and Nachum Dershowitz. 2015. 'Computer Source Criticism of Biblical Texts'. *Journal of Biblical Literature* 134 (2): 253–71. doi.org/10.15699/jbl.1342.2015.2754.

Dorobantu, Marius. 2022. 'Imago Dei in the Age of Artificial Intelligence: Challenges and Opportunities for a Science-Engaged Theology'. *Christian Perspectives on Science and Technology*, n.s., 1: 175–96. doi.org/10.58913/KWUU3009.

Driver, Samuel Rolles. 1913. *An Introduction to the Literature of the Old Testament*. 9th rev. ed. Edinburgh: T&T Clark.

Dyk, Janet W. 2016. 'How do Hebrew Verbs Differ? A Flow Chart of Differences'. In *Contemporary Examinations of Classical Languages: Valency, Lexicography, Grammar*, edited by Timothy Martin Lewis, Alison G. Salvesen, and Beryl Turner, 33–51. Perspectives on Linguistics and Ancient Languages 8. Piscataway, NJ: Gorgias.

Dyk, Janet, Oliver Glanz, and Reinoud Oosting. 2013. 'Het belang van valentiepatronen voor het vertalen van Bijbels

Hebreeuwse werkwoorden'. *Met Andere Woorden* 32 (2): 23–35.

Dyk, Janet W., and Percy S. F. van Keulen. 2013. *Language System, Translation Technique, and Textual Tradition in the Peshitta of Kings*. Monographs of the Peshitta Institute Leiden 19. Leiden: Brill.

Erwich, Christiaan M. 2021. 'Who is Who in the Psalms? A Computational Analysis of Participants and Their Networks'. PhD dissertation, Vrije Universiteit Amsterdam.

Gurry, Peter J. 2016. 'How Your Greek NT is Changing: A Simple Introduction to the Coherence-Based Genealogical Method (CBGM)'. *Journal of the Evangelical Theological Society* 59 (4): 675–89.

Hamidović, David, Claire Clivaz, and Sarah Bowen Savant (eds). 2019. *Ancient Manuscripts in Digital Culture: Visualisation, Data Mining, Communication*. Digital Biblical Studies 3. Leiden: Brill, 2019.

Hardmeier, Christof Felix. 1970. 'Die Verwendung von elektronische Datenverarbeitungsanlagen in die alttestamentliche Wissenschaft: Neue Möglichkeiten der Forschung am Alten Testament'. *Zeitschrift für die alttestamentliche Wissenschaft* 83: 175–85.

Holmstedt, Robert D., and John A. Cook. 2018. 'The Accordance Hebrew Syntactic Database Project'. *Journal of Semitics* 27 (1) [23 pages]. doi.org/10.25159/1013-8471/3010.

Jurafsky, Dan, and James H. Martin. 2021. *Speech and Language Processing*. 3rd ed. Draft. https://web.stanford.edu/~jurafsky/slp3/, accessed 4 May 2023.

Kaajan, Marianne. 2019. 'Is Biblical Hebrew a Non-Configurational Language? Reconsidering the Evidence from Discontinuous Phrases'. *HIPHIL Novum* 5 (2): 45–69.

Kingham, Cody. 2018. 'Data Creation (Updated version 03.04.18)'. http://www.etcbc.nl/datacreation/, accessed 23 May 2023.

Kingham, Cody, Etienne van de Bijl, Sandjai Bhulai, and Wido van Peursen. 2018. 'A Probabilistic Approach to Linguistic Variation and Change in Biblical Hebrew'. https://github.com/ETCBC/Probabilistic_Language_Change, accessed May 23, 2022.

Kingham, Cody, and Wido van Peursen. 2018. 'The ETCBC Database of the Hebrew Bible'. *Journal for Semitics* 27 (1) [13 pages]. doi.org/10.25159/1013-8471/2974.

Kittel, Gerhard, and Gerhard Friedrich (eds). 1933–79. *Theologisches Wörterbuch zum Neuen Testament*. Stuttgart: Kohlhammer.

Kroeze, Jan H. 2013. 'Computational Information Systems: Biblical Hebrew'. In *Encyclopedia of Hebrew Language and Linguistics* 1: 527–34, edited by Geoffrey Khan. Leiden: Brill.

Longacre, Robert E. 1989. *Joseph: A Story of Divine Providence*. Winona Lake, IN: Eisenbrauns.

Mealand, David. 1988. 'Computers in New Testament Research: An Interim Report'. *Journal for the Study of the New Testament* 33 (2): 97–115.

Meeuse, Bas. 2021. 'SHEBANQ Tutorial 2021. How to Start Using the BSHA Database'. https://github.com/ETCBC/Tutorials/blob/master/SHEBANQ%20tutorial%202021.pdf, accessed 23 May, 2022.

Miller-Naudé, Cynthia L., and Jacobus A. Naudé. 2018. 'New Directions in the Computational Analysis of Biblical Hebrew Grammar'. *Journal for Semitics* 27 (1) [17 pages]. doi.org/10.25159/1013-8471/4628.

Naaijer, Martijn. 2020. 'Syntactic Variation in Clause Structure in Biblical Hebrew'. PhD dissertation, Vrije Universiteit Amsterdam.

Naaijer, Martijn, and Wido van Peursen 2022. 'Parsing Hebrew and Syriac Morphology using Deep Learning: State-of-the-art Technology Meets Ancient Literature'. https://blog.esciencecenter.nl/parsing-hebrew-and-syriac-morphology-using-deep-learning-cb6832bb6685, accessed 23 May, 2022.

Oosting, Reinoud. 2016. 'Computer-Assisted Analysis of Old Testament Texts: The Contribution of the WIVU to Old Testament Scholarship'. In *The Present State of Old Testament Studies in the Low Countries: A Collection of Old Testament Studies Published on the Occasion of the Seventy-Fifth Anniversary of the Oudtesta-mentisch Werkgezelschap*, edited by Klaas Spronk, 192–209. Oudtestamentische Studiën 69. Leiden: Brill.

Porter, Stanley E., Christopher D. Land, and Francis G. H. Pang. 2019. *Linguistics and the Bible: Retrospects and Prospects*. McMaster New Testament Studies 9. Eugene, OR: Pickwick Publications.

Postma, Ferenc, Eep Talstra, and Marc Vervenne. 1983. *Exodus: Materials in Automatic Text Processing*. Amsterdam: VU Boekhandel.

Poswick, R. Ferdinand. 2010. 'From Louvain-la-Neuve (1985) to El Escorial in Madrid (2008): 25 Years of AIBI'. In *Computer Assisted Research on the Bible in the 21st Century*, edited by Luis Vegas Montaner, Guadalupe Seijas de los Ríos-Zarzosa, and Javier del Barco, 3–11. Bible in Technology 3. Piscataway, NJ: Gorgias.

Roorda, Dirk. 2018. 'Coding the Hebrew Bible'. *Research Data Journal for the Humanities and Social Sciences* 3 (1): 27–41. doi.org/10.1163/24523666-01000011.

Sanborg-Petersen Ulrik. 2011. 'On Biblical Hebrew and Computer Science: Inspiration, Models, Tools, and Cross-Fertilization'. In *Tradition and Innovation in Biblical Interpretation: Studies Presented to Professor Eep Talstra on the Occasion of his Sixty-Fifth Birthday*, edited by Willem Th. van Peursen and Janet W. Dyk, 261–76. Studia Semitica Neerlandica 57. Leiden: Brill.

Siebesma-Mannens, Femke. 2014. 'Continuity and Discontinuity. A Study in Biblical Hebrew on the Variation of the Prepositions אֶל and לְ Occurring with the Verb אמר'. MA thesis, Vrije Universiteit Amsterdam.

Smend, Rudolf. 1978. *Die Entstehung des Alten Testaments*. Stuttgart: Kohlhammer.

Talstra, Eep. 2010. 'In the Beginning, when Making Copies used to Be an Art…: The Bible among Poets and Engineers'. In *Text Comparison and Digital Creativity: The Production of Presence and Meaning in Digital Text Scholarship*, edited by Wido van Peursen, Ernst D. Thoutenhoofd, and Adriaan van der Weel, 31–56. Scholarly Communication 1. Leiden: Brill.

Talstra, Eep and Janet W. Dyk. 2006. 'The Computer and Biblical Research: Are there Perspectives beyond the Imitation of Classical Instruments?'. In *Text, Translation, and Tradition: Studies on the Peshitta and Its Use in the Syriac Tradition Presented to Konrad D. Jenner on the Occasion of his Sixty-Fifth Birthday*, edited by W. Th. van Peursen and R. B. ter Haar Romeny, 189–203. Monographs of the Peshitta Institute Leiden 14. Leiden: Brill.

van Altena, Vincent Paul. 2022. 'What has Athens to Do with Jerusalem: The Potential of Spatial-Temporal Analysis Methods to Interpret Early Christian Literature'. PhD dissertation, Technical University Delft.

van der Schans, Yanniek, David Ruhe, Wido van Peursen, and Sandjai Bhulai. 2020. 'Clustering Biblical Texts Using Recurrent Neural Networks'. In *Proceedings of the Network Institute Academy Assistants program 2018/2019*, edited by Victor de Boer, Antske Fokkens, Christine Moser, and Ivar Vermeulen. doi.org/10.5281/zenodo.4003509.

van der Weel, Adriaan. 2011. *Changing our Textual Minds: Towards a Digital Order of Knowledge*. Manchester: Manchester University Press.

Van Hecke, Pierre. 2018. 'Computational Stylometric Approach to the Dead Sea Scrolls: Towards a New Research Agenda'. *Dead Sea Discoveries* 25 (1): 57–82.

Van Hecke, Pierre, and Johan de Joode. 2021. 'Promises and Challenges in Designing Stylometric Analyses for Classical Hebrew'. In *Hebrew Texts and Language of the Second Temple Period: Proceedings of an Eighth Symposium on the Hebrew of* the Dead Sea Scrolls and Ben Sira, edited by Steven Fassberg, 349–74. Studies on the Texts of the Desert of Judah 134. Leiden: Brill.

van Peursen, Willem Th. 2007. *Language and Interpretation in the Syriac Text of Ben Sira: A Comparative Linguistic and Literary Study*. Monographs of the Peshitta Institute Leiden 16. Leiden: Brill.

———. 2010. 'Text Comparison and Digital Creativity: An Introduction'. In *Text Comparison and Digital Creativity: The Production of Presence and Meaning in Digital Text Scholarship*, edited by Wido van Peursen, Ernst D. Thoutenhoofd, and Adriaan van der Weel, 1–27. Scholarly Communication 1. Leiden: Brill.

———. 2015. 'Mathematical Rigour and Scholarly Intuition: Some Reflections on Andersen's and Forbes' *Biblical Hebrew Grammar Visualized*'. *Ancient Near Eastern Studies* 52: 298–307. doi.org/10.2143/ANES.52.0.3082875.

———. 2018. 'Introduction: Linking Syriac Geographic Data'. https://medium.com/pelagios/introduction-linking-syriac-geographic-data-3e7a8f88dede, accessed 4 May 2023.

———. 2020a. 'Tracing Text Types in Biblical Hebrew'. *Vetus Testamentum* 70 (1): 140–55. doi.org/10.1163/15685330-12341430.

———. 2020b. 'De computer en de Geest: Digital Humanities en het verstaan van de Bijbel'. *Radix* 46 (4): 298–308.

van Peursen, W. T., and J. G. Veldman. 2018. *Linking Syriac Liturgies*. DANS. doi.org/10.17026/dans-26t-hhv7.

Verhaar, Peter. 2016. 'Affordances and Limitations of Algorithmic Criticism'. PhD dissertation, Leiden University.

Vlaardingerbroek, Hannes. 2017. 'Do You See What I Am Talking About? Towards a Topic Visualizer for Syriac Texts' Project Report'. https://www.academia.edu/30737774/Do_you_see_what_I_am_talking_about, accessed 23 May 2022.

Wachtel, Klaus 2019. 'The Development of the Coherence-Based Genealogical Method (CBGM), its Place in Textual Scholarship, and Digital Editing'. In *The Future of New Testament Scholarship*, edited by Garrick V. Allen, 435–46. Wissenschaftliche Untersuchungen zum Neuen Testament 417. Tübingen: Mohr Siebeck.

EMERGING FROM SILOS OF ANALYSIS: A COMPLEXITY THEORY APPROACH TO THE STUDY OF BIBLICAL TEXTS

Sophia L. Pitcher

Language is a complex system (Larsen-Freeman 1997; Larsen-Freeman and Cameron 2008; Ellis and Larsen-Freeman 2009a). Together, the many dimensions of language comprise an intricate nexus of heterogenous components that often interact in surprising ways. Some of the dimensions of language—grammar, orthography and the written transmission of texts, language acquisition, and language variation—comprise complex systems in themselves. For example, language acquisition, or more precisely an individual's developing proficiency in a language (see Larsen-Freeman and Cameron 2008, 157; Dörnyei 2009; Ellis and Larsen-Freeman 2009b; Naudé 2012, 64), involves dynamic interactions between multiple agents. Speech communities, in constant flux, are comprised of individuals at various levels of proficiency who exhibit varying patterns of language use (see Mufwene 2008, 3; Beckner et al. 2009, 12–15; Naudé 2012, 67–68, 69). Language variation is similarly complex, as it encompasses variation manifested synchronically and diachronically. Synchronic language variation happens in real time at the level of individual speakers (viz. idiolects) and communities of speakers (viz. dialects; see Mufwene 2008, 15–28; Beckner et al. 2009, 7, 9, 12–15; Blythe and Croft 2009, 48; Naudé 2012, 67–68), while diachronic language variation involves the interplay between culturally transmitted linguistic structures that "persist for millennia" (Naudé 2012, 73) and those that do not, resulting in the "renovation of morphosyntactic structure" (Givón 2009, 43; Naudé 2012, 73) over time (see also Beckner and Bybee 2009).

Higher-level dimensions of language can be reduced to reveal complex components at lower levels of organisation. For example, the components of the grammar of a language include syntax, morphology, phonology, semantics, and discourse-pragmatics. These components interface at various levels and to varying degrees, forming dynamic and often nonlinear phenomena. For example, the phonological dimension not only includes a language's sound system as represented by its consonants, vowels, and lexical tones (if present) but also prosodic phonology, with its own array of constituent features that interact with morphological, syntactic, semantic, and discourse-pragmatic domains.

Conceptualised as a complex system, language consists of multi-dimensional layers that are distinct but nonetheless interrelated—each layer influencing the other, while simultaneously shaping the system as a continuously evolving whole. This hierarchical interconnectedness characterises the nature of complex systems. As Baicchi (2015, 10) describes, complex systems are "heterogeneous entities that, interacting with each other and with their environment, generate multiple layers of collective structure exhibiting hierarchical self-organization without centralized control." Characterising language in such a way encourages analyses that are also multi-dimensional and that seek to account for linguistic phenomena as they exist within the system. Although a complex systems approach may threaten analysis with a bewildering degree of variability, it offers two clear and compelling benefits: (1) an awareness of the empirical nature of the object of study, which includes the presence of other phenomena that share its nexus, and (2) theoretical grounding that aims to provide greater analytical integration of seemingly disparate factors operating within the system.

In other words, a complex-systems approach to language recognises that isolated analyses artificially simplify and often obscure the object of study (see Larsen-Freeman 1997; Larsen-Freeman and Cameron 2008, 9; Schwartzhaupt 2013, 262). Perhaps more fundamentally, it "offers greater coherence in explaining what [is] already know[n]" (Larsen-Freeman and Cameron 2008, 11). It is for these reasons that a complexity approach to language is beginning to influence the way language phenomena are understood within certain subfields of linguistics. This systems view is also beginning to impact the way biblical scholars analyse, teach, and translate biblical texts.

To introduce the merits of a complexity approach to the study of biblical texts, this paper will discuss the origins of Complexity Theory (CT) and its historical development within the field of linguistics (§1), the seven core attributes of complex systems (§2), and the ways in which a complexity approach has been fruitfully applied to biblical scholarship (§3).

1.0. Complexity Theory: Origins and Historical Development

Baicchi (2015, 10) identifies the ancient Greek philosopher Heraclitus (ca 500 BCE) as articulating the earliest philosophical expressions on the dynamism and unity of natural phenomena (see also Larsen-Freeman and Cameron 2008, 6). Heraclitus described the material world as interconnected and in continuous flux. This perspective challenged a static philosophy of the material world, "which described reality as if it were composed of static individuals and the state of being as conceptually 'simple', internally unchangeable and undifferentiated" (Baicchi 2015, 10). Baicchi (2015, 10) also cites the 'process philosophy' of Alfred Whitehead as advancing Heraclitus' notion of dynamicity and originating 'systems thinking' in the early twentieth century. In his essay *Process and Reality*, Whitehead (1929) argues for a philosophical balance between "the metaphysics of substance… and the metaphysics of flux" (1929, 209). Whitehead does this by postulating that a "particular existent" or entity is characterised by the notion of concrescence—a "fluency inherent in [its] constitution" (1929, 210). He argues that "the real internal constitution of a particular existent" (1929, 210) is an interconnected, dynamic process of a larger whole (1929, 211, 214–215):

> 'Concrescence' is the name for the process in which the universe of many things acquires an individual unity in a determinate relegation of each item of the 'many' to its subordination in the constitution of the novel 'one'. The most general term 'thing'—or, equivalently, 'entity'—means nothing else than to be one of the 'many' which find their niches in each instance of concrescence. Each

> instance of concrescence is itself the novel individual 'thing' in question.... The notion of 'organism' is combined with that of 'process' in a twofold manner. The community of actual things is an organism; but it is not a static organism. It is an incompletion in process of production.... In this sense, an organism is a nexus. Secondly, each actual entity is itself only describable as an organic process. It repeats in microcosm what the universe is in macrocosm. It is a process proceeding from phase to phase, each phase being the real basis from which its successor proceeds towards the completion of the thing in question. Each actual entity bears in its constitution the 'reasons' why its conditions are what they are. These 'reasons' are the other actual entities objectified for it.... Thus each actual entity, although complete so far as concerns its microscopic process, is yet incomplete by reason of its objective inclusion of the macroscopic process.

Whitehead understands an individual category or entity to be the perception of a process at a particular moment in time. Furthermore, he concludes that an individual entity or occasion may be analysed, but the analysis is by nature transitory.

While these philosophical antecedents of complexity are noteworthy, Larsen-Freeman and Cameron (2008, 2–3) credit mid-twentieth century scientists with formulating the most influential precursors of CT. They cite Conrad Waddington's description of embryogenesis in 1940 as a pivotal systems description. Within this conceptual framework, an embryo is not fully determined by genetic information, but rather (Larsen-Freeman and Cameron 2008, 2):

> each step in the process of development creates the conditions for the next one. In other words, "the form of the

body is literally constructed by the construction process itself—and is not specified in some pre-existing full instruction set, design or building plan…" (van Geert 2003, 648–649).

In a similar vein, in 1950, biologist Ludwig von Bertalanffy proposed a general systems theory that described "an entity as the sum of the properties of its parts" (Larsen-Freeman and Cameron 2008, 2). In doing so, he eschewed reducing an entity to any one of its parts, underscoring the importance of the "relationships among the parts which connect them to the whole" (Larsen-Freeman and Cameron 2008, 3).

Over the next three decades, scientists continued to develop a systems approach to natural phenomena (see Larsen-Freeman and Cameron 2008, 3–4).[1] In the 1980s, this field of research culminated in the founding of the Santa Fe Institute. The institute quickly became the hub for exploring the nature of complex adaptive systems, where CT was formalised and multidisciplinary research flourished (Larsen-Freeman and Cameron 2008, 3). The application of CT has been extended to such diverse fields (see Larsen-Freeman and Cameron 2008, 3–7; see also Pearce and Merletti 2006) as business management (Battram 1998), physics (Gell-Mann 1994), epidemiology (Pearce and Merletti 2006), psychology (Spivey 2007), economics (Arthur 2013), and translation and development studies (Marais, 2014).

---

[1] Marais (2014, 19) also cites chaos theory as an influential precursor to the development of CT. Chaos theory is a branch of mathematics that explores the underlying order of systems that exhibit random states of disorder and irregular patterns (e.g., the weather as demonstrated by the butterfly effect [Gleick 1987, 9–31; Dooley 2009]).

At the close of the century, Larsen-Freeman pioneered a complexity approach to applied linguistics, exploring the merits of a complexity model for language acquisition and second language instruction. Her primary hope for developing complexity thinking within her field was that "the dynamics of complex nonlinear systems [would] discourage reductionist explanations" (Larsen-Freeman 1997, 142). For Larsen-Freeman, much of the theoretical appeal of CT lies in the dynamic and holistic metaphor that it engenders, enabling researchers to perceive fundamental properties and interactions of language phenomena that remain opaque to traditional theoretical frameworks. She argues that the insights that emerge from a complexity approach are not equally accessible to these frameworks because at their core they reduce or isolate the object of study, and in doing so obscure it.

According to Larsen-Freeman and Cameron (2008, 6), linguists have typically taken a binary approach to the description of language phenomena, as either an inner perspective of the mind (see Chomsky 1965), or an outer perspective of the world (see Weinreich et al. 1968). Linguists who take the inner perspective typically investigate "mental competence rather than performance" (2008, 6), while those who have taken the outer perspective often seek to create "a model of language which accommodates the facts of variable usage" (2008, 6). Larsen-Freeman and Cameron (2008, 6) assess the deficiencies of these polar approaches to language theory in the following way:

> Applied linguists have... preferr[ed] to explain the facts of language... either through an appeal to a mental competence... or by taking language use factors into account, showing patterns in variability.... But mental competence,

when it is seen to be "irreducibly self-contained, cannot meaningfully relate to the world outside" (Leather and van Dam 2003, 6)—which applied linguists must do—and the hybridity of more socially-oriented approaches have tended to treat the world (context) as an independent variable that influences linguistic form, not as a dynamic system itself. Here, perhaps, Complexity Theory may contribute to a resolution.

A complexity approach to language resolves the tension of this dichotomy by rejecting the view that the environment is "external to and independent from the organism" (Larsen-Freeman and Cameron 2008, 7) and advancing the view that the dimensions of language "emerge from interrelated patterns of experience, social interaction, and cognitive mechanisms" (Beckner et al. 2009, 2).

Perhaps most fundamentally, Larsen-Freeman (2013, 370) understands CT to be a metatheory "still necessitating object theories" (viz. discipline theories). According to Larsen-Freeman, it is precisely this characteristic that endows CT with one of its greatest advantages—transdisciplinarity: CT "avoids the splintering of disciplinary knowledge and creates instead new forms of knowledge, which are thematic, cutting across disciplinary boundaries" (2013, 370). In fact, Marais (2014, 18) considers the trajectory of Western scholarship towards interdisciplinarity and complexity frameworks to be inevitable:

> In a sense, complexity thinking seems to be inevitable. The whole program of Western science has focused on analyzing the parts of reality in order to understand them better…. Now, the realization is dawning on scholars that analysis can only take you so far, because only a small part

of reality is to be explained by the way parts are, or only a small part of reality can be understood by understanding the parts of it. Much of reality is to be explained not by the parts themselves but by the way in which they relate to one another or by the way in which they are becoming, the way in which constituent parts form wholes... The focus has thus shifted from an analysis of parts to a focus on the relationships and connections between parts and between parts and wholes. Also, the focus has shifted from an interest in phenomena to an interest in processes, that is, the way in which phenomena are the result of the interaction of their constituent parts.

Marais is also quick to point out that while the notions of movement, process, and interdisciplinary synthesis factor into the descriptions of complex systems, they are not of primary importance. For Marais (2014, 18), stasis, being, and disciplinary analysis are equally important notions since they too characterise reality:

> The philosophical problems of stasis and movement, and of how both constitute reality, are within the purview of complexity thinking. Let me hurry to say that I do not suggest replacing analysis with synthesis or being with process. I hope to incorporate these binaries in a complexity view in which both sides of the binary find their rightful place in thinking about a particular phenomenon.

2.0. Seven Core Characteristics of Complex Systems

CT is chiefly concerned with the description and modelling of the relationships between the components of complex systems—particularly, the relationships that emerge from changing and often unexpected interactions among the components. According to Larsen-Freeman and Cameron (2008), seven core attributes characterise complex systems: 1) dynamism, 2) heterogeneity, 3) openness, 4) interconnectedness, 5) emergence, 6) nonlinearity, and 7) adaptation.

First, complex systems are dynamic. The dynamism of a complex system refers to its non-static nature; it is a system in constant flux (Larsen-Freeman and Cameron 2008, 29–30). In fact, Larsen-Freeman and Cameron assert that dynamism is likely the defining feature of language as a complex system (2008, 25) because "language, language use, and language development are continuously in action" (2008, 29).

Second, unlike simple systems (e.g., a traffic light; see Larsen-Freeman and Cameron 2008, 27) that are comprised of "a small set of similar components… connected in predictable and unchanging ways" (2008, 27), complex systems embody a multiplicity of dynamic, heterogeneous components.

Third, complex systems are open. Unlike closed systems, those that are open allow energy, matter, or other influences to enter from the outside (Larsen-Freeman and Cameron 2008, 32). For example, a closed highway system would be one with a fixed number of vehicles and a fixed road capacity. However, in an open road system (2008, 31) where traffic continually increases but road capacity remains static, the roads will eventually "reach equilibrium in the form of gridlock" (2008, 32). Such a result initiates pressure to add road capacity, thereby influencing the context of the system. So, in an open highway system, free-flowing equilibrium can only be maintained by introducing additional road capacity to the system. This means that open systems "not only adapt to their contexts but also initiate change in those contexts; these systems are not just dependent on context but also influence context" (Larsen-Freeman and Cameron 2008, 34).

A linguistic example of this attribute is provided in the lexicon—a subsystem of language that exhibits varying degrees of openness. Certain classes of words in the lexicon are more open than others; the addition or attrition of nouns, for example, is greater than that of prepositions. Furthermore, as an open system, the lexicon can undergo transformation generated by the interaction of lexical inputs and other dimensions of language. For example, the loss of case in Biblical Hebrew (see Waltke and O'Connor 1990, §8.1.c), a morphological change, initiated a phonological process that changed the vowel structure of segolate nouns. Specifically, the loss of the vocalic case marker resulted in a consonant cluster, triggering an epenthetic vowel, which then effected vowel harmony in the first syllable (e.g. *malk > malek > melek 'king'; see Blau 2010, 54).

This leads to the fourth attribute of complex systems—interconnectedness. Complex systems exhibit interconnectedness between their numerous components, dimensions, and contextual factors. A linguistic example of this attribute is illustrated in the morphophonemics of the Biblical Hebrew conjunction *waw*. As is well known, the coordinating *waw* morpheme has multiple allophones depending on its phonological context. However, Revell (2015, 43; 2016, 75–76) and Scheumann (2020, 58–59) observe that the proclitic allophones of *waw* are also determined by their prosodic contexts—particularly, the position of *waw* within a phrase segmented by a disjunctive *ṭaʿam*.

> Conjunction *waw* takes a [*qameṣ*] before the second conjunct of each pair that has an initial accent [viz. an accent on the first syllable] [לַיְלָה וָיוֹם 1 Kgs 8.29].... Conversely, when a *waw* is attached to the first conjunct in each pair, it takes a schwa, even though these conjuncts also have an initial accent [וְיוֹם וָלַיְלָה Gen. 8.22].... The phonetics of the accented syllable do not play a decisive role for this vocalisation of *waw*.... The vocalic change cannot be explained by phonetic assimilation or dissimilation rules. Rather, the distribution of the allophone וָ is determined by prosody (Scheumann 2020, 58–59).

Moreover, scholars have proposed additional factors (see Scheumann 2020, 59–60) that may influence the phonological realisation of the conjunction *waw* with *qameṣ*, including syntactic distribution (see Gesenius 1910; Revell 1981; Waltke and O'Connor 1990; Joüon and Muraoka 2006; van der Merwe et al. 2017), semantics (Waltke and O'Connor 1990; van der Merwe et al. 2017; see also Revell 2015; 2016), and rhythm (Gesenius 1910; Joüon and Muraoka 2006).

The fifth attribute of complex systems is emergence. Complex systems exhibit emergent behaviour when dynamic interactions between lower-level components and dimensions of the system give rise to new phenomena that contribute to the nature of the system (Larsen-Freeman and Cameron 2008, 58–60; Marais 2019b, 47–49). For example, "subatomic particles give rise to atoms, atoms to molecules, molecules to organisms; or phonemes to words, words to propositions, propositions to discourses" (Reid 2021, 33). In each case, the whole of the system—organism or discourse—is not simply the sum of its parts, but what emerges when the parts of the system interact. Ellis and Larsen-Freeman (2009a, 14–15) describe both idiolects and dialects as characteristically emergent:

> Language exists both in individuals (as idiolect) and in the community of users (as communal language). Language is emergent at these two distinctive but interdependent levels: An idiolect is emergent from an individual's language use through social interactions with other individuals in the communal language, whereas a communal language is emergent as the result of the interaction of the idiolects.

The sixth attribute of complex systems is nonlinearity. Larsen-Freeman and Cameron (2008, 31) define this feature as "change that is not proportional to input" (2008, 31; see also Beckner et al. 2009, 16). An idiom is perhaps a simple example of nonlinearity because it is semantically non-compositional—the meaning of the whole expression (viz. output) cannot be derived from the meaning of its individual parts (viz. input; van den Heever 2013, II:106–110, 178).[2] For example, the input of בקש ('seek') and את־נפש ('the life') yields an semantic output of 'to want or try to kill someone', not 'to look for someone's life' (van den Heever 2013, 189–90).

---

[2] Idioms (and their formation) constitute complex phenomena in themselves (see van den Heever 2013). Van den Heever defines semantic non-compositionality as a complex concept "whose global meaning is a semantic extension of the combined meanings of its constituent elements" (2013, 178).

Another illustration of linguistic non-linearity is the process of grammaticalisation whereby a lexical item loses its semantic content and develops a grammatical function. For example, there is abundant cross-linguistic evidence for the diachronic grammaticalisation of the copula into a focus marker (see Heine and Reh 1984; Harris and Campbell 1995; Heine and Kuteva 2002; Lehmann 2015; Khan 2019). One of the pathways to grammaticalisation of the copula (viz. input) begins with cleft sentences, and over time, in some languages, the copula ceases to serve as a verb (viz. output), and instead is interpreted as a particle marking focus.[3] For the languages where this has not occurred, Lehmann (2015, 125) states that the very existence of the "autonomous pattern" of the cleft sentence demonstrates that "the communicative function of focus is already minimally grammaticalized."[4]

Finally, complex systems are adaptive. Larsen-Freeman and Cameron (2008) define adaptation as "the process in which a system adjusts itself in response to changes in its environment"

---

[3] In many languages, the cleft sentence is the most explicit way of marking focus (Lehmann 2015, 123–24). An example of a cleft construction in English is the sentence 'It is X that Y', where X is the focused NP and Y is the comment regarding the NP: *It is JOHN that loves Mary* (Khan 2019, 14).

[4] In some languages, cleft sentences exhibit evidence of further grammaticalisation as the syntactic complexity of the construction simplifies through the loss of certain morphemes, such as the relativiser introducing the subordinate clause: 'It is X Y' (Khan 2019, 15; see also Lehmann 2015, 124). Khan (2019, 15) provides examples of this type of cleft sentence in Israeli Hebrew and Syriac.

(2008, 33). This attribute is evident in the written transmission of sacred texts, where editors adapt their translations to accommodate a variety of editorial considerations (see Naudé and Miller-Naudé 2019, 201, 182–83; Reid 2021, 38–41). For example, Samaritan scribes chose to continue to use the paleo-Hebrew script instead of adopting the Aramaic square script. By doing so, they created an immediate visual distinctive for readers of the Samaritan Pentateuch (Reid 2021, 53). According to Reid (2021, 53), the social schism between the Judean Jews and Samaritan Jews encouraged the use of a different script, which "transformed the visual impact of the manuscript and gave it a Samaritan identity" (2021, 53).

3.0. Complexity Thinking in Biblical Scholarship

This section provides an overview of complexity thinking as applied to five distinct areas of biblical scholarship. Naudé and Miller-Naudé have pioneered this approach, exploring complexity models for diachrony (§3.1), language pedagogy (§3.2), and the translation of sacred texts (§3.3). This framework has been extended to include a complexity model for the Masoretic accents of the Tiberian Masoretic Reading Tradition (Pitcher 2020; §3.5), a complexity approach to syntactic coordination in Biblical Hebrew (Scheumann 2020; §3.4), and a paradigm for understanding the Samaritan Pentateuch as an intralingual translation (Reid 2021; §3.3).

3.1. Diachrony

Naudé (2012) models a complexity approach to the description of language change and diffusion in Biblical Hebrew. His stated aim for this approach (2012, 61) is to promote "viewing the diverse aspects of language change holistically (that is, understanding the causal dependencies and emergent processes among the elements that constitute the whole system) rather than viewing them partially and in isolation." Naudé enumerates four fundamental dimensions of language change and diffusion that must be accounted for in any substantive systems description of diachrony: (1) the dimension of the individual idiolect, (2) the social dimension within a community of speakers, (3) the dimension of the process of chronological change over time, and (4) the development of written texts. He argues that an understanding of the dynamic interplay between each of these dimensions renders "the simple linear model of Ancient Biblical Hebrew, Early Biblical Hebrew, Late Biblical Hebrew, and Mishnaic Hebrew" untenable, yielding a more accurate and complex model of the language development (2012, 71).

Within his system of diachrony, Naudé (2012, 72) describes the dimension of the individual as a domain where the formation of idiolects arises from the "innate grammar of an individual speaker." He states that language change at this level reflects the differences between the grammar of the individual and "that of the input source (for example, child versus parents)." Change at this level is ongoing throughout the individual's life and "always emergent" (2012, 72) as cognition develops and continues to shape the individual's competencies in the use of grammar (2012, 70, 72; see also Givón 2009).

The social dimension of diachrony encompasses the changes that emerge within the dialects of communities of speakers. In this dimension, the diffusion of idiolects is at work, as "one differing grammar becomes dominant and gains acceptance by the local speech community and later by society at large" (Naudé 2012, 72). Naudé notes that diffusion always involves multiple idiolects that are at once competing with and being influenced by the standard language.

The dimension of time recognises that language change and diffusion are processes that develop chronologically and often in observable patterns (2012, 72–73; see also Pintzuk 2003). According to Naudé (2012, 73), linguistic structures accumulate through the daily communicative interactions of speakers in a community, many of which are culturally transmitted to future generations in the form of "fossilized linguistic structures." The complex process by which some linguistic structures (e.g., morphological, phonological, syntactic) "persist for millennia," while other structures simplify or completely erode, is called the "diachronic cycle." It is through this cycle that language undergoes "deep structured changes."

The fourth dimension of diachrony is the development of written texts. In order to account for this dimension, Naudé (2012, 73) asserts that the differences between speech and writing must be identified. One fundamental difference is that "writing is secondary to speech and employs special forms... for its unique purposes (for example, the use of devices for the organization of discourse)." Understanding these differences includes accounting for the use of the text and the context out of which it arises.

For example, for Biblical Hebrew, it is important to understand the context of the Ancient Near East, where the written text was often used as an administrative tool and did not necessarily reflect "a connection with spoken language" (Naudé 2012, 73); this was an "advantage for [outstretched empires] and linguistically unrelated agents." Naudé (2012, 74–75) argues that this contextual description must also consider the socio-cultural nature of the epigraphic and biblical texts, including scribal culture; the political and economic circumstances at the time of composition or redaction; the types of discourses produced (viz. royal, history, law, prophecy) and the audiences they address (viz. the monarchy, the people, personal second person versus impersonal third person). Furthermore, biblical texts have an added layer of complexity because "they were transmitted through multiple editors and copyists, rather than archaeologically excavated straight from their original context" (2012, 74). Naudé maintains that all these factors must be considered when explaining the process of diachrony in biblical languages.

Naudé (2012, 75) illustrates the complexity of the diachronic cycle that "began in Biblical Hebrew, escalated in Qumran Hebrew, and was finished in Mishnaic Hebrew" using data "on the *waw*-consecutive and distribution of the independent personal pronouns in Biblical and Qumran Hebrew." He traces the chronological use of consecutive *waw* with perfective verb forms and notes that this form is statistically more prevalent in Biblical Hebrew than Qumran Hebrew, and almost completely absent in Mishnaic Hebrew (2012, 76–77). While changes in these verbal forms throughout the various stages of Hebrew have been well-documented (2012, 77, n. 2), the theory of diachrony that Naudé (2012, 77–78) develops explains their significance:

> In the biblical period, the change occurred in one or more idiolects. The change then diffused so that, by the time of Qumran, there were fewer examples of the consecutive form and more examples of conjunctive *waw*. The examples of consecutive forms that remained were stylistic fossils. By the time of the Mishnah, the cycle of change was complete: the consecutive forms occurred only in biblical quotations, and the vernacular language was structurally different from the language in the Bible.

The system of diachrony advanced in Naudé (2012) moves traditional descriptions of language development beyond notions that characterise the various forms and stages of biblical languages according to the "synchronic styles available to biblical authors" (2012, 71).

3.2. Language Pedagogy

Miller-Naudé and Naudé (2014) present a complex systems approach to teaching and learning Biblical Hebrew by *reading* the biblical text—an approach that systematises some of the best teaching practices for Biblical Hebrew instruction. The methodology they employ is based on pedagogical complexity models, which assume a theory of second language development that is multi-dimensional and involves "a process of dynamic adaptation"

(2014, 95; see Larsen-Freeman and Cameron 2008; Ellis and Larsen-Freeman 2009a).[5]

Miller-Naudé and Naudé (2014, 92) select the act of reading as the basis of an effective complexity model for teaching biblical languages because the act of reading requires a range of complex skills ranging from "lower-level visual processing involved in decoding the print to higher-level skills involving syntax, semantics, and discourse, and even to skills of text representation and integration of ideas with the reader's global knowledge" (Nassaji 2009, 173). Furthermore, they argue that the socio-political context of their classroom at a South African university itself provides grounds for developing such an approach. Their description of "the 'new' South Africa (since 1994)" (2014, 92) celebrates a country with twelve official languages and the integration of peoples who were once rigidly separated from one another. Accordingly, one key dimension of their pedagogical approach has been to hire a multi-cultural and multi-lingual teaching staff that is able not only to teach in multiple languages (viz. Afrikaans, English, Sesotho), but also to provide parallel linguistic examples and explanations of Hebrew linguistic structures in these diverse languages.

Another key contextual dimension that Miller-Naudé and Naudé's (2014) pedagogical model accounts for is the manner in which South Africa's national teaching requirements train

---

[5] The model of language development proposed here contrasts with models of language acquisition which describe learners accessing a fixed "mental architecture of language" (Miller-Naudé and Naudé 2014, 95).

students to learn new information. They observe that these modes of learning tend to conflict with traditional methods for teaching Biblical Hebrew. Particularly, they have found that South Africa's outcomes-based educational system is focused "too much on the application of knowledge" (2014, 93):

> As a result, students/learners typically have not acquired the skills for memorization. Traditionally, the teaching of Biblical Hebrew has relied upon memorization for the acquisition of vocabulary and verbal paradigms, but this method is almost impossible for students whose previous academic experience has exclusively relied on Outcomes Based Learning (2014, 93).

The six dimensions of Miller-Naudé and Naudé's (2014) complexity model for teaching Biblical Hebrew are as follows: (1) the use of a typological framework for introducing grammatical features, (2) the use of the five complex cognitive skills that must be developed when learning to read, (3) building students' vocabulary, (4) reading, singing, listening, and simplified speaking, (5) increasing students' understanding of the cultural context of the biblical text, and (6) the application of exegesis and theology to the biblical text.

The first dimension of the model involves establishing a typological framework for teaching the grammatical features of the biblical language. A typological framework is particularly suited for this because it classifies languages that are "genetically unrelated and that have no geographical proximity" (2014, 96) according to "shared formal characteristics" (Whaley 1997, 7). Miller-Naudé and Naudé argue that language typology is a key pedagogical feature because it allows instructors "to describe the grammatical features of [the biblical language] to speakers with different mother tongues" (2014, 96). For example, they observe that English- and Afrikaans-speaking students often find the Hebrew construct phrase more difficult to grasp because in these languages "the genitive precedes the noun… a predominant pattern among the world's languages" (2014, 96). However, speakers of African languages such as Sesotho quickly grasp this concept because the noun-genitive pattern in these languages corresponds to the pattern found in Hebrew. Miller-Naudé and Naudé (2014, 96–97) state that these types of conceptual difficulties with the features of a biblical language can be mitigated by explaining them in terms of the typological differences found among the languages of the world.

The second dimension of the model is quite complex in itself because it incorporates the five following cognitive skills of reading (2014, 97–98): (1) learning to interpret and pronounce the orthography; (2) developing the ability to visually process words (viz. learning to identify a word by recognising the string of consonants); (3) developing reading comprehension skills by learning to "[select] the meaning of the word that is relevant to the context" (2014, 98); (4) learning to identify discourse-level features;[6] and (5) learning to interpret "culturally relevant

---

[6] According to Miller-Naudé and Naudé (2014, 98), discourse-level features include "compound sentences, identification of the narrative structures of on-line and off-line information, volitive chains, the embedding of direct and indirect speech, and genre-specific features such as poetic lineation and poetic word pairs."

information for processing the pragmatic inferences of biblical texts" (2014, 97).

The third dimension of the model encompasses the teaching of vocabulary. For Miller-Naudé and Naudé (2014, 100), vocabulary instruction includes equipping students with not only sound files for hearing and pronouncing words but also the culturally relevant information needed to understand them in their textual contexts.

The fourth dimension of the model involves several key activities—reading, singing, listening, and simplified speaking—that all reinforce new skills and allow students to integrate and practise the concepts that they are being taught. For example, reading activities include both an intensive and an extensive component. Intensive reading "involves close, deliberate study of short texts with attention to vocabulary, grammar and discourse of the text" (2014, 102), while extensive reading "involves a wide range of texts of different genres, text structures and language patterns." Additionally, students are provided with audio files of their classroom materials, which affords them ample opportunity to listen to the biblical language. Finally, singing biblical verses and performing simplified oral drills and dialogues reinforces "specific morphological forms, syntactic constructions and vocabulary items" (2014, 101) in engaging ways.

The fifth dimension of the model provides students with the necessary cultural information regarding the ancient biblical world so that they can "bridge the gap between their cultural context… and that of ancient Israel" (2014, 100).

Finally, the sixth dimension of the model involves the application of exegesis and theology to the biblical text. For Miller-Naudé and Naudé (2014, 100), this is the "ultimate goal of Biblical Hebrew language teaching" and the reward for students within the religious context of their institution. This dimension enables students to apply and appreciate their growing knowledge of the language and culture of the biblical text.

3.3. Translation Theory

Marais (2019b, 43; see also 2014) describes translation as a complex process that emerges out of cause-and-effect relationships among a variety of dimensions, including "linguistics, pragmatics, culture, society, ideology, power, a brain, a human personality and meaning" (2019b, 46–47). Marais (2019b, 44) argues that the process of translation—that is, "the process of making meaning"—is fundamentally a sign-process (viz. semiosis), entailing the interrelatedness of three elements: (1) the sign, (2) a mental representation of the referent triggered by the sign, and (3) the actual referent, "either an idea of something or the thing itself." Conceptualising translation as a process means that the mental construct is only relevant for "a particular moment in the semiosis"—that is, the mental construct is "not absolutely final, only pragmatically final" (2019b, 44).

Furthermore, Marais (2019b, 43, 46) argues that the incipient text is as much an emergent phenomenon as the subsequent text, and that the process of translating is not linear or binary—there is no direct line from incipient text to subsequent text. For Marais (2014; 2019b, 46), a complexity model for translation not only means that the translation process is recursive but also that the 'turns' of translation are not mutually exclusive. As such, previous translations of a text are not invalidated by subsequent ones, but instead are viewed as "complementary perspectives that contribute to a fuller understanding of the complexity of translation" (2019b, 46; see also Robinson 2017).

Naudé and Miller-Naudé (2019) explore Marais' complexity model using the Book of Ben Sira in the Septuagint as a case study. Their complexity framework for Ben Sira serves as an alternative to the frameworks that are utilised in two recent modern translations—namely, the *Septuaginta Deutsch* project (LXX.D) and the *New English Translation of the Septuagint* project (*NETS*).[7] Naudé and Miller-Naudé (2019, 181) consider these translations to be reductionist approaches because the former domesticates the text, while the latter renders it foreign to the reader. For example, *NETS* employs a literal translation of the Greek and incorporates transliterated terms. They observe the opposite, but equally reductionist, phenomenon with LXX.D as it veers too heavily in the direction of favouring German culture at the expense of the culture of the incipient text (2019, 181). Marais (2014, 40) describes the pull of these types of reductionist translation models as either being "too strongly biased toward the direction of the target [text]," as in the case of LXX.D, or "too strongly biased toward the source [text]," as in the case of *NETS*.

Naudé and Miller-Naudé argue that their complexity approach to Ben Sira resolves this stark dichotomy by both

---

[7] See Ross (2021) for an overview of the range of recent Septuagint translation projects.

"respecting its alterity" (2019, 203) and being sensitive to "issues of intelligibility and representation." They accomplish this by identifying two sets of dimensions that are inherent in sacred writings and incorporating them into the production of the translated text, largely in the form of footnotes.

The first set of dimensions characterise the religious nature of sacred texts. These dimensions explore the psychological and sociological aspects of religion, as well as the influence that the oral-writing traditions of the text have wielded over time. The psychological dimension "influences how individuals perceive and react to the environment in which they live," while the sociological dimension encompasses a complex nexus of "intercultural and interlinguistic communication influenced by socio-cultural, organizational, and situational factors that result in self-critical corrections, adaptations, and apologies in religious discourse and practice" (2019, 182). Naudé and Miller-Naudé (2019, 181–182) observe:

> Sacred writings, which are texts beyond everyday life that inspire awe, respect, and even fear, are associated with religion and have various special functions or roles within a religious context (Sawyer 1999). As a complex phenomenon, religion and its sacred writings form an inextricable part of culture. Religion is a central part of human experience, influencing how individuals perceive and react to the environments in which they live (Giddens 1993, 456).

Naudé and Miller-Naudé (2019, 182) describe the oral-writing tradition of sacred texts as the words, texts, and language used in public worship, "which are the result of complex processes of canonization and translation." They also recognise that most religious communities require translated versions of their sacred texts, and that these texts "quickly assume the status of incipient (source) texts and become central to the religious domain."

> Sacred writings, then, exhibit complex webs of interaction between numerous emergent, complex adaptive systems—the religious communities who produce and use sacred writings, the sacred writings as emergent incipient (source) texts, the sacred writings as emergent subsequent (target) texts, and in some instances, subsequent (target) texts as emergent sacred writings (Naudé and Miller-Naudé 2019, 183).

The second set of contextual dimensions for the complexity model accounts for the complex nature of the Septuagint and the place of Ben Sira within it. According to Naudé and Miller-Naudé (2019, 183–84), the Septuagint is itself a complex adaptive system for the following historical, text-critical, editorial, and socio-cultural reasons: (1) it has a complex history of origin and transmission; (2) the source text(s) for the translated texts of the Septuagint are pluriform and emergent "in that it did not reach its final, canonical form until many centuries later" (see also Ulrich 2015); (3) the Septuagint comprises "multiple translations (e.g., into Latin and Syriac) and revisions (e.g., by Aquila and Symmachus)" that were produced to serve the "needs and concerns of various religious communities, especially since the Protestant Reformation;" (4) although originally produced for Jews, they subsequently rejected it after it was adopted by Christians as their sacred text.[8] Furthermore, according to Naudé

---

[8] For an alternative view regarding this claim, see De Lange et al. 2009.

and Miller-Naudé, while "research on the Septuagint has been driven primarily by the needs of textual criticism and modern philology, either as a search for the Vorlage or Urtext (earliest) or as a search for the best or most authoritative final text," a new philology approach to the Septuagint views each individual manuscript "as a meaningful, historical artifact, and variants found in these manuscripts are viewed... interesting in their own right."[9]

Naudé and Miller-Naudé argue that a complexity model for Ben Sira, then, considers and incorporates these multiple dimensions. One of their strategies for avoiding foreignising or domesticating the text is by making use of footnotes in order to both provide the modern reader with access to the alterity (viz. foreignness) of the Hebrew incipient text and make this alterity comprehensible.

For example, Ben Sira 24.13–17 depicts Lady Wisdom in terms of "a variety of flora that are mentioned in their ecological contexts" (2019, 189). According to Naudé and Miller-Naudé (2019, 190), since this portion of text lacks a Hebrew incipient text, these terms must be translated with respect to "both the cultural world of ancient Israel and the appropriation of those cultural terms in metaphorical contexts." In this poetic passage, they

---

[9] Naudé and Miller-Naudé (2019, 184) state that "new philology as a philological perspective within the larger field of editorial theory provides a model broadly conceived for understanding texts, text production, and transmission—and for exploring texts in their manuscript contexts." Note that Brill's *Septuagint Commentary Series* assumes this approach (see Porter 2021 for a description).

provide three examples where the *NETS* translation chooses an English term whose referent either is not found in Israel or does not fit the metaphorical function of the plant in the passage, or both (2019, 190–93). Furthermore, in instances where additional information is needed to fill out a modern reader's understanding of the term, footnotes "open up the cultural world of the text to the modern reader by indicating both the botanical characteristics and the social functions of the plant. The alterity of the text is retained and respected but without domestication of its foreignness" (2019, 193). For Naudé and Miller-Naudé (2019, 193), footnotes are powerful metatexts that help retain the complexity of text by making the alterity of the incipient text accessible and intelligible to a modern reader.

Following Marais (2014; 2019a; 2019b) and Naudé and Miller-Naudé's (2019) models for translation, Reid (2021) demonstrates a similar use of complexity principles in his analysis of the Samaritan Pentateuch as an intralingual translation—that is, a rewording or reinterpretation of a text in the same language. Reid presents a paradigm for understanding the Samaritan Pentateuch, particularly, the variants found in the text, "the choices made by the editors... the context they worked in, and the reason they embarked on the project" (2021, 2). Unlike interlingual translations that "might be done simply to facilitate communication between speakers of different languages" (2021, 50), Reid argues that "intralingual translations must be done for a particular reason or *skopos*, as the original material is already accessible in the target language."[10] Reid concludes that the *skopos* for the Samaritan Pentateuch is rooted in a particular set of scribal interventions that emerge from a complex interaction of multiple texts—e.g., proto-Masoretic, pre-Samaritan, Septuagint (2021, 10–22, 71)—and multi-dimensional factors, including (1) the diachronic development of the Samaritan dialect and inter-dialectic variants (2021, 59–60); (2) editorial considerations, e.g., choosing to preserve the paleo-Hebrew script (2021, 53) and substituting archaic grammatical forms for those that were more commonly used (2021, 58); and (3) the "cultural rich points" that differentiate the Jewish and Samaritan traditions, e.g., the correct place of worship, Gerizim versus Jerusalem, (2021, 60–64).

3.4. Syntax

Scheumann (2020) applies complexity thinking to the grammatical feature of phrasal coordination in Biblical Hebrew because he recognises that "semantic observations of clausal coordination" do not yield a comprehensive description of coordination, and that a purely syntactic analysis is equally insufficient (2020, 11). His complexity approach provides a metatheory for the Minimalist Programme (see Chomsky 1995) that undergirds his syntactic analysis, allowing for other relevant dimensions of language to be considered (2020, 6, 10):

---

[10] In accordance with Vermeer (2004), Reid defines *skopos* as "the aim or purpose of a translation" (Vermeer 2004, 227; see also Reiss and Vermeer 2014; Nord 2018).

> I approach [Biblical Hebrew] language as a connected whole with the interacting levels of syntax, semantics, prosody, morphophonology, and discourse.... Moreover, because coordination is so pervasive in the Pentateuch, it requires a grasp of many areas of [Biblical Hebrew] syntax that intersect with phrasal coordination: prosody, pronoun binding, information structure, word order, null elements, ellipsis, differential object marking, prepositions, negation, markedness, apposition, subordination, and verbal agreement.

Using cross-linguistic data to support his claim for the syntactic structure of coordination in Biblical Hebrew, Scheumann (2020, 30–32, 56) proposes an asymmetric, hierarchical structure based on the following complex features: (1) asymmetric prosodic breaks exhibiting the segmentation between conjuncts at the phrasal and clausal levels (2020, 30); (2) the cliticisation of the coordinating particle to one of the conjuncts (2020, 30–31); (3) syntactic constraints on the locus of a coordinator within a clause (2020, 31); (4) constraints on which conjuncts are able to do the joining or binding within a clause (2020, 32); and (5) asymmetries between verbal agreement and the structure of coordination (2020, 224–25).

Scheumann observes that his hierarchical model for coordination has implications for understanding instances of partial verbal agreement and conjoined subjects (e.g., 2 Sam. 2.12). He concludes that partial agreement is the default pattern when the coordinate complex is post-verbal (e.g., Gen. 33.7), and that "the verb always agrees with the initial conjunct (e.g., Exod. 21.4), whether the coordinate complex is post-verbal or pre-verbal" (2020, 227).

While Scheumann determines that syntax is the primary factor for understanding coordination and verbal agreement asymmetries, he recognises that syntactic analysis alone is insufficient to explain the different types of asymmetries that are found in Biblical Hebrew (2020, 238, 261). Having established the underlying syntactic structure for coordination, he determines (2020, 246–49, 261) that the role discourse plays in the partial agreement of verbs with coordinated subjects is more accurately understood when considered together with other factors such as conjunct word order, conjunct binding (viz. a coreferential pronoun that binds to the second conjunct [2020, 84]), and the subsequent use of pro-drop (2020, 262):

> We have seen that in sentences with a post-verbal coordinate structure headed by a pronoun, the number of the verb is noteworthy. The compound is not the subject, but functions as a [quantifier phrase] that modifies the subject. A singular verb, thus, has discourse significance, because the subject is singular, which is coreferential with the pronoun conjunct. In this way, the pronoun referent is the principal actor because, syntactically, it is the only actor in terms of subjecthood. The prominence of the pronoun is highlighted further with conjunct binding and with a subsequent singular pro-drop verb. Conversely, a plural verb does not mark the conjuncts as equally-prominent actors. While both conjuncts in the [quantifier phrase] explicate the plural pro subject reference, the initial conjunct in the [quantifier phrase] can still be discourse-prominent, much like how the first conjunct in a compound subject can be the principal actor, whether the verb is singular or plural.

3.5. Masoretic Accents of the Tiberian Masoretic Reading Tradition

The current accepted analytical model for the Masoretic accents of the Tiberian Masoretic Reading Tradition is rooted in a nineteenth-century philological algorithm known as the Law of Continuous Dichotomy (LCD, Wickes 1887), which reduces (i.e., artificially simplifies) the accents to a system of pausal segmentation. However, Pitcher's (2020; 2023; see also 2021) model for the accentual system departs from the LCD as a tool of analysis in order to advance a complexity approach that integrates the system's features, structures, and functions within a wholly linguistic framework. Pitcher argues that LCD-based analyses cannot appropriately account for or accommodate the complex linguistic data represented by the accentual system, and should, therefore, be replaced by a cross-linguistic complexity model for six main reasons: (1) LCD-based algorithms were designed to reconstruct the 'correct' sequences of accents in a verse (Wickes 1881, Preface, 5–7; see also Pitcher 2023), not to identify and explain the complex linguistic data that they represent; (2) scholars have long acknowledged the prosodic nature of the system (Spanier 1927; Lazarus 1942; Avenary 1963; Janis 1987; Dresher 1994; Strauss 2009; DeCaen and Dresher 2020; Park 2020), but the LCD does not treat the accents as natural speech phenomena; (3) the LCD is a philological algorithm with no theoretical basis outside of itself; (4) the LCD reduces the accentual system to pausal segmentation; (5) a cross-linguistic complexity model provides a more accurate description of the accentual system, integrating its seemingly disparate features (viz. melody, stress, prosodic phrase structure, syntax interface, and meaning); and (6) a cross-linguistic complexity model provides the necessary theoretical framework to test and substantiate the complex dimensions of the accentual system's features, structures, and functions. At its core, a cross-linguistic complexity model for the accentual system recognises that the multifaceted dimensions of language—including tonal and metrical structure, syntax, semantics, and discourse-pragmatics—comprise a prosodic system, and this model seeks to account for these dimensions within a comprehensive linguistic analysis.

The basis for this new analysis is partly grounded in the oral orientation of traditional descriptions of the accents and the notion of recitation found therein (see Spanier 1927, 9–17; Crowther 2015, 54–63; Eldar 2018, 53–56; Shoshany 2022, 23–24, 27–28; see also Khan 2013, 37, 43, 47; Khan 2020a, 1–3, 49–53), as well as the system's close association with the vocalic phonology of the orally performed text (Khan 2013, 37–65; Eldar 2018, 85–88; Khan 2020a, 96–97, 2020b, 1–3; Posegay 2021, 25–26, 38–42, 82–84, 131; see also Crowther 2015, 50–51, 62–63). Furthermore, according to Yeivin (1980, 158), the accents are traditionally understood to perform three functions: (1) to represent the melodies that accompany the reading of the text, (2) to mark the locus of lexical stress, and (3) to mark semantic units (1980, 158)—that is, to contribute to the meaning of the text. A cross-linguistic complexity model unifies these functions within the theoretical framework of prosodic phonology. Within this model, the accentual graphemes constitute a prosodic orthography, where conjunctive and disjunctive graphemes are iconic representations of pitch accents at three levels of contrastive pitch—low, high, and extra high (Pitcher 2023; see also Wickes 1887, 13–14; Lazarus 1942, 283–86; Pitcher 2020, 145–58, 189–92;)—embedded within two domains of prosodic phrase structure. In other words, the orthography of the accents represents pitch fluctuations in the flow of speech that are associated with the locus of lexical stress, with disjunctive accents additionally indicating the locus of two types of cross-linguistically distinct phrasal boundaries—namely, those of the intermediate phrase (φ) and the intonational phrase (ι).

This cross-linguistic complexity model, however, not only identifies the precise nature of the accentual system but also provides a way to assess its functional semantic features. For example, relative clauses, which have attested cross-linguistic prosodic features (Nespor and Vogel 2007, 188), provide an accessible syntactic domain to test how the prosodic system represented by the accents contributes to the meaning of the biblical text. Semantically non-restrictive relative clauses, which provide supplemental information for an already identifiable referent, form intonational phrases separate from their head nouns. Semantically restrictive relative clauses, which modify the head noun by restricting the identification of the referent, form cohesive intonational phrases with their head nouns.[11]

---

[11] The prosodic data of relative clauses within the 21 Books of the Hebrew Bible also include prosodic formats that are prosodically ambiguous with regard to restriction (Pitcher 2020, 333–55). Note that this type of prosodic ambiguity has been attested in Birkner's (2012) study on the prosodic realisations of relative clauses in German. Birkner's

These cross-linguistic prosodic features, which distinguish the semantic restriction of relative clauses, are present in the prosodic record of the Masoretic Text. Example (1) illustrates a Tiberian Hebrew relative clause that is semantically restrictive, where the head noun (בֵּן) shares a cohesive intonational phrase (ι) with its relative clause (אֲשֶׁר־יָלְדָה הָגָר):

(1) ((וַתֵּלֶד הָגָר) φ (לְאַבְרָם) φ (בֵּן) φ)ι
((וַיִּקְרָא אַבְרָם שֶׁם־בְּנוֹ) φ (אֲשֶׁר־יָלְדָה הָגָר) φ (יִשְׁמָעֵאל:) φ)ι

((and.she.bore Hagar)φ (to.Abram)φ (son)φ)ι
((and.he.called Abram name.of-his.son)φ (whom-she.bore Hagar)φ (Ishmael)φ)ι

'And Hagar bore to Abram a son. And Abram called the name of his son whom Hagar bore, Ishmael.' (Gen. 16.15)

Example (2) illustrates a Tiberian Hebrew relative clause that is semantically non-restrictive, where the proper head noun (יְהוָה) and relative clause (אֲשֶׁר הוֹצִיאֲךָ) constitute separate intonational phrases (ι).

(2) ((הִשָּׁמֶר לְךָ֫) φ)ι
((פֶּן־תִּשְׁכַּח) φ (אֶת־יְהוָה) φ)ι
((אֲשֶׁר הוֹצִיאֲךָ) φ (מֵאֶרֶץ מִצְרַיִם) φ (מִבֵּית עֲבָדִים:) φ)ι

((be.guarded for.yourself)φ)ι
((lest-you.forget)φ (ACC-LORD)φ)ι
((who he.brought.you)φ (from.land.of Egypt)φ (from.house.of slaves)φ)ι

---

study demonstrates that these prosodic realisations are "more heterogeneous than... presented in grammar books, complying neither with dichotomous semantics nor with the two postulated formats" (2012, 20).

'Guard yourselves, lest you forget the LORD, who brought you out of the land of Egypt, from the house of slavery.' (Deut. 6.12)

Another example of the semantic feature of the Masoretic accentual system involves the disambiguation of tripartite verbless clauses from verbless clauses with left dislocation. Using a cross-linguistic framework, Naudé and Miller-Naudé (2017, 233) note that syntactic left dislocation "involves a gap at the boundary between the dislocated constituent and the matrix sentence," which can be realised by a pause, interjection (Berman-Aronson and Grosu 1976), or intonational contour (Korchin 2015, 14–15). Naudé and Miller-Naudé use this gap feature to disambiguate the subject NP of a tripartite verbless clause from a left-dislocated NP construction. They observe that a left-dislocated NP in the biblical text is phonologically characterised by a disjunctive accent that separates it from the matrix clause, while the pronoun of a tripartite clause (PRON) is phonologically conjoined to the subject NP. The prosodic formats of these two types of constructions confirm this analysis.

Example (3) exhibits the prosodic format of a left-dislocated verbless construction, where a prosodic phrase boundary separates the 3ms subject pronoun (הוּא) from the topicalised NP (וְחָ֨ם).

(3) ⸤(φ(וְחָ֨ם))
⸤(φ(:אֲבִ֥י כְנָֽעַן) φ(הוּא))

((and.Ham)φ)⸤
((he)φ (father.of Canaan)φ)⸤
'As for Ham, he was the father of Canaan.' (Gen. 9:18)

Example (4) exhibits the prosodic format of a tripartite construction, where the 3ms pronoun (הוּא, i.e., PRON) shares the same internal intermediate phrase with the subject NP (הָאָשָׁם).[12]

(4) ((כִּי)φ (כְּחַטָּאת)φ (הָאָשָׁם הוּא)φ (לַכֹּהֵן)φ)ι

((for)φ (as.the.sin-offering)φ (the.guilt-offering PRON)φ (to.the.priest)φ)ι

'For just like the sin-offering, the guilt-offering belongs to the priest.' (Lev. 14:13)

These examples demonstrate that a cross-linguistic complexity approach to the Masoretic accents can more precisely identify and unify what is already known about the system, while also providing scientific avenues for exploring its semantic and discourse-pragmatic functions.

4.0. Conclusion

This chapter introduced Complexity Theory, a metatheory whose principles provide a framework for understanding language as a complex system, in order to introduce the merits and budding developments of complexity thinking in the study of biblical texts. The core attributes of a complex system were presented along with an overview of the ways in which complexity thinking has been applied thus far to five areas of biblical scholarship: diachrony, language pedagogy, translation theory, syntax, and the Masoretic accents of the Hebrew Bible. These studies have demonstrated the fruitful outcomes of such an approach and

---

[12] Naudé and Miller-Naudé (2017, 223) describe the pronoun in a tripartite verbless clause as a "last resort syntactic strategy" for disambiguating the subject NP.

provide models for pursuing similar complexity approaches to linguistic research in biblical studies.

Complexity Theory treats an object of study as part of an integrated and dynamic whole, not as an isolated or self-contained phenomenon. Within the domain of language and culture, this metatheory aims to describe the complex nature of linguistic phenomena as shaped by the interaction of multiple internal dimensions and external influences, rather than as contained within a particular autonomous analytical silo. Most crucially, a complexity approach to biblical scholarship provides the researcher with a model for thinking about the impact of adjacent and interrelated phenomena on the object of study, and for understanding how aspects of biblical languages and texts fit into larger systems of language and culture, ultimately offering "greater coherence in explaining what [is] already know[n]" (Larsen-Freeman and Cameron 2008, 11). A complexity approach, then, can serve as a counterbalance to the powerful scholarly inclination to isolate one's object of study, encouraging the development of a research programme that takes into account the larger systems in which the phenomenon occurs.

5.0. Further Reading

5.1. Dynamic Processes, Chaos Theory, and Complexity Theory

1. Gleick (1987)
2. Waldrop (1992)
3. Lorenz (1994)
4. Van Geert (2003)

5. Dooley (2009)

5.2. Complexity Approach to Applied Linguistics

1. Larsen-Freeman (1997; 2013)
2. Larsen-Freeman and Cameron (2008)
3. Ellis (2008)
4. Ellis and Larsen-Freeman (2009a)
5. Beckner et al. (2009)

5.3. Complexity Approach to Translation and Biblical Studies

1. Marais (2014; 2019a; 2019b)
2. Naudé (2012)
3. Naudé and Miller-Naudé (2017; 2019)
4. Miller-Naudé and Naudé (2014; 2020)
5. Pitcher (2020)
6. Scheumann (2020)
7. Reid (2021)

References

Arthur, W. Brian. 2013. *Complexity and the Economy*. Oxford: Oxford University Press.

Avenary, Hanoch. 1963. *Studies in the Hebrew, Syrian, and Greek Liturgical Recitative*. Tel Aviv: Israel Music Institute.

Baicchi, Annalisa. 2015. *Construction Learning as a Complex Adaptive System: Psycholinguistic Evidence from L2 Learners of English*. SpringerBriefs in Education Series. London: Springer.

Battram, Arthur. 1998. *Navigating Complexity: The Essential Guide to Complexity Theory in Business and Management*. London: The Industrial Society.

Beckner, Clay, Richard Blythe, Joan Bybee, Morten H. Christiansen, William Croft, Nick C. Ellis, John Holland, Jinyun Ke, Diane Larsen-Freeman, and Tom Schoenemann. 2009. 'Language Is a Complex Adaptive System: Position Paper'. In *Language as a Complex Adaptive System*, edited by Nick C. Ellis and Diane Larsen-Freeman, 1–26. Chichester, UK: John Wiley & Sons Ltd.

Beckner, Clay, and Joan Bybee. 2009. 'A Usage-Based Account of Constituency and Reanalysis'. In *Language as a Complex Adaptive System*, edited by Nick C. Ellis and Diane Larsen-Freeman, 27–46. Chichester, UK: John Wiley & Sons Ltd.

Berman-Aronson, Ruth, and Alexander Grosu. 1976. 'Aspects of the Copula in Modern Hebrew'. In *Studies in Modern Hebrew Syntax and Semantics*, edited by Peter Cole, 265–85. Amsterdam: North-Holland.

Birkner, Karin. 2012. 'Prosodic Formats of Relative Clauses in Spoken German'. In *Prosody and Embodiment in Interactional Grammar*, edited by Bergmann, J. Brenning, M. Pfeiffer, and E. Reber, 19–39. Berlin: De Gruyter.

Blau, Joshua. 2010. *Phonology and Morphology of Biblical Hebrew: An Introduction*. Winona Lake, IN: Eisenbrauns.

Blythe, Richard A., and William A. Croft. 2009. 'The Speech Community in Evolutionary Language Dynamics'. *Language Learning* 59 (1): 47–63.

Chomsky, Noam. 1965. *Aspects of a Theory of Syntax*. Cambridge, MA: The MIT Press.

———. 1995. *The Minimalist Program*. Cambridge, MA: The MIT Press.

Chomsky, Noam, and Morris Halle. 1968. *The Sound Pattern of English*. New York: Harper and Row.

Crowther, Daniel J. 2015. 'The Relevance of the *Te'amim* to the Textual Criticism, Delimitation and Interpretation of Biblical Poetic Texts with Special Reference to the Song of David at Psalm 18 and 2 Samuel 22'. PhD thesis, Trinity College, University of Bristol.

DeCaen, Vincent, and B. Elan Dresher. 2020. 'Pausal Forms and Prosodic Structure in Tiberian Hebrew'. In *Studies in Semitic Vocalisation and Reading Traditions*, edited by Aaron D. Hornkohl and Geoffrey Khan, 331–77. Cambridge Semitic Languages and Cultures 3. Cambridge: Open Book Publishers.

De Lange, N. R. M., Julia G. Krivoruchko, and Cameron Boyd-Taylor (eds). 2009. *Jewish Reception of Greek Bible Versions: Studies in their Use in Late Antiquity and the Middle Ages*. Texts and Studies in Medieval and Early Modern Judaism 23. Tübingen: Mohr Siebeck.

Dooley, Kevin J. 2009. 'The Butterfly Effect of the "Butterfly Effect"'. *Nonlinear Dynamics, Psychology, and Life Sciences*. 13 (3): 279–88.

Dörnyei, Zoltán. 2009. 'Individual Differences: Interplay of Learner Characteristics and Learning Environment'. In *Language as a Complex Adaptive System*, edited by Nick C. Ellis and Diane Larsen-Freeman, 230–48. Chichester, UK: John Wiley & Sons Ltd.

Dresher, B. Elan. 1994. 'The Prosodic Basis of the Tiberian Hebrew System of Accents'. *Language* 70 (1): 1–52.

Eldar, Ilan. 2018. קריאת לפי "הקורא הורייה" ספר של המקרא טעמי תורת הי"א במאה ארץ־ישראל. Jerusalem: Bialik Institute.

Ellis, Nick C. 2008. 'The Dynamics of Second Language Emergence: Cycles of Language Use, Language Change, and Language Acquisition'. *The Modern Language Journal* 92 (2): 232–49.

Ellis, Nick C., and Diane Larsen-Freeman (eds). 2009a. *Language as a Complex Adaptive System*. Oxford: Blackwell.

———. 2009b. 'Constructing a Second Language: Analyses and Computational Simulations of the Emergence of Linguistic Constructions'. In *Language as a Complex Adaptive System*, edited by Nick C. Ellis and Diane Larsen-Freeman, 90–125. Chichester, UK: John Wiley & Sons Ltd.

Gell-Mann, Murray. 1994. *The Quark and the Jaguar: Adventures in the Simple and the Complex*. New York: W.H. Freeman and Company.

Gesenius, Wilhelm. 1910. *Gesenius' Hebrew Grammar*. 2nd ed. Edited by E. Kautzsch and A. E. Cowley. Oxford: Clarendon Press. Electronic Edition.

Giddens, A. 1993. *Sociology*. 2nd ed. Cambridge: Polity Press.

Givón, Thomas. 2009. *The Genesis of Syntactic Complexity: Diachrony, Ontogeny, Neuro-cognition, Evolution*. Philadelphia: Benjamins.

Gleick, James. 1987. *Chaos: Making a New Science.* New York: Viking Penguin.

Harris, Alice C., and Lyle Campbell. 1995. *Historical Syntax in Cross-Linguistic Perspective.* Cambridge: Cambridge University Press.

Heine, Bernd, and Tania Kuteva. 2002. *World Lexicon of Grammaticalization.* Cambridge: Cambridge University Press.

Heine, Bernd, and Mechtild Reh. 1984. *Grammaticalization and Reanalysis in African Languages.* Hamburg: Helmut Buske Verlag.

Janis, Norman. 1987. 'A Grammar of the Biblical Accents'. PhD thesis, Harvard University.

Joüon, Paul, and Takamitsu Muraoka. 2006. *A Grammar of Biblical Hebrew.* 2nd ed. Rome: Pontifical Biblical Institute.

Khan, Geoffrey. 2013. *A Short Introduction to the Tiberian Masoretic Bible and Its Reading Tradition.* 2nd ed. Piscataway, NJ: Gorgias Press.

———. 2019. 'Copulas, Cleft Sentences and Focus Markers in Biblical Hebrew'. In *Ancient Texts and Modern Readers: Studies in Ancient Hebrew Linguistics and Bible Translation*, edited by Gideon R. Kotze, Christian S. Locatell, and John A. Messarra, 14–62. Leiden: Brill.

———. 2020a. *The Tiberian Pronunciation Tradition of Biblical Hebrew.* Vol. 1. Cambridge Semitic Languages and Cultures 1. Cambridge: Open Book Publishers.

———. 2020b. *The Tiberian Pronunciation Tradition of Biblical Hebrew.* Vol. 2. Cambridge Semitic Languages and Cultures 1. Cambridge: Open Book Publishers.

Korchin, Paul. 2015. 'Suspense and Authority Amid Biblical Hebrew Front Dislocation'. *Journal of Hebrew Scriptures* 15, article 1. doi.org/10.5508/jhs.2015.v15.a1.

Larsen-Freeman, Diane. 1997. 'Chaos/Complexity Science and Second Language Acquisition'. *Applied Linguistics* 18 (2): 141–65.

———. 2013. 'Complexity Theory: A New Way to Think'. *Revista Brasileira de Linguística Aplicada* 13 (2): 369–73.

Larsen-Freeman, Diane, and Lynne Cameron. 2008. *Complex Systems and Applied Linguistics*. Oxford: Oxford University Press.

Lazarus, Harris M. 1942. 'The Rationale of the Tiberian Graphic Accentuation (XXI Books)'. In *Essays in Honour of the Very Rev. Dr. J.H. Hertz, Chief Rabbi of the United Hebrew Congregations of the British Empire, on the Occasion of His Seventieth Birthday, September 25th 1942*, edited by Isadore Epstein, Ephraim Levine, Cecil Roth, and Joseph H. Hertz, 271–91. London: Edward Goldston.

Lehmann, Christian. 2015. *Thoughts on Grammaticalization*. 3rd ed. Classics in Linguistics 1. Berlin: Language Science Press.

Leather, Jonathan, and Jet van Dam (eds). 2003. *Ecology of Language Acquisition*. Dordrecht: Kluwer Academic Publishers.

Lorenz, Edward N. 1994. *The Essence of Chaos*. Seattle: University of Washington Press.

Marais, Kobus. 2014. *Translation Theory and Development Studies: A Complexity Theory Approach*. New York: Routledge.

———. 2019a. *A (Bio)Semiotic Theory of Translation: The Emergence of Social-Cultural Reality*. London: Routledge.

———. 2019b. 'Translation Complex Rather Than Translation Turns? Considering the Complexity of Translation'. *Syn-Théses: Interdisciplinarity and Translation Studies* 9–10: 43–55.

Miller-Naudé, Cynthia L., and Jacobus A. Naudé. 2014. 'A Typological, Complex Systems Approach to the Teaching of Biblical Hebrew Reading'. In *Discourse, Dialogue, and Debate in the Bible: Essays in Honour of Frank H. Polak*, edited by Athalya Brenner-Idan, 92–106. Sheffield: Sheffield Phoenix Press.

———. 2020. 'A Programmatic Proposal for the Study of Biblical Hebrew as a Language'. *Journal for Semitics* 29 (2): 1–29.

Mufwene, Salikoko S. 2008. *Language Evolution: Contact, Competition and Change*. London: Continuum.

Nassaji, Hossein. 2009. 'Issues in Second-Language Reading: Implications for Acquisition and Instruction'. *Reading Research Quarterly* 46: 173–84.

Naudé, Jacobus A. 2012. 'Diachrony in Biblical Hebrew and a Theory of Language Change and Diffusion'. In *Diachrony in Biblical Hebrew*, edited by Cynthia L. Miller-Naudé and Ziony Zevit, 61–81. Linguistic Studies in Ancient West Semitic 8. Winona Lake, IN: Eisenbrauns.

Naudé, Jacobus A., and Cynthia L. Miller-Naudé. 2017. 'At the Interface of Syntax and Prosody: Differentiating Left Dislocated and Tripartite Verbless Clauses in Biblical Hebrew'. *Stellenbosch Papers in Linguistics* 48: 223–38.

———. 2019. 'Sacred Writings and Their Translations as Complex Phenomena: The Book of Ben Sira in the Septuagint as a Case in Point'. In *Complexity Thinking in Translation Studies: Methodological Considerations*, edited by Kobus Marais and Reine Meylaerts, 180–215. New York: Routledge.

Nespor, Marina, and Irene Vogel. 2007. *Prosodic Phonology*. Berlin: Mouton de Gruyter.

Nord, Christiane. 2018. *Translation as a Purposeful Activity: Functionalist Approaches Explained*. 2nd ed. London: Routledge.

Park, Sung Jin. 2020. *The Fundamentals of Hebrew Accents: Divisions and Exegetical Roles Beyond Syntax*. Cambridge: Cambridge University Press.

Pearce, Neil, and Franco Merletti. 2006. 'Complexity, Simplicity, and Epidemiology'. *International Journal of Epidemiology* 35 (3): 515–19.

Pintzuk, Susan. 2003. 'Variationist Approaches to Syntactic Change'. In *The Handbook of Historical Linguistics*, edited by Brian D. Joseph and Richard D. Janda, 509–28. Malden, MA: Blackwell.

Pitcher, Sophia. 2020. 'A Prosodic Model for Tiberian Hebrew: A Complexity Approach to the Features, Structures, and Functions of the Masoretic Cantillation Accents'. PhD thesis, University of the Free State.

———. 2021. 'Towards a Prosodic Model for Tiberian Hebrew: An Intonation-based Analysis'. *Stellenbosch Papers in Linguistics Plus* 63: 1–27.

———. 2023. 'The Medieval Prosodic Orthography of the Tiberian Masoretic Reading Tradition'. *Journal of Semitic Studies*. https://doi.org/10.1093/jss/fgad009.

Porter, Stanley E. 2021. 'The Septuagint: A Greek-Text-Oriented Approach'. In *The T&T Clark Handbook of Septuagint Research*, edited by William A. Ross and W. Edward Glenny, 363–37. London: T&T Clark.

Posegay, Nick. 2021. *Points of Contact: The Shared Intellectual History of Vocalisation in Syriac, Arabic, and Hebrew*. Cambridge Semitic Languages and Cultures 10. Cambridge: Open Book Publishers.

Reid, Phil. 2021. 'A Preliminary Investigation into the Samaritan Pentateuch as an Intralingual Translation'. MA dissertation, University of the Free State.

Revell, Ernest J. 1981. 'Syntactic/Semantic Structure and the Reflexes of Original Short a in Tiberian Pointing'. *Hebrew Annual Review* 5: 75–100.

———. 2015. *The Pausal System: Divisions in the Hebrew Biblical Text as Marked by Voweling and Stress Position*. Edited by Raymond de Hoop and Paul Sanders. Sheffield: Sheffield Phoenix Press.

———. 2016. 'Terminal Markers in the Masoretic Text'. *Journal of Semitic Studies* 61 (1): 67–84.

Reiss, Katharina, and Hans J. Vermeer. 2014. *Towards a General Theory of Translational Action: Skopos Theory Explained*. Translated by Christiane Nord. London: Routledge.

Robinson, Douglas. 2017. *Schleiermacher's Icoses: Social Ecologies of the Different Methods of Translating*. Bucharest: Zeta Books.

Ross, William A. 2021. 'The Septuagint and Modern Language Translations'. In *The T&T Clark Handbook of Septuagint*

Research, edited by William A. Ross and W. Edward Glenny, 329–34. London: T&T Clark.

Sawyer, John F. A. 1999. *Sacred Languages and Sacred Texts*. Religion in the First Christian Centuries. London: Routledge.

Scheumann, Jesse. 2020. 'A Syntactic Analysis of Phrasal Coordination in Biblical Hebrew'. PhD thesis, University of the Free State.

Schwartzhaupt, Bruno Moraes. 2013. 'Conceiving Language as a Complex Adaptive System: A Problem for SLA Researchers?'. *SIGNO* 38 (65): 261–72.

Selkirk, Elisabeth. 1981. 'On Prosodic Structure and Its Relation to Syntactic Structure'. In *Nordic Prosody II*, edited by Thorstein Fretheim, 111–40. Trondheim: Tapir.

———. 2011. 'The Syntax-Phonology Interface'. In *The Handbook of Phonological Theory*, 2nd ed., edited by John Goldsmith, Jason Riggle, and Alan Yu, 435–83. Oxford: Blackwell.

Shoshany, Ronit. 2022. למסורת בהשוואה הבבלית: במסורת המקרא טעמי הטברנית. Jerusalem: The Ben-Zvi Institute.

Spanier, Arthur. 1927. *Die Massoretischen Akzente*. Berlin: Akademie-Verlag.

Spivey, Michael. 2007. *The Continuity of Mind*. Oxford Psychology Series 40. Oxford: Oxford University Press.

Strauss, Tobie. 2009. 'חלוקת על אחרים וגורמים פרוזודיים גורמים השפעת ספרים א"כ טעמי'. PhD dissertation, The Hebrew University of Jerusalem.

Ulrich, Eugene. 2015. *The Dead Sea Scrolls and the Developmental Composition of the Bible*. Supplements to Vetus Testamentum 169. Leiden: Brill.

Van den Heever, Cornelius M. 2013. 'Idioms in Biblical Hebrew: Towards Their Identification and Classification with Special Reference to 1 and 2 Samuel'. PhD dissertation, Stellenbosch University.

Van der Merwe, Christo H. J., Jacobus A. Naudé, and Jan H. Kroeze. 2017. *A Biblical Hebrew Reference Grammar*. 2nd ed. London: Bloomsbury.

Van Geert, Paul. 2003. 'Dynamic Systems Approaches and Modeling of Developmental Processes'. In *Handbook of Developmental Psychology*, edited by J. Valsiner and K. Connolly, 640–72. London: Sage.

Vermeer, Hans J. 2004. 'Skopos and Commission in Translational Action'. In *The Translation Studies Reader*, 2nd ed., edited by Lawrence Venuti, 227–38. London: Routledge.

Von Bertalanffy, Ludwig. 1950. 'An Outline for General Systems Theory'. *British Journal for the Philosophy of Science* 12 (1): 134–65.

Waddington, Conrad H. 1940. *Organisers and Genes*. Cambridge: Cambridge University Press.

Waldrop, M. Mitchell. 1992. *Complexity: The Emerging Science at the Edge of Order and Chaos*. New York: Simon & Schuster.

Waltke, Bruce K., and Michael O'Connor. 1990. *An Introduction to Biblical Hebrew Syntax*. Winona Lake, IN: Eisenbrauns.

Weinreich, Uriel, William Labov, and Marvin Herzog. 1968. 'Empirical Foundations for a Theory of Language Change'. In *Directions for Historical Linguistics: A Symposium*, edited by W.P. Lehmann and Y. Malkeil, 95–195. Austin, TX: University of Texas Press.

Whaley, Lindsay. 1997. *Introduction to Typology: The Unity and Diversity of Language*. Thousand Oaks, CA: Sage Publications.

Whitehead, Alfred N. 1929. *Process and Reality: An Essay in Cosmology*. New York: Macmillan.

Wickes, William. 1881. *A Treatise on the Accentuation of the Three So-Called Poetical Books of the Old Testament, Psalms, Proverbs, and Job*. Oxford: Clarendon Press.

———. 1887. *A Treatise on the Accentuation of the Twenty-One So-Called Prose Books of the Old Testament*. Oxford: Clarendon Press.

Yeivin, Israel. 1980. *Introduction to the Tiberian Masorah*. Translated and edited by E. J. Revell. Missoula: Scholars Press.

GLOSSARY

Ablaut
    Morphological vowel alternations in Indo-European languages.

Adjunct
    An optional or omissable constituent in a predication (contrast *complement*).

Alveolar
    A place of articulation behind the upper teeth.

Anaphor
    A grammatical element without independent reference, which gains its reference from an antecedent within the same structure (i.e., reflexive pronouns, reciprocal pronouns).

Artificial Intelligence
    Techniques that enable computers to perform intellectual tasks normally performed by humans.

Bilabial
    A place of articulation between the lips.

Case Structure
    Case (capitalised) refers to the assignment of abstract grammatical relations (Cases) within syntactic structure.

Comment
    The material of a sentence that is the main point. Typically, it is new information. In Topic-Comment analysis, the Topic is the foundation on which the Comment is shared.

Glossary

Complement

A required constituent in a predication (e.g., direct object; contrast *adjunct*).

Computer Linguistics

Any form of linguistic analysis with computational methods.

Concatenative Morphology

The interweaving of vowel and consonant morphology in Semitic languages.

Constituent Negation

Negation with scope only over a constituent (contrast *sentential negation*).

Contextualising Constituent

Or Topic Constituent, part of a sentence that specially signals a point of connection with the context.

Copies

See *traces*.

Coronal

A class of consonants articulated with the forward portion of the tongue.

Corpus Linguistics

Linguistic analysis based on text corpora. It studies the language as it is expressed in a corpus, be it a purposefully designed corpus (such as, e.g., the British National Corpus) or a corpus that has come down to us through tradition (such as the Old and New Testaments).

Debuccalisation

The loss of a place of articulation.

Deep Structure

The underlying structure of language.

Degemination

The shortening of consonantal articulation.

Deep Learning

Extraction of patterns from data with the help of neural networks. A subgroup of machine learning.

E-Language

External language (see *language performance*).

Empty Category

A category that is not overtly present in surface structure but is present in the underlying (deep) structure (see also *null constituent*).

Extraposition

The movement of a constituent to the right (final) edge of the sentence (see also *topicalisation* and contrast *right dislocation*).

Focus

This term may indicate (1) the salient information of a sentence; (2) for generic emphasis, covering both Topic and Focus in Functional Grammar, including either part of a sentence or a whole sentence itself; or, in Functional Grammar, (3) specially marked salient information. The Focus may be marked by word order positions, intonation, or lexically.

Functional Categories

Categories within Universal Grammar whose members are items with no descriptive content, namely, D(eterminer),

T(ense), Asp(ect), M(ood) C (complementiser/coordinator; contrast *lexical categories*).

Fricative
A class of consonants articulated with a narrow opening in the vocal tract.

Geminate
The lengthening of consonantal articulation.

Generative Linguistics
A model of linguistic analysis developed by Noam Chomsky that considers grammar as a set of rules that generates grammatical sentences in any given language from an innate universal grammatical structure.

Glottal
A class of consonants articulated with the glottis.

Grammaticalisation
The process by which a lexical item loses its semantic content and develops a grammatical function.

Heavy Extraposition
The movement of a constituent to the right (final) edge of construction across a sentence boundary.

Heavy Topicalisation
The movement of a constituent to the left (initial) edge of a construction across a sentence boundary.

I-Language
Internal language (see *language competence*).

Information Structure
The way a message is presented to an audience so that new information is built upon presumably shared information,

which may be explicit or implicit. The basic terms of information packaging are part of Topic-Comment analysis.

Interdental

A place of articulation between the teeth and the tongue.

Intermediate Phrase

The intermediate phrase is the minor phrase domain of the prosodic hierarchy above the prosodic word. The intermediate phrase organises words into a cohesive prosodic unit. It is the main prosodic domain of the syntax-phonology interface.

Intonational Phrase

The intonational phrase is the major phrase domain of the prosodic hierarchy above the intermediate phrase. The intonational phrase is primarily associated with post-lexical meaning (viz. meaning above the word).

Isogloss

A linguistic innovation linking two or more speech communities.

Language Competence

The finite internal language knowledge of speakers that allows them to produce an infinite number of sentences and their meanings.

Language Diffusion

A diachronic process by which a dominant language spreads.

Language Typology

A cross-linguistic comparison and classification of languages and their components according to shared features.

Language Performance

An individual speakers' use of language knowledge in acts of communication, namely, speech production and speech perception.

Laryngeal

A class of sounds hypothesised for Proto-Indo-European with direct reflexes in Hittite.

Last Resort

The principle that a grammatical operation applies only when there is no other means of satisfying a grammatical requirement.

Left Dislocation

A constituent that occurs before the left (initial) edge of the sentence and is represented within the sentence with a resumptive element (see also *right dislocation* and contrast *topicalisation*).

Lexical Categories

Categories within Universal Grammar whose members are items with descriptive content, namely, N(oun), V(erb), A (adjective/adverb), and P(reposition; contrast *functional categories*).

Linked Data

A method for publishing structured data using vocabularies that allow for interlinking with other data and useful semantic queries.

Logical Form

The underlying semantic representation of grammatical structure.

Machine Learning
>Algorithms that enable computers to learn without being explicitly programmed; a subgroup of Artificial Intelligence.

Merge
>Movement of elements within the Minimalist Programme.

Morpheme
>The minimal discrete unit of meaning in language.

Move α
>Movement of elements within Principles-and-Parameters.

Natural Language Processing
>The design and analysis of algorithms for processing and representing natural human language.

Null Constituent
>A clause constituent that is present in the deep structure but not realised in the surface structure (also called *zero constituent*; see also *empty category*).

Null Head
>The head of a phrase that is present in the deep structure but not realised in the surface structure.

Null Subject Parameter
>A parameter present in some languages allowing a finite verb to occur without an overt subject in surface structure (also called *pro-drop parameter*).

Open Science
>A movement that aims at more open scholarly practices, in which research data, software and publications are made available for reuse.

Palatal

A class of consonants articulated with the palate.

Parameter

A language feature that may have different 'settings' in different languages (e.g., the pro-drop parameter is present in some languages and absent in other languages).

Pharyngeal

A class of consonants articulated with the pharynx.

Phone

Any distinct sound unit.

Phoneme

The minimal sound unit; a building block for morphemes.

Phonological Form

The final, phonological shape of language at surface structure.

Pitch Accents

Pitch fluctuations in the flow of speech that are associated with accented syllables.

Pro-Drop Parameter

See *null subject parameter*.

Prosodic Hierarchy

The prosodic hierarchy is an abstract structure for conceptualising the phonological organisation of constituent domains within the flow of speech (e.g., higher-level constituents include the prosodic word, intermediate phrase, intonational phrase, and utterance). Since prosodic domains are organised from syntactic structures, the prosodic hierarchy mediates an indirect syntax-phonology interface.

Prosodic Orthography

A conventionalised writing system of the phrase structure and key phonological and phonetic features (e.g., intonation, stress, segmentation) of a prosodic system.

Prosodic Phonology

A subfield of linguistics that provides the cross-linguistic theoretical framework for understanding the complex systems of sounds and interfaces that govern the organisation of speech.

Prosodic Phrase Structure

The grouping of words in an utterance, characterised by smaller units embedded in larger ones.

Prosodic System

A complex system (viz. interfacing with other dimensions of language including phonology, syntax, and discourse-pragmatics) that regulates the way spoken language is realised. The phonetic features of a prosodic system are pitch, stress, segmentation, and voice quality.

Prosodic Word

Any word in an utterance that bears stress. In the prosodic orthography of Tiberian Hebrew (viz. the Masoretic accentual system), prosodic words are marked by either conjunctive or disjunctive graphemes.

Proto-Indo-European

The reconstructed ancestor of the Indo-European family of languages.

Proto-Language

A reconstructed common ancestor of a family of languages.

Right Dislocation

A constituent that occurs beyond the right (end) edge of the sentence and is represented within the sentence with a resumptive element (see also *left dislocation* and contrast *extraposition*).

Role and Reference Grammar

A model of linguistic analysis developed by William A. Foley and Robert D. Van Valin, in which language is conceived as a system of communicative social action and which focuses on the communicative functions of grammatical structures.

Sentential Negation

Negation with scope over the entire sentence.

Sibilant

A class of fricatives with acoustically prominent amplitude and pitch.

Spirantisation

The change from a stop articulation to a fricative.

Structuralism

A model of linguistic analysis developed building on the works of Ferdinand de Saussure, in which language is conceived as a self-contained system whose elements are defined by their relationship to other elements within the system.

Stop

A class of consonants produced by a momentary obstruction of airflow in the vocal tract.

Surface Structure

The overt realisation of language structure.

Supervised Learning

A form of machine learning in which the machine learns from human-labelled examples.

Suppletive Morphology

A paradigm with phonemically unrelated morphemes.

Suprasegmental

Phonetic features that map across multiple segments.

Syntax-Phonology Interface

The syntax-phonology interface refers to the interaction of syntactic constituents with phonological constituents. It is primarily observed in the phonological rules that reference syntactic constituents as the domains for their application.

Tagmemics

A model of linguistic analysis developed by Kenneth Pike, which takes the tagmeme as the basic unity of grammatical description, a tagmeme being defined as the correlation of a grammatical slot and the class of words by which it can be filled.

Topicalisation

The movement of a constituent to the left (initial) edge of the sentence (see also *extraposition* and contrast *left dislocation*).

Theme/Rheme

Alternate names for Topic and Comment, respectively.

Thetic
> Sentences where the whole sentence is presented as Comment material, without shared orientating information. May answer an implied question, 'What happened?'

Topic
> This term may indicate (1) the subject matter of a text; (2) information assumed to be shared and that becomes the introduction to material in a sentence that is the main message, called the Comment; or, in Functional Grammar, (3) a pragmatic function that can activate word order placement rules.

Traces
> The original positions of moved elements in the underlying structure.

Transformational Grammar
> Part of the theory of generative linguistics, that refers to the transformations that are used to produce sentences.

Triphthong
> A sequence of vowels flanking an intervocalic glide in Semitic languages.

Universal Grammar
> Part of the theory of generative linguistics that refers to the hypothesised common properties of language shared by all natural languates.

Unsupervised Learning
> A form of machine learning in which the machine has to detect patterns in the unlabelled data by itself.

Velar

The place of articulation between the velum and tongue body.

INDICES

Index of Passages Cited

Bible

Acts
  2.9–11, 255
Amos
  4.10, 33
1 Chron.
  15.1, 38
2 Chron.
  15.11, 42
Dan.
  11.20, 33
  11.45, 194–95
Deut.
  1.30, 34
  6.12, 309
Eccl.
  1.4, 85
Exod.
  10.13, 40
  11.4, 28
  21.4, 303
Ezek.
  11.23, 147
  16.15, 138
  16.58, 34
Ezra
  2.64, 40

Gen.
  1.2–3, 98
  1.29, 40
  3.14, 40
  3.24, 147
  4.1, 94, 96
  4.15, 250
  44.3–4, 101
  45.8, 40
  6.9, 79
  8.22, 284
  9.18, 309
  10.22, 195
  14.5, 80
  14.8–9, 32–33
  15.14, 84
  16.15, 308
  20.5, 80
  22.1, 97
  22.2, 36
  22.2–16, 98
  24.66, 43
  27.45, 43
  29.16, 44
  31.17, 20, 99
  31.18–19, 100
  31.32, 82
  31.43, 34
  33.7, 303
  34.31, 29
  37.28, 99

37.36, 99
39.1, 99
45.3, 102
Isa.
  41.12, 32
  48.17, 45
  58.2, 82
Jer.
  1.11–12, 83
  2.20, 138
  7.26, 45
  23.21, 39
  30.20, 147
  48.19–20, 89
Job
  23.8, 145
Joel
  2.1, 137
John
  1.1, 106
  1.2-5, 107
Jonah
  1.4, 95
  1.5, 99
  4.5, 132
Josh.
  9.8–9, 81
Judg.
  5.1, 250
  5.11, 213
  18.31, 40
1 Kgs
  1.14, 93
  3.5, 81

8.29, 284
Lam.
  1.18, 36
Lev.
  7.20, 34
  14.13, 310
Luke
  8.51, 151
Mark
  1.34, 151
  2.4, 9, 11–12, 198
  4.21, 198
  5.9, 15, 198
  6.27, 37, 198
  6.55, 198
  7.3–4, 198
  12.14, 16–17, 198
  12.15, 198
  12.42, 198
  13.17, 198
  14.5, 198
  14.21, 198
  15.15–16, 198
  15.39, 44–45, 198
Matt.
  6.12, 150
  8.22, 151
  12.31, 150
  16.5–8, 135
  16.12–13, 141
  18.27, 150
Neh.
  13.5, 38

Num.
  9.15, 80
  13.32, 28
Prov.
  8.22, 147
Ps.
  29.11, 103
  51.18–19, 153
  51.5, 102
  90.4, 138
  139.5, 145
  140.3, 40
Rev.
  11.9, 151
1 Sam.
  1.16, 81
  4.1, 82
  4.16–17, 90
  9.10–11, 92
  17.14, 35
  20.23, 35
2 Sam.
  2.12, 303
  3.24–25, 91
  6.22, 31
  6.23, 30
  24.3, 31
Zech.
  6.10, 30

Dead Sea Scrolls

1QIsa[a]
  XL:23, 45

4Q506
  131–132.IV.13, 45

Index of Authors

Abbegg, Martin, Jr., 224
Abney, Steven, 21–22
Allen, Rutger, 216
Andersen, Francis, 223, 226–27, 241, 247, 262
Aquinas, Thomas, 225
Arthur, W. Brian, 278
Atkinson, Ian, 89, 110
Avenary, Hanoch, 305
Babbage, Charles, 225
Bach, Emmon, 48
Baicchi, Annalisa, 274, 276
Barr, James, 238
Battram, Arthur, 278
Beckner, Clay, 273–74, 280, 285, 312
Bennett, Phil, 148
Berman-Aronson, Ruth, 35, 309
Berman, Joshua, 263
Bickerton, Derek, 87
Birdsell, Brian, 139
Blau, Joshua, 216
Blevins, James, 122
Bloomfield, Leonard, 121
Blythe, Richard, 274
Boas, Franz, 121
Bod, Rens, 232–33, 262
Bopp, Franz, 185
Borer, Hagit, 24, 27, 48
Bosman, Hendrik-Jan, 249

Brettler, Marc, 152
Briggs, Charles, 254
Broccias, Cristiano, 149
Brown, Francis, 254
Brugmann, Karl, 179, 186
Busa, Robert, 225
Bybee, Joan, 3, 175, 274
Cameron, Lynne, 273, 275–80, 282–84, 285–86, 292, 311–12
Campbell, Lyle, 120, 121–22, 217, 286
Canu Højgaard, Christian, 247, 254
Carnie, Andrew, 48
Chadwick, John, 176
Chantraine, Pierre, 216
Chomsky, Noam, 7–27, 48, 68, 122–23, 125, 241, 243–44, 279, 302
Cienki, Alan, 134
Clark, Alexander, 262
Clarke, David, 124
Clivaz, Claire, 262
Colston, Herbert, 131
Cook, John A., 3, 224, 243–44, 262
Cowper, Elizabeth, 44
Croft, William, 126–27, 128, 129, 149, 150, 157, 274
Crowther, Daniel, 306
Cruse, D. Alan, 126–27, 129, 150, 157

Cuykens, Hubert, 118, 125, 128, 157
D'hulst, Lieven, 47
Dąbrowska, Ewa, 157
Dancygier, Barbara, 157
de Blois, Reinier, 155
de Groot, A. D., 239
de Joode, Johan, 245, 249
De Maurio, Tullio, 120
de Saussure, Ferdinand, 3, 120–21, 123, 175, 178
DeCaen, Vincent, 44, 305
Delbrück, Berthold, 179
Den Dikken, Marcel, 47
Dershowitz, Idan, 248, 251, 252, 263
DesCamp, Mary Therese, 152
Descartes, René, 9
Dik, Simon, 67–69, 73, 76, 77–78, 105, 110
Dilthey, Wilhelm, 232
Dirven, René, 158
Divjak, Dagmar, 157
Dooley, Kevin, 312
Dőrnyei, Zoltán, 273
Dorobantu, Marius, 240
Doron, Edit, 36
Dresher, B. Elan, 305
Driver, S. R., 214, 252, 254
Dyk, Janet, 250, 254
Eco, Umberto, 120
Ehrensvärd, Martin, 213–14
Eldar, Ilan, 306
Ellis, Nick, 273, 285, 292, 312

England, Barbara, 47
Evans, Vyvyan, 127–28, 131, 134, 137, 140, 143, 145, 150, 157–58
Everaert, Martin, 47
Fassberg, Steven, 212
Fauconnier, Gilles, 139–40, 142–43, 158
Fillmore, Charles, 134, 149
Fodor, Jerry, 12, 15
Forbes, A. Dean, 223, 226–27, 229, 241, 242, 243, 247, 249, 253, 262
Formigari, Lia, 120
Fortson, Benjamin, 173, 217
Fox, Chris, 262
Freidin, Robert, 122
Fresch, Christopher, 215
Friberg, Barbara, 258
Friberg, Timothy, 258
Fritz, Matthias, 217
Gambier, Yves, 47
Gaon, Saadya, 195
García Ureña, Lourdes, 154
Geeraerts, Dirk, 118, 125–29, 145, 157–58
Gell-Mann, Murray, 278
Gentry, Peter, 216
Gesenius, Wilhelm, 212, 284
Gibbs, Raymond, Jr., 131
Givón, Talmy, 70, 274, 289
Glanz, Oliver, 250, 260
Gleick, James, 311
Goldberg, Adele, 149–50

Grady, Joseph, 137
Green, Joel B., 152
Green, Melanie, 127–28, 131, 134, 137, 140, 143, 145, 150, 152, 158
Grohmann, Kleanthes, 48
Grosu, Alexander, 35, 309
Groves, J. Alan, 227
Gurry, Peter, 260
Gzella, Holger, 217
Haegemann, Liliane, 48
Hamidović, David, 260–61
Hardmeier, Christof, 226–27
Harris, Alice, 286
Harris, Randy, 121
Heine, Bernd, 286
Hengeveld, Kees, 69
Hetzron, Robert, 182
Hock, Hans, 217
Hoftijzer, Jaap, 224
Holmstedt, Robert, 31, 37, 42–44, 224, 243–44, 262
Hornkohl, Aaron, 86, 88, 110, 214
Hornstein, Norbert, 48
Horrocks, Geoffrey, 217
Howe, Bonnie, 124, 151–52, 157
Huehnergard, John, 183, 217
Hurvitz, Avi, 212, 215
Hyams, Nina, 20
Jackendoff, Ray, 14–15, 48
Janda, Laura, 119, 126
Janis, Norman, 305
Jasanoff, Jay, 180

Johnson, Mark, 124, 130, 136, 151
Jones, William, 173
Joseph, Brian, 217
Joseph, John, 120
Joüon, Paul, 284
Jurafsky, Dan, 262
Katz, Jerrold, 12–16, 48
Kay, Paul, 149
Khan, Geoffrey, 88, 90, 92, 195, 286, 306
Kingham, Cody, 224, 242, 245, 263
Kittel, Gerhard, 238
Klein, Jared, 217
Kogan, Leonid, 216
Korchin, Paul, 309
Kraft, Robert, 258
Kroeze, Jan, 45, 155, 262
Kurylowcz, Jerzy, 217
Kuteva, Tania, 286
Lakoff, George, 14–15, 124, 136, 144, 151, 158
Langacker, Ronald, 124, 148, 158
Langslow, David, 217
Lappin, Shalom, 262
Larsen-Freeman, Diane, 273, 275–80, 282–84, 285, 286, 292, 311–12
Lasnik, Howard, 18, 21
Lazarus, Harris, 305, 307
Leather, Jonathan, 280
Lehmann, Christian, 286

Leibniz, Wilhelm, 226
Lewandowska-Tomaszczyk, Barbara, 145
Littlemore, Jeanette, 157
Longacre, Robert, 242
Lorenz, Edward, 311
Marais, Kobus, 278, 280, 281, 284, 296–97, 301, 312
Martin, James, 262
Mayrhofer, Manfred, 217
McKenzie, J. Lachlan, 69, 110
Meeuse, Bas, 250, 261, 263
Merletti, Franco, 278
Miller-Naudé, Cynthia L., 7, 31, 33–35, 38–39, 44–45, 47, 122, 213, 241, 262, 286, 287, 291–301, 309, 312
Mink, Gerd, 260
Moser, Amalia, 216
Moshavi, Adina, 110, 213
Mufwene, Salikoko, 273–74
Muraoka, Takamitsu, 284
Naaijer, Martijn, 245, 250
Nassaji, Hossein, 292
Naudé, Jacobus A., 7, 27, 29–31, 33–34, 35, 36–39, 44–45, 47, 122, 155, 241, 262, 273, 274, 287–301, 309, 312
Nerlich, Brigitte, 124
Nespor, Marina, 307
Noonan, Benjamin, 199, 216
Nord, Christiane, 47
Notarius, Tania, 213
Nunes, Jairo, 48

Nuyts, Jan, 123
O'Connor, Michael, 283–84
Oakley, Todd, 131
Olender, Maurice, 120
Oosting, Reinoud, 250, 262
Osthoff, Hermann, 186
Pagliuca, William, 3
Park, Sung Jin, 305
Pat-El, Na'ama, 183, 217
Pearce, Neil, 278
Perkins, Revere, 3
Pike, Kenneth, 241
Pintzuk, Susan, 289
Pitcher, Sophia, 287, 305, 307, 312
Pollock, J.-Y., 21
Porter, Stanley, 259, 263
Posegay, Nick, 306
Postal, Paul, 12–14, 16, 48
Poswick, R. F., 227, 262
Radford, Andrew, 46, 48
Rashi, 96
Rask, Rasmus, 185
Reh, Mechtild, 286
Reid, Paul, 285, 287, 301, 302, 312
Rendsburg, Gary, 39, 214
Revell, Ernest, 283–84
Rezetko, Robert, 213–14
Richter, Wolfgang, 224
Rix, Helmut, 216
Rizzi, Luigi, 21–22
Robar, Elizabeth, 154
Robins, R. H., 120–21

Robinson, Douglas, 297
Robinson, Peter, 260
Rosch, Eleanor, 144
Ross, William A., 153–54
Rubin, Aaron, 183, 217
Runge, Steven, 104–05, 106, 110, 154, 215–16
Russell, Bertrand, 226
Sáenz-Badillos, Angel, 217
Sandborg-Petersen, Ulrik, 250
Sapir, Edward, 121
Sasse, Hans-Jürgen, 90
Schechter, Solomon, 212
Scheumann, Jesse, 37, 283–84, 287, 302–04, 312
Schleicher, August, 185
Schmid, Hans-Jörg, 134, 137, 150, 158
Schneider, Wolfgang, 224
Schwartzhaupt, Bruno, 275
Sells, Peter, 47
Shoshany, Ronit, 306
Siebesma-Mannens, Femke, 249
Sinclair, Cameron, 44
Snyman, F. P. J., 39
Spanier, Arthur, 305–06
Speelman, Dirk, 249
Spivey, Michael, 278
Strauss, Tobie, 305
Suchard, Benjamin, 216
Sullivan, Karen, 130
Sweetser, Eve, 124, 151–52
Talmy, Leonard, 158
Talstra, Eep, 227, 236, 238, 247

Tan, Randall, 259
Tauber, James, 258
Taylor, John, 124, 144, 145, 148, 157
Tov, Emanuel, 227
Turner, James, 120
Turner, Mark, 139, 143, 158
Ulrich, Eugene, 299
Ungerer, Friedrich, 134, 137, 150, 158
van Altena, Vincent, 255, 256
van Dam, Jet, 280
van den Heever, Cornelius, 285
van der Merwe, Christo, 45, 88, 90, 92, 153, 155, 284
van der Schans, Yanniek, 245
van der Weel, Adriaan, 226, 262
van Geert, Paul, 278, 311
van Gelderen, Elly, 45, 48
Van Hecke, Pierre, 245
van Keulen, Percy, 250
van Peursen, Wido, 224, 232, 235, 241–42, 250, 255, 262–63
van Riemsdijk, Henk, 11, 15, 17, 47–48
Van Valin, Robert, Jr., 70, 123
van Wolde, Ellen, 154
Vegas Montaner, Luis, 231
Veldman, J. G., 255
Ventris, Michael, 176
Verhaar, Peter, 253
Vern, Robyn, 209
Verspoor, Marjolijn, 158

Vervenne, Marc, 227, 231
Veselinova, Ljuba, 45
Vlaardingerbroek, Hannes, 245
Vogel, Irene, 307
von Bertalanffy, Ludwig, 278
von Humboldt, Wilhelm, 8
Wachtel, Klaus, 260
Waddington, Conrad, 277
Waldrop, M. Mitchell, 311
Waltke, Bruce, 283–84
Webelhuth, Gert, 47
Weinreich, Uriel, 279
Weinrich, Harald, 224
Whaley, Lindsay, 293
Whitehead, Alfred, 276–77
Wickes, William, 305, 307
Williams, Edwin, 11, 15, 17, 48
Wilson-Wright, Aren, 183
Wilson, Daniel, 44–45
Wittgenstein, Ludwig, 12
Wu, Andi, 259
Yeivin, Israel, 306
Young, Ian, 213, 214
Zeichmann, Christopher, 197, 198
Zevit, Ziony, 213

Subject Index

adaptation, 282, 286–87
analogy, 208–11
Anatolian, 176–77, 178–79
Andersen-Forbes database, 223, 226, 229, 241, 242, 253, 262

Association Internationale Bible et Informatique, 227
author clustering, 247, 251–53
Avoid Pronoun principle, 27–28
Biblical Aramaic, 30, 175, 180
Biblical Greek, 103–09, 154, 172, 175–77, 215, 216, 259
Biblical Hebrew, 21–22, 26, 30, 37–38, 42, 78–79, 80–82, 83–85, 96, 109, 152–53, 172, 175, 180, 210, 235–36, 246, 249, 283, 287–88, 290–93, 302–04
binding theory, 20
Borer-Chomsky conjecture, 24
bounding theory, 20
Canaanite, 209–10
Case theory, 20
Cognitive Grammar, 148–49
Cognitive Linguistics, 2–4, 17, 117–71, 224
Coherence-Based Genealogical Method, 260
comparative linguistics, 200–04
Complexity Theory, 2, 4, 273–323
computational linguistics, 2–3, 223–72
conceptual blending, 139–41
conceptual metaphor theory, 136–37
Conceptual-Intentional system, 23
Construction Grammar, 149–50, 243
contextualisation, 94–100
control theory, 20
cross-linguistic complexity model, 305–07
Dead Sea Scrolls, 212, 249
deep structure, 13–14, 17–18
Determiner Phrase Hypothesis, 22
diachrony, 3, 119, 121, 274, 288, 289, 290, 291
discourse analysis, 4, 85–86
dislocation, 30, 32–35
Documentary Hypothesis, 251–52
domains, 136–37, 138
dramatic pause, 100–02
dynamism, 282
Eep Talstra Centre for Bible and Computer database, 224, 227, 229, 238, 241–42, 247, 255
embodied cognition, 125–26, 130
emergence, 284–85
extraposition, 32–33
Focus, 73–74, 80–87, 94, 106, 108
form-meaning pairings, 125–28
frame semantics, 133–36, 142–43
fronted constituents, 86–93
Functional Grammar, 2–3, 67–116, 123–124
general systems theory, 278

generative grammar, 7–8, 12, 18, 36, 38, 68, 122
generative linguistics, 2–3, 4, 6ff, 118–19, 124, 224
generative semantics, 13–16, 123
generative syntax, 23
geospatial data, 255–56
Government and Binding theory, 19–20, 28, 243–44
grammaticalisation, 286
heterogeneity, 282
historical linguistics, 2–3, 4, 7–10, 45, 172–222, 212, 276–77
Holmstedt-Abbegg database, 229, 243–44
image schemas, 129–32
Indo-European languages, 173–80
interdisciplinarity, 2, 280–81
I[nternal]-language and E[xternal]-language, 9–10
Katz-Postal hypothesis, 14
language acquisition, 9
language branching, 190–93
language change, 45, 184–90
language pedagogy, 291–96
language software, 224, 228–29, 234, 258, 260
Latinisms, 197–98
Law of Continuous Dichotomy, 305
lenition, 204–05
lexical categories, 38–39

lexical semantics, 143, 144, 155
lexicalist position, 16, 75
linguistic borrowing, 196–99
linguistic reconstruction, 186–90
linguistic theory, 1–4, 6, 276–81
linguistics, 2, 119
  see also Cognitive Linguistics, comparative linguistics, computational linguistics, generative linguistics, historical linguistics, typological linguistics
linked data, 255–56
loanwords, 197, 199
Logical Form, 20
machine learning, 3, 240, 244–45
Masoretic accents, 305–10
mental spaces, 139–41
Merge, 23–25, 29
Minimalist Programme, 22–26, 28, 46
morphology, 10, 187–188
Natural Language Processing, 3
negation, 39–40
nonlinearity, 285
null elements, 20–21, 43–44, 75
open systems, 282–83
orality, 306
orthography, 306–07
parent language, 174
participles, 83–85

philology, 1, 119, 193–96
phonemes, 187–88
Phonetic Form, 20, 23
phonology, 186–89, 204–07
Plato's problem, 8–9
pragmatics, 67–68, 71–73, 76–77, 102–03, 105–06
Principles and Parameters approach, 17–22, 26–29
pro-drop parameter, 20
prototypes, 143–48
quantifiers, 39–42
Qumran Hebrew, 27, 30
reductionist translation models, 297
relative clauses, 42
rule-based machine translation, 233–35
Samaritan Pentateuch, 287, 301–02
semantic extension, 143–44, 145, 146–47
semantics, 11, 14–17, 71, 129, 253–54
    see also frame semantics, generative semantics, lexical semantics
Semitic languages, 180–83
Septuagint, 297, 299–300
Society of Biblical Literature, 152
speech communities, 190–93
Split Complementiser Phrase, 22
Split Inflection Hypothesis, 21

Standard Theory Model, 12–18
structuralism, 2–4, 121
surface structure, 17, 19
synchrony, 4, 121, 273–74
syntactic structure, 12, 15, 26
syntactical databases, 3, 249–50
syntax, 10–12, 16, 26, 35–38, 68–69, 71–73, 122, 155, 243, 253–54, 302–04
    see also generative syntax
textuality, 289–90
theta theory, 20
thetic sentences, 88–93
Tiberian Masoretic Reading Tradition, 287, 305–10
Tiberias Stylistic Classifier, 251
Topic, 73–74, 80–81, 82, 83–87, 94–95, 106, 108
topicalisation, 29, 31
transdisciplinarity, 280
transformational grammar, 68, 122
transformations, 14–15, 68, 75
translation theory, 296–302
typological linguistics, 2–3, 293
Ugaritic, 209–10
Universal Grammar, 19, 25, 38
verbal valence patterns, 254
wayyiqtol, 22, 27–28, 87, 89, 92, 94–99, 101, 154, 208
Werkgroep Informatica Vrije Universiteit, 226–27

Westminster Leningrad Codex, 227

yiqtol, 27–29, 96, 182, 2

About the Team

Alessandra Tosi was the managing editor for this book and provided quality control.

Anne Burberry performed the copyediting of the book in Word. The main fonts used in this volume are SIL Charis, SBL Hebrew, and SBL Greek.

Cameron Craig created all of the editions — paperback, hardback, and PDF. Conversion was performed with open source software freely available on our GitHub page (https://github.com/OpenBookPublishers).

Jeevanjot Kaur Nagpal designed the cover of this book. The cover was produced in InDesign using Fontin and Calibri fonts.

Cambridge Semitic Languages and Cultures

General Editor Geoffrey Khan

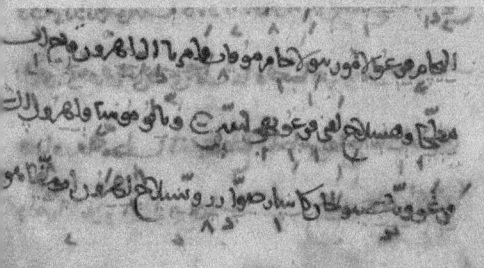
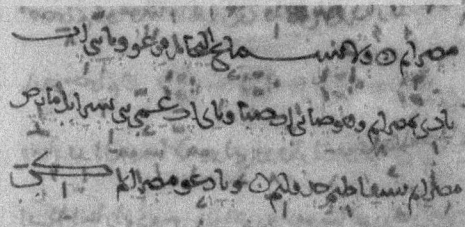
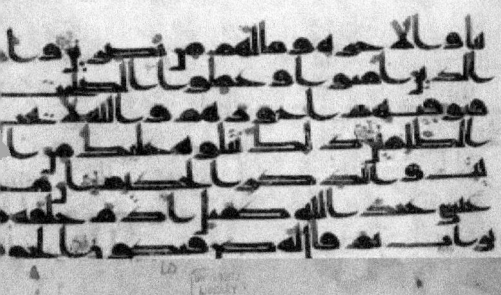

Cambridge Semitic Languages and Cultures

About the series

This series is published by Open Book Publishers in collaboration with the Faculty of Asian and Middle Eastern Studies of the University of Cambridge. The aim of the series is to publish in open-access form monographs in the field of Semitic languages and the cultures associated with speakers of Semitic languages. It is hoped that this will help disseminate research in this field to academic researchers around the world and also open up this research to the communities whose languages and cultures the volumes concern. This series includes philological and linguistic studies of Semitic languages and editions of Semitic texts. Titles in the series will cover all periods, traditions and methodological approaches to the field. The editorial board comprises Geoffrey Khan, Aaron Hornkohl, and Esther-Miriam Wagner.

This is the first Open Access book series in the field; it combines the high peer-review and editorial standards with the fair Open Access model offered by OBP. Open Access (that is, making texts free to read and reuse) helps spread research results and other educational materials to everyone everywhere, not just to those who can afford it or have access to well-endowed university libraries.

Copyrights stay where they belong, with the authors. Authors are encouraged to secure funding to offset the publication costs and thereby sustain the publishing model, but if no institutional funding is available, authors are not charged for publication. Any grant secured covers the actual costs of publishing and is not taken as profit. In short: we support publishing that respects the authors and serves the public interest.

This book was copyedited by Anne Burberry.

Other titles of the series

An Introduction to Andalusi Hebrew Metrics
José Martínez Delgado
doi.org/10.11647/OBP.0351

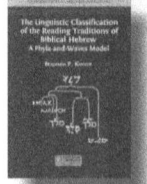

The Linguistic Classification of the Reading Traditions of Biblical Hebrew: A Phyla-and-Waves Model
Benjamin Paul Kantor
doi.org/10.11647/OBP.0210

Faculty of Asian and Middle Eastern Studies

More information and a complete list of books in this series can be found at:
https://www.openbookpublishers.com/series/2632-6914

www.ingramcontent.com/pod-product-compliance
Lightning Source LLC
Chambersburg PA
CBHW051535230426
43669CB00015B/2604